Canadian Federalism
and Quebec Sovereignty

American University Studies

Series X
Political Science

Vol. 47

PETER LANG
New York • Washington, D.C./Baltimore • Boston • Bern
Frankfurt am Main • Berlin • Brussels • Vienna • Oxford

Christopher Edward Taucar

Canadian Federalism and Quebec Sovereignty

PETER LANG
New York • Washington, D.C./Baltimore • Boston • Bern
Frankfurt am Main • Berlin • Brussels • Vienna • Oxford

JL
27
.T395
2000

Library of Congress Cataloging-in-Publication Data

Taucar, Christopher Edward.
Canadian federalism and Quebec sovereignty / Christopher Edward Taucar.
p. cm. — (American university studies. Series X, Political science; vol. 47)
Includes bibliographical references and index.
1. Federal government—Canada. 2. Federal government—Québec (Province).
3. Québec (Province)—History—Autonomy and independence movements.
I. American university studies. Series X, Political science; v. 47.
JL27.T395   320.471'049—dc21   00-020960
ISBN 0-8204-4952-0
ISSN 0740-0470

Die Deutsche Bibliothek-CIP-Einheitsaufnahme

Taucar, Christopher Edward:
Canadian federalism and Quebec sovereignty / Christopher Edward
Taucar –New York; Washington, D.C./Baltimore; Boston; Bern;
Frankfurt am Main; Berlin; Brussels; Vienna; Oxford: Lang.
(American university studies: Ser. 10, Political science; Vol. 47)
ISBN 0-8204-4952-0

Printed in the United States of America

Preface

The issue of Quebec sovereignty has almost become a perennial feature of the Canadian federalism landscape. It is characterized, at times, by high drama, exposure and even nervousness given the outcome can decide the future of a very polity and country. The very consequences of a sovereignty outcome and its implications for Quebecers and all Canadians alike make it imperative for its supporters to justify its necessity. Certainly, many criticisms have been made of Canadian federalism and bold assertions have been made of its failure and unworkability. These assertions must be vigorously tested. Similarly and surprisingly, little has been publicly discussed as to the very fundamental successes of the Canadian federation.

In order to answer the question on Quebec sovereignty, the essential inquiry must be whether or not Canadian federalism has been fundamentally working successfully, especially with respect to Quebec. If it has worked to provide or allow for the most basic interests and needs of Quebecers, then there exists nothing (or very little) in support of secession. The only way to critically assess the issue is to take a detailed look at the workings of the Canadian federation. Therefore, this book is as much (or more) about Canadian federalism as anything else. Although federalism keeps changing and new events arise, the core principles remain.

In undertaking a study of this type, one cannot help but be reminded of the multitude of people who have made significant contributions to furthering the knowledge of Canadian federalism and of Quebec society. A comprehensive list of the same is not possible here, save to mention the inspirational examples of people such as Peter H. Russell and J. Stefan Dupré. Of course, I take responsibility for the contents of this book.

If the result of this book is a major argument against Quebec separatism, it is simultaneously no more comforting to any who may believe Quebec should be "put in its place". Simply put, neither approach is the way of federalism.

CET

Table of Contents

Introduction

Rational validity for the outcome of separatism and sovereignty in Quebec requires the proponents of that political view, who are proposing a radically different political structure that may drastically affect the lives of Quebecers and all Canadians, to justify the need for such action. In turn, it becomes the obligation of Quebecers voting in a referendum on separatism or sovereignty to rationally assess those justifications. The real question in any such referendum for Quebec is whether or not reasonable and substantial grounds exist justifying separatism or sovereignty for the people of Quebec in the context of Canada. It is, also, necessary that all Canadians have a basic understanding about the workings of Canadian federalism in order to make assessments about its workings, the improvements that may be necessary, and even the possible responses to a sovereignty 'yes' vote.

Reference is made to both 'separatists' and 'sovereignists'. The term 'sovereignist' is used to denote supporters of sovereignty-association (political independence, together with economic association with Canada); whereas, 'separatists' do not see economic association as necessary. Both groups are really by definition separatists as each seek to establish Quebec as an independent state, however, sovereignists attempt to repackage that separatism.

Several themes underlie the basis for arguments in support of separatism or sovereignty. First, many supporters of separatism or sovereignty state that Quebec must be allowed to affirm itself, which is not possible in Canada. Quebecers and other Canadians are said to hold such great differences in views that a new political order must be created as Canada's vision is apparently not compatible with Quebec's reality. A second theme underlying such justifications is that without sovereignty, Quebec francophone society may become assimilated or cannot flourish within Canada. The third theme is that some separatists or sovereignists argue that Canada is illegitimate, or parts of its constitution are, particularly the *Constitution Act, 1982*, which, in turn, justifies Quebec sovereignty. Although not a 'theme' *per se*, other arguments are forwarded in favour of separatism/sovereignty. The first is that secession is a rational goal and justified in Quebec because it has received increased support in recent times. The second argument is that Canadian federalism functions too inefficiently, or generates too much competition.

Such perceptions and views, giving rise to an apparent justification for secession, will be critically examined to determine the extent to which they actually reflect reality in Canada and to assess the actual significance of such justifications in order to determine whether or not there exist reasonable and substantial grounds for separatism or sovereignty for Quebec.

On the journey towards this ultimate aim, we will have traversed the landscape of Canadian federalism, both past and present. The approach of this book is, first and foremost, to situate and analyse the separatism/sovereignty debate within the entire context of Canadian federalism. Without taking such a global perspective, important aspects of the issues will be obscured. To take account only of partial or selective elements of the entire subject area may give rise to misperceptions, or may obscure the analysis and identification of what may, in fact, be a problem area within the federation, or may lead to the search for solutions in all the wrong places and by all the wrong means, and so on. At the very least, any other approach risks never fully addressing the separatist/sovereignist issue resulting in the difficulties outlined, and includes the risk that the issue may never be discussed constructively because the dialogue is constantly being held at cross-purposes; one side never really communicates with the other. This dialogue at cross-purposes is furthermore complicated by the fact that the workings of federalism are not always readily apparent and are multifaceted. In particular, many important issues are or may be satisfactorily resolved without resort to the highly visible, high politics approaches that some might otherwise expect to see or upon which they evaluate federalism.

Federalism is the common ground which provides both the context and structure for the discussion. Accordingly, it is only through this thorough view of the Canadian federalism landscape that one may assess whether or not grounds for separatism or sovereignty truly exist, let alone whether or not the Canadian federal system is broken, or beyond repair. The two topics are inextricably linked.

The analysis is divided into three Parts containing one or more Chapters. Each Part and Chapter will build on previous Parts and Chapters until a complete view of Canadian federalism, including its form, processes and history is provided. In Part I, the basic elements that make up Canadian federalism are outlined, including its form and processes, underlying societal interests, the role of the judiciary, and conclusions that may be thereby drawn.

Part II deals with the perceptions and the grounds postulated in support of secession held by many Quebec citizens. It examines these views with respect to Canadian federalism, its workings, and the reasons for which those views may be held. Chapter 2 reminds us that while constituting a majority in Quebec and a minority in Canada and North America, the overriding concern of Quebecers is to preserve the French language and to promote the flourishing of its francophone society. In a sense, the former is one aspect of the latter since part of the flourishing of francophone society must be to live and work in the French language. As well, the latter includes economic flourishing and the expression of francophone culture.

Chapter 3 examines the political-historical background of Canada as it relates to Quebec. Events from the imperial and colonial conflicts of France and Britain up to the FLQ crisis will be outlined. These historical conflicts show that even with Confederation, political union did not necessarily always ensure social unity or harmony. Secondly, more and more, Quebecers looked to their provincial level of government to best reflect their interests.

The contemporary constitutional history of Canada may be characterized by wrangling and discord from the attempts at patriating the Constitution and establishing an amending formula, to the processes occurring after Patriation. Nothing seemed to work very well in amending the terms of the written constitutional text of the Canadian constitution, and it may have appeared to some that Quebec's needs and concerns were not being addressed within the federation.

Finally, and, perhaps, most importantly, prior to the late 1970's, Quebec's economy was largely controlled by Canadian anglophones and Americans. As a result, much resentment arose because francophones, who while constituting a majority in Quebec, did not share more equally in the development of their own province. Furthermore, given the modernization, industrialization and urbanization of Quebec society, an anglophone dominated business world posed serious threats to the robust survival of the French language and francophone society, at least in certain areas of Quebec.

Without understanding Canadian federalism as a whole, one may believe that Canadian federalism does not work very well. By focusing on certain events and by not giving adequate consideration to Canadian federalism in its entirety, a powerful sense may be created that only Quebec can truly represent the interests of francophone Quebecers and that federalism is inadequate to protect their needs and concerns.

However, Part III of this book tells another story. It examines in greater depth the form, processes and history of Canadian federalism to demonstrate that Canadian federalism can and does address the needs and concerns of Quebecers and Canadians alike. Chapter 6 confronts the crucial issues by demonstrating that the province of Quebec and Quebecers have the ability and willingness to protect the French language and to promote the flourishing of francophone society within the context of Canadian federalism. This Chapter discusses the Quebec business world, workplace and government in the post-1980's reflecting francophone dominance, both linguistically and structurally. Quebec's policies sensitive to its demographic position, including incentives to raise its birth rate, policies in relation to immigration and other policy areas affecting language, such as the language of work, the language of education, the "French face" of outdoor and commercial advertising, and, finally, the policy area of culture will be examined. Once it is shown that Quebecers and the Quebec government possess the ability (and willingness) to protect the French language and to promote the flourishing of francophone society within Canada, there remains little else in reason to support separatism or sovereignty.

Chapter 7 discusses the constitutional aspects of federalism relating to questions of whether further accommodation or distinct society recognition in written constitutional text is necessary *vis-à-vis* Quebec, and whether or not the *Constitution Act, 1982* is legitimate. Quebec already possesses sufficient powers to protect language and to promote the flourishing of its francophone society. In fact, a careful examination of the Constitution demonstrates that the province of Quebec enjoys considerable distinct society recognition and that the 'distinctiveness' of that society has been flourishing within the scope of the Constitution as it exists.

Irrespective of the foregoing, the symbolism of Quebec not being a signatory to the *Constitution Act, 1982* remains a powerful weapon that is used against Canada in the attempt to demonstrate that the Canadian Constitution and federalism do not work well. The crucial events leading up to the agreement of that Amendment will be outlined to determine what was truly happening at that time. Confronted will be the issues of whether or not Quebec was betrayed or stabbed in the back, whether or not the Amendment process was proper by observing the necessary legal rules of the time, and whether or not the process was nevertheless legitimate.

Furthermore, despite the fact that few amendments occurred to the text of the written Constitution, substantial changes and accommodations have taken place often in favour and at the behest of Quebec. These modifications and accommodations comprise the substance of Chapter 8. Canadian federalism is a creature far more decentralized than its origins would suggest. It progressed to become a true federation, and a decentralized one at that, through constitutional convention, judicial decisions, constitutional amendments and intergovernmental relations.

Perhaps the most significant and substantial decentralization of all occurred through highly successful intergovernmental relations in the area of government revenues and expenditures, or fiscal federalism. Furthermore, as can be observed in Chapter 9, the evolution of fiscal federalism demonstrates that the workings of Canadian federalism changed dramatically, and bears witness to many significant accommodations, including balancing the needs and concerns of both levels of government, as well as those of the province of Quebec in particular.

These significant accomplishments of Canadian federalism, once known, cannot be downplayed or minimized. All these successes occurred within Canadian federalism and in a context of only minimal changes occurring in written constitutional text. The true purpose of a constitution is to limit and channel government authority, thereby, reflecting the fundamental values of a society and to provide a framework in which the role of government may be adapted in light of future circumstances. However, instead of assessing how the Canadian constitution has been meeting the needs of Canadians in reality, it is judged by many on a symbolic level, while constitutionalism in Canada has degenerated into a game of symbolism and 'status seeking' in written constitutional text, and an attempt by others to address their own 'status anxieties'. As a result, constitutional amendment becomes practically impossible. This process both created the impetus and sounded the death knell for the Meech Lake and Charlottetown Accords.

The analysis becomes more abstract again in Chapter 11, in order to better explain the forces behind the significant and far reaching changes that occurred in Canadian federalism and to better explain the nature of federalism in Canada. First and foremost, federalism as a form of government allows national and territorial communities to exist and to affirm their identities within common boarders by giving salience to both, and also gives rise to a symbiotic relationship between those communities. However, federalism has as much to do with governments as with the communities they represent. The forces which generated provincial assertiveness and enhanced intergovernmental competition were the territorial division of power ordained by the *Constitution Act, 1867*,[1] the theoretical and practical overlap of these jurisdictional powers giving rise to an interdependence between the two orders of government, the Cabinet-Parliamentary system of government, the political economy of Canada, and, finally, the existence of a compartmentalized dual citizenship giving rise to the ability of each level of government to draw upon the same citizen support for different purposes. Its long term implication is the competition between both orders of government over jurisdiction and over citizen conceptions of community. The province of Quebec is no different from any other province in the sense of engaging in this process of competition, but is often the most assertive one. Indeed, Ontario was the first real activist province. Overlapping jurisdictions of the federal and provincial levels of government will also be examined to determine their relationship, if any, to separatism or sovereignty justifications.

The structure of power within a certain level of government and the structure of relationships between governments also have important effects on whether relations between the two orders of government will be competitive or co-operative. Another variable affecting the nature of relations in Canada is that of party politics and government leaders in Quebec. The first implication of this variable of party politics and government leaders in Quebec is that it contributed to a disproportionate public and intergovernmental focus on explicit constitutional reform. Secondly, it has become an embedded game in the politics of Quebec that parties seek some form of special status and demand decentralization. Finally, individual personalities can play an important role with some Quebec government leaders being more successful than others in promoting the separatist or sovereignist agenda in Quebec.

Federal-provincial competition is a dynamic element inherent in Canadian federalism and is not just confined to battles over jurisdiction. It includes battles over the conceptions of community that citizens hold. Although it is not surprising that Quebecers demonstrate a natural affinity towards the province of Quebec and often look to that level of government to pursue their interests, what is surprising is that for a significant proportion of Quebecers who are sovereignists and separatists, there is not a simultaneously strong sense of community towards Canada and the national level of government.

History, played a significant role in this state of affairs, along with the media and education in Quebec, as does the importance of provincial jurisdiction for the flourishing of francophone society. Another large element explaining the rise of separatist or sovereignist sentiment and the corresponding decline of nationhood bonds relates to the visibility to Quebecers of the successes of Canadian federalism and the importance of the federal government and the Canadian national community in the lives of Quebecers. In this respect, the federal government has been outcompeted with the result that the national community is not properly represented to all Quebecers.

In examining the form, process and history of Canadian federalism thoroughly, phrases such as Quebec and Canada do not see 'eye to eye' and cannot live together ultimately make little or no sense. A thorough examination of Canadian federalism demonstrates that the grounds in support of separatism and sovereignty once perhaps seemingly strong and unshakeable now illuminate a far less credible content.

Indeed, to the contrary, reasonable and substantial grounds support the province of Quebec remaining in Canada. Although inadequately depicted as such, Canadian federalism allows for and works to produce the affirmation of the French language, as well as of the Québécois community and identity within Canada. Within the Canadian federation as it exists today, the province of Quebec possesses enough power to protect the French language and to provide for the flourishing of their francophone society. Secondly, Canadian federalism involves a symbiotic relationship between territorial and national communities and the governments that represent them. The fundamental needs and concerns emanating from the province of Quebec are recognized and balanced, often at the behest of Quebec governments, in the course of the significant and far reaching changes and evolution occurring within the Canadian federation. The actual workings of the constitution have reflected the ultimate values within Canadian federalism and have been successfully adapted in light of contemporary circumstances to meet the needs of its participants and citizens.

Perhaps the next set of discussions about Canadian federalism will involve practical issues such as fine-tuning its workings and managing its interdependencies so that further benefits may result for governments and citizens alike.

PART I
The Basic Elements of Canadian Federalism

Chapter 1
The Canadian Constitution, Federalism and the Judiciary

In order to assess Quebec separatism or sovereignty adequately, the issue must be placed within the broader context of the Canadian polity and, particularly, Canadian federalism. Only by understanding the Canadian system as a whole can one assess its workability, successes and shortcommings in addressing the issues the country faces, including with respect to the needs and concerns of Quebecers. Chapter 1 provides basic principles and the overview for this book. The first section examines constitutions and constitutionalism. The second section outlines the basic elements that comprise Canada and Canadian federalism.

Constitutions and Constitutionalism

One writer has put the matter very well when he said:

> In a sense all law is constitutional. Even the most particular law and legal decision must be legitimate in the sense that their validity can be traced to first principles of the constitution.[1]

Constitutions empower government by setting out bodies with authority, their powers and limits on that authority, if any, and in this way set out the common values within a geographical area comprising the state. Constitutionalism purely defined, on the other hand, is an unwritten limitation on the government's use of constitutional powers, arising from demands made upon government to observe certain constitutional limits. Constitutionalism may also give rise to specific conventions or practices, which are not legal in nature, but, governmental actors will nevertheless see themselves bound by them. Although Constitutionalism is usually thought of in terms of limiting or influencing the use of government powers, it may also come to mean a pursuit to influence and/or redefine the explicit or symbolic values of a constitution. It may very well be that a country has a constitution but lacks constitutionalism.

Constitutions may be written as in the United States and may be contained in one or more documents, or, they may be wholly or largely unwritten as in the United Kingdom. The Canadian constitution is a mixture of written and unwritten sources, the written portions of which are contained in several documents and may even encompass Orders-in-Council. The exercise of constitutional powers may be limited or influenced by constitutionalism, but, are also limited by such matters as democracy, social pluralism, various practical constraints that may arise relating to federalism, economic and social considerations, and judicial review of legal limits.

The Canadian constitution can be said to reflect certain values. The written Constitution creates Parliamentary democracy in Part IV of the *Constitution Act, 1867*, and which, furthermore, states that executive power is vested in the Queen and Privy Council. With the development of convention, or the unwritten constitution, Canada observes the rule of responsible government, with Parliament and the Legislatures exercising true or *de facto* power, particularly through the driving force of the political executive as represented by the Prime Minister or Premier, and Cabinet.

The second pillar of the Constitution is federalism, which reflects the need to preserve national and regional differences through the existence of national and provincial levels of government. Federalism is embodied concretely in the division of jurisdiction sections of the Constitution and as interpreted in judicial decisions, but, is also reflected in or modified by unwritten rules, such as constitutional convention.

The third pillar of the Constitution, arising in 1982, is the Charter of Rights and Freedoms. This document sets out various rights Canadians hold as against government interference, with recourse to the courts to provide a remedy for its violation.

The fourth pillar of the Constitution involves judicial review of government action, which is implicit in federalism and the rule of law. The function of the rule of law is to provide for a predictable and ordered society, and not arbitrary state action. Judicial review is also provided for in the Charter. The 1982 *Constitution Act* states:

> **s. 51(1)** The Constitution of Canada is the supreme law of Canada, and any law that is inconsistent with the provisions of the Constitution is, to the extent of the inconsistency, of no force or effect.

s. 24(1) Anyone whose rights or freedoms, as guaranteed by this Charter, have been infringed or denied may apply to a court of competent jurisdiction to obtain such remedy as the court considers appropriate and just in the circumstances.

Finally, there is a fusion of the executive and legislative functions in the Cabinet-Parliamentary system of government. The judiciary is separate and largely independent of the executive and legislature.

It is always important to bear in mind that what a constitution says or appears to say in its written text is not necessarily how it, in fact, operates. It is the way in which the constitution actually operates, or evolves to operate that is important as it is this aspect that affects the daily lives of citizens. Therefore, a constitution can only be properly assessed by how it works, in reality, to address the needs, concerns and challenges faced by the country, and not by any other standard. One may desire certain provisions to be entrenched in a constitution, but, the success, or lack thereof, in entrenching such visions must ultimately be judged by a constitution's operational aspects and effects.

The Basic Elements of Canadian Federalism

The basic elements that comprise Canada and Canadian federalism will be outlined in this section. Without understanding these basic elements and how they interrelate, one cannot truly understand the events arising within the system. Taking an event or numerous events in isolation may very well give rise to a misperception regarding the meaning and/or significance of such event(s), or even of the entire system. An examination of the basic elements comprising Canadian federalism reveals that a dynamic of competition between the federal and provincial governments is inherent within the federal system.

Canadian Federalism—Form and Process

Aside from Democratic values, the *Constitution Act, 1867* ordained a territorial division of power in which there are two levels of government, federal and provincial, exercising authority within their respective spheres of power. The basic division of power is contained in sections 91 and 92 of that Act, with other features, the more significant of which relating to education, old age pensions and agriculture and immigration being contained in sections 93, 94A and 95 respectively. As such, power is divided between the federal and provincial governments.

It must also be noted that public officials have a significant degree of autonomy from societal constraints, and the way in which power is structured within the government system has an important independent effect on the behaviour of those officials and the allocative outputs of the system.[2] Thus, although public officials may be influenced by elements outside government, they operate under a significant degree of autonomy.[3] The government system itself will influence the way in which those officials make decisions and it will influence the decision itself. It is the very apparatus of government that gives government much of its strength and which allows it, once established, to act as an independent force to shape and influence the environment. In short, a government structure takes on a life of its own.

The essential dynamic that arises from this element is that governments and bureaucracies will seek to expand their responsibilities and compete with other governments and bureaucracies to expand and to fight challenges to their 'jurisdiction'. If demands for their services decline, they must find new justifications to exist. Their jurisdiction and the expertise of these organizational complexes constitute their power and create their permanence. The politics of competitive organizations affects relations not only within a specific level of government (intragovernmental relations), it also affects the interaction between different governments within a polity (intergovernmental relations, either among provincial governments, or, between federal and provincial governments). This process holds profound implications for the relations between the different levels of constitutionally recognized governments, namely, the federal and provincial levels of government, and not just for their bureaucracies.

Federal and provincial bureaucratic pyramids are headed by political authorities that are protectionist and expansionist. These executive and legislative institutions are formally subordinated to their respective Cabinets, through the constitutional convention of responsible government.[4] The Cabinets constitute the main engine driving each level of government in a Parliamentary system of government due to the relatively predictable support of a Parliamentary majority and, therefore, are able to translate their policy initiatives into legislation.[5] Given that the federal and provincial governments are supreme within their respective spheres of power, relations between the two are somewhat analogous to a mini-international system.[6] The result is a dynamic for competition and conflict between the interdependent federal and provincial levels of government to expand and protect jurisdiction, as well as to gain "credit, status and importance and to avoid discredit and blame," especially in highly visible areas.[7]

Secondly, the Cabinet-Parliamentary system of government within a federation tends to produce a compartmentalized dual citizenship. Citizens' attitudes and decisions regarding the federal and provincial levels of government are governed by different considerations. This explains why Quebecers could vote for René Lévesque and Pierre Trudeau at the same time. Therefore, both federal and provincial governments can draw on the same citizen support for different purposes.

Furthermore, due to the Cabinet-Parliamentary form of government and party discipline, it is difficult for central government policies to be adjusted by territorially sensitive M.P.s in the governing party. In addition, since the Canadian national government lacks an effective bicameral legislature or upper house, it is difficult for federal-provincial adjustment to be made intrastate and so is often conducted through interstate federalism.[8]

In other words, the system of government created by the Constitution is such that, often, federal-provincial adjustments and compromises must be conducted through federal-provincial relations. This relationship is so because, from an institutional perspective, the federal government lacks bodies that permit effective representation of territorial interest. All of this is not to say that Parliament or the federal government are not sensitive to territorial interests when making policy. Cabinet, itself, for example, plays a role in bringing regional interests to bear on policy-making. However, such sensitivity must be represented informally, rather than through formal structures that may give particular salience to such views.

The conclusion then that one may draw from this structure is that a further element is added creating a dynamic of competition and tension between the federal and provincial governments within the federalism system. In their role as standard bearers of territorial interests, provinces seem to acquire a sense of legitimacy in competing with the federal government for more power, whether or not the federal government is, in a given case, acting in a manner sensitive to territorial interests.

In addition to the institutional dynamic of two levels of government, dividing jurisdiction in a federal system will always give rise to difficulties of interpretation when it is applied to the variety and complexities of social and economic relationships, particularly those which do not correspond to the neat logical divisions found in the Constitution. Secondly, the Constitution, itself, does not provide clear guidelines regarding the division of jurisdiction, especially when one considers the relevance of the federal powers of the

Constitution Act, 1867, s. 91(2) Trade and Commerce, s. 91(27) Criminal law, peace order and good government; and, the provincial powers of s. 92(13) Property and Civil Rights in the Province, and s. 92(16) Generally all Matters of a merely local or private Nature in the Province. Such general powers lack a clear, legal meaning and conceptually overlap with each other. Interpreting the powers of one level of government expansively can easily render the other level of government's powers without efficacy. For example, the federal power over Trade and Commerce could mean that the provinces can have little or no say over matters of business under its powers over "Property and Civil Rights" or with respect to local matters.

The dynamic for competition is enhanced by further factors. First, there is the inherent overlapping of powers contained in the Constitution, as discussed. Second, there was an explosion of government involvement in society and the economy, especially after the Second World War. Third, emerging issues in contemporary times could not have been foreseen in 1867, and were not contemplated in the drafting of the Constitution. Finally, such issues involve an overlapping of federal-provincial jurisdictions in which both levels of government have capacity to act. This overlap created an increased degree of interdependence between the two levels and a corresponding need for and emphasis on co-ordinating policies.

The Constitution, then, can be seen as having the effect of structuring the federal-provincial game primarily along the lines of the division of jurisdiction and interstate federalism. Up to this point, the form of the Constitution and its effect of creating an institutional dynamic of competition between the two levels of government were outlined, as well as the process aspect of the Constitution, that is, the structuring effect on that federal-provincial dynamic.

Canadian Federalism—Underlying Societal Interests

In addition to the form and processes of the Constitution, there is a deeper level of interests sought to be protected. Not all interests finally triumph. Federalism gives particular salience to territorial cleavages demarcated by constitutionally guaranteed boundaries.

In Canada there is no typical province or region. Each has its own unique resource base, location, history and distinct population characteristics, which dictate, in part, the interests each seeks to protect and, hence, its relationship with the rest of Canada.

The Western provinces are rich in agriculture and natural resources like oil, gas, potash and, in British Columbia, forestry. Its regional identity is based on recurring issues Westerners experience regarding property and resource development, especially, oil and gas prices, freight rates, tariffs, the cost of supplies and the sale of products. In the past, due to the tariff structure, the West bought manufactured goods at above international market prices, while having to sell its products in the open international marketplace. Part of Western alienation sees the political system favouring central Canada, and as not sufficiently acknowledging the West's contribution to the national economy.

Ontario and Quebec are more diversified from an economic perspective, especially in relation to industries like manufacturing, and contain the largest financial centres. Quebec has a disproportionate share of 'declining' manufacturing industries, such as clothing and textiles. Ontario being more vulnerable to high energy prices supported initiatives that stabilize prices, like the National Energy Policy (NEP). At the same time, Ontario has been traditionally more cautious about free trade with the United States than the West, at least until the mid to late 1980's. Quebec was more welcoming of free trade seeing it as integral to the flourishing of its francophone society since its domestic economy is too small to sustain that flourishing economically. Due to their size, wealth and bureaucratic sophistication, Ontario and Quebec are in a position to compete vigorously with the federal government.

The Atlantic provinces rely more heavily on the fisheries and seasonal work. Their economies are not as strong as the rest of Canada. Equalization payments have been a major source of federally financed province-building. The prospects of offshore oil and gas for Newfoundland and Nova Scotia may change the outlook for these provinces.

Not only do the various provinces and territories display differing interests and circumstances, but, within provinces themselves, sub-provincial regionalism can exist. In Quebec there is a sizable anglophone and allophone population centred in the Montreal area. Southern Ontario is more economically prosperous and diversified than Northern Ontario. Within each province, urban areas have different interests and concerns than rural ones, and so on.

Citizen Conceptions of Community

Furthermore, and related to what was said thus far, are the conceptions held by Canadian citizens at a given time with respect to which level of government they view as 'natural' or deserving of citizen loyalty, and which level of government, if any, they see as 'extensive' or merely artificial and only valued for convenience. A citizen's identification with the nation or local territory, or both, as representing their community will determine their views on whether a certain level of government is seen as 'natural' or 'extensive'. In a truly federal state, citizens will, therefore, have a natural affinity for both levels of government. Confederalism regards only the local government as the natural one; whereas, in a unitary state, only the national government is seen as properly representing the citizen's natural community.

On a conceptual and practical level, there are various views held about the Canadian community. In the pan-Canadian definition of community, there is a strong affinity towards the nation and a recognition that there are diverse elements in the Canadian polity. However, the central government is regarded as being best capable of representing and accommodating this diversity. The "provincialist" ideal represents a strong provincial affinity and generates division-of-powers proposals that are the flip side of those advanced under the pan-Canadian ideal. This ideal sees the provincial government as being best able to represent and reflect local concerns. Quebec encompasses the added elements of a distinct language and a majority francophone population within the province, while constituting a minority outside the province. Indeed, many citizens of Quebec, in past and present, looked not to the nation or Ottawa, but, to Quebec and the Quebec government as the 'natural' territory and government. Conceptions of national or local communities are, of course, not the only ones that unify, divide, or are otherwise of concern to or shape ideas of what Canadians see as pertaining to their life and society. Yet, it is the federalism aspect that poses the most serious threat to Canada.

Accordingly, governments in Canada use citizen conceptions of loyalties as political resources in their competition with one another. The ultimate resource in any such competitions is the threat of separatism, and the perception of a lack of affinity by citizens of a territory with respect to the federation can also be a powerful weapon.

The Judiciary

Among its other functions, the judiciary plays the role of umpire in the federal system, adjudicating disputes regarding the constitutionality of legislation enacted by either level of government. Initially, the legal basis of this power was derived from the doctrine of paramountcy, and since the *Constitution Act, 1867* was in form a British statute, any colonial law inconsistent with that Act would be held to be without jurisdiction, or *ultra vires*, and of no force or effect. Since the repealing of the *Colonial Laws Validity Act*, the Court has continued to play the umpire role between federal and provincial governments. Judicial review, then, did not evolve as an instrument of imperial control over Canadian affairs, but, rather a practical device for delineating powers respecting the two levels of government. The Supreme Court of Canada itself recognized this role of controlling the limits of the respective sovereignty lines.[9]

As alluded to earlier, there is no clear division of jurisdiction between the federal and provincial governments. The powers read broadly in either s. 91 or s. 92 would render the other set of powers nugatory and, therefore, one set of powers must be read in light of the other set of powers in an effort to maintain some form of acceptable balance in light of contemporary circumstances.

The legal results of court decisions must always be borne in mind by legislatures or their laws risk being struck down by courts. Restrictive decisions affecting one level of government could have the result of frustrating attempts to deal with important issues. It is precisely this type of criticism which was levied against the decisions of the British Judicial Committee of the Privy Council, for example, in striking down federal New Deal legislation enacted in response to the Depression. An *ultra vires* ruling, if not evaded by more careful legislative drafting, might exclude that level of government from a policy field. Secondly, even if it does not, it will certainly influence the choice of instruments available to government in any given field.

To be sure, the legal results of judicial decisions are not the only significant aspect of such decisions and may not even be the most important factor influencing Canadian federalism. If one speaks of the purely legal consequences of judicial decisions, one must keep in mind D.V. Smiley's conclusion that "[t]he federal aspects of the Canadian constitution, using this term in its broadest sense, have come less to be what the courts say they are than what the federal cabinets and bureaucracies in a continuous series of formal and informal interactions determine them to be."[10] W.R. Lederman pointed out, however, that judicial interpretation remains important in a context where federal and provincial governments cannot agree on a particular measure of co-operative action.[11] The courts may then be called upon to decide which legislative body has power to do what.

Secondly, judicial decisions are a "primary element in defining the bargaining power of the federal government on the one hand, and the provincial governments on the other."[12] It is observed by P.H. Russell that whether won or lost, constitutional cases representing constitutional power become a resource for bargaining governments just as popularity or a good international climate are resources, and in the proliferation of constitutional litigation after 1975, both levels of government attempted to strengthen their bargaining positions against one another by resorting to the courts.[13] In short, "executive federalism" (the political aspect of federalism) and "judicial federalism" (the legal aspect of federalism) are not mutually exclusive processes.

Conclusion and Goals

It is clear that inherent in Canadian federalism as in all successful federations there is a tension between the federal and provincial levels of government, in part, due to the territorial division of power and structure of government ordained by the Constitution and, in part, as a result of the territorial interests themselves underlying the form and processes of the Constitution. In addition to such differing interests as economic base and the regional identities that may thereby arise, Quebec encompasses the added 'peculiarisms' of language, history and of containing a majority francophone population within its borders while constituting a minority outside of that province. This state of affairs shapes its perspective with respect to the other parts of Canada.

However, in the end, the goal of a federalism is to balance successfully the interests contained within itself. In Canada, this balancing comprehends the national or pan-Canadian interests with the provincialist views, as well as those from Quebec, and the views and interests of citizens at large. The most fundamental goal for Quebecers is to protect the French language and to promote the flourishing of its francophone society. In reality, these diverse interests can be and have been successfully balanced, while, at the same time, an illusory perception may exist that the elements have not been properly balanced and that federalism is not working.

PART II
Perceptions and the Grounds for Secession

Whether or not federalism is functioning well, in practice, by successfully balancing the elements that make up Canadian federalism, may be irrelevant to whether or not it is *perceived* to be working well, or whether or not and to what extent the citizens of a territory within the federation feel an affinity towards the national level and its representative government.

One must always bear in mind that it is not all, or even a majority, of Quebecers who take from their history and situation within the federation a need or desire to separate or become sovereign. Indeed, a very large percentage of Quebecers, including francophones, are federalists. The idea of federalism and of identifying with the Canadian community is deeply entrenched in Quebec and the rejection of sovereignty/separatism in two referendums, 1980 and 1995, further demonstrates this attachment.

A tour through Part II of this book will reveal three main themes underlying the bases on which support for separatism or sovereignty is rooted. The arguments marshalled against Canadian federalism can overlap these themes and can be relevant to or reflect them in varying ways and to varying extents.

The first global theme is essentially that Quebecers and Canadians just do not see 'eye to eye' on many highly important issues. These differing views, or visions of the country, are said to be so fundamental that the two 'peoples' really should live apart to some large degree. For example, François Rocher writes that Canada is a federal regime that is now incompatible with the principles of federalism that Quebec understands and desires, particularly since it less and less recognizes and respects diversity.[1]

The second theme is 'assimilation' in which the protection of the French language and the promotion of the flourishing of francophone society are thought not to be possible within Canada. The quality of francophone life in Quebec encompasses the flourishing of francophone society, a major component of which is the ability of francophones to live and work in the French language, as well as involving economic and cultural flourishing. The implicit assumption, therefore, is that the way in which Canadian federalism operates is not and cannot successfully provide for these worthy goals.

Third, is a legitimacy argument. Under this view, Canada is or parts of the Canadian structure or Constitution are seen as illegitimate insofar as Quebec is concerned. This illegitimacy either supports or compels a move towards separation or sovereignty. The underlying assumption of the legitimacy argument is either an imposition was made upon Quebec without the consent of Quebec, or resulted from a procedure which itself was improper, or that a state of affairs exists within Canada operating fundamentally to the detriment of Quebecers.

Although not a theme underlying Quebec secession *per se*, one argument advanced is that secession has become a rational goal and justified for Quebec because it has received increased popular support in recent times. The final argument is an efficiency based argument. The efficiency argument is that federalism is simply too costly and ineffective to run, including in terms of public policy formation, due to the problem of overlapping jurisdictions and the interdependencies between the two levels of government. Presumably, the inefficiencies are so great as to in themselves or in combination with other reasons, like the amount of perceived competition occurring in the federalist system, compel a re-ordering of the fundamental structure of Canada.

One must note that the arguments of different writers criticizing the Canadian federation may reflect one theme more than another, or, indeed, may reflect a combination of themes in various ways. The purpose is not to characterize the arguments of the various writers individually. Rather, these general themes serve a useful organizational and analytical function when considering the workings of the Canadian federation as a whole and the further question of whether or not on the basis of reason one ought to choose secession in a popular referendum.

Focusing on specific aspects of the political, business, economic, and constitutional history of Quebec, without taking full account of the workings and history of Canadian federalism as a whole, including the entire history of Quebec and the progression of that history, may very well give rise to misperception.

Part II of this book explores the arguments or themes characterizing the bases in support of separatism or sovereignty as applied to the historical background of federalism relating to Quebec. Chapter 2 outlines the overriding demographic concern of francophone Quebecers. This concern relates to language and the existence of a majority francophone population in Quebec, while constituting a minority within Canada and North America. Chapter 3 outlines specific events in the political history of Quebec, which help to provide an indication of why some francophone Quebecers might see only the provincial level of government as worthy of affinity. The Constitution has been the major area of grievance for many Quebecers. Chapter 4 deals with this Constitutional-historical background. Chapter 5 provides an outline of the business and economic history of Quebec.

One will quickly discover how these facts, when taken in isolation, can create a sense within many Quebec francophones that only Quebec can truly represent the interests of that group, and that the structure of federalism is inadequate to protect their interests. The apparent conclusion is that only the territorial government is deserving of citizen affinity within that country. The corollary may be that Quebec must become a sovereign or independent nation.

Furthermore, as one progresses through Part II, one may lose sight of the federalist system and its workings. It is at this point that the misperceptions pertaining to the workability and desirability of Canadian federalism arise. The greatest problem is that the entire federalism history has not been made explicit and taken into consideration by all Canadians alike.

Chapter 2
Quebec: Demography, Language and Society

In Canada the majority of the population is English speaking. The overriding concern of francophone Quebecers must then be, and historically has been, to preserve the French language and to provide for the flourishing of francophone society. From a linguistic perspective, two main concerns are the birth rate of francophone Quebecers and of immigration enlarging the ranks of anglophones within the province. This Chapter provides an overall demographic picture of Quebec, as well as the significant transformation of Quebec society that occurred.

Quebec's Demographic Landscape
Birth Rate and Immigration

The birth rate of francophone Quebecers has been consistently dropping and has reached a level that represents the lowest in the Western world.[1] Between 1956 and 1961, the francophone birth rate was 4.2 percent, dropping to 2.3 percent between 1966–1971, and falling to 1.5 percent for the period of 1981–86, where it remained from 1986 to 1991.[2] Some assume a birth rate of 2.1 percent to assure the long term rejuvenation of the francophone population.[3]

It is hoped that through immigration, the French speaking portion of Quebec will be maintained or augmented. In the twenty years encompassing 1969 to1988, the average level of immigration was about 23,000.[4] However, since 1990, the numbers increased dramatically, varying from between 40,842 and 51,707, returning in 1994 to the more familiar number of 27,102 new immigrants.[5] Some, like Stéphan Dion, argue that, in reality, Quebec's birth rate is now comparable to the other regions of Canada when one factors into the calculation these more recent immigrants.[6]

Overall Demographics and Sub-Regions

In terms of overall numbers, francophone Quebecers constitute a great majority within the province of Quebec. The following figures give a basic overall linguistic picture. The percentage of Quebecers whose maternal language was French (i.e. language first learned in the home and still understood) dropped, from 82.5 percent in 1951 to 80.7 percent in 1971, and has since climbed back to the 1951 level.[7] One study revealed the following about maternal language and language most often spoken at home, in 1991, in Quebec: 82.2 percent of Quebecers were of the French maternal language, whereas, 83 percent of Quebecers most often spoke French at home; 9.7 percent were of the English maternal language, while 11.2 percent most often spoke English in the home; and 8.1 percent had neither English or French as their maternal language (allophone), and 5.8 percent spoke neither English or French most often in the home.[8] The population of Quebec in 1991 was 6,895,960.[9] A great majority of the population, consisting of 93.5 percent, affirmed that they were capable of carrying on a conversation in French.[10] Furthermore, 58.1 percent are unilingually French, 35.4 percent are bilingual, 5.5 percent are unilingually English and 1 percent understand neither English nor French.[11]

However, as one begins to focus on the Metropolitan region and Island of Montreal, the weight of francophones as a proportion of the population is not as great. In the region of Montreal,[12] in 1991, 68.5 percent were of the French maternal language, while 69.4 percent most often spoke French in the home; whereas, 15.7 percent were of the English maternal language and 19.3 percent most often spoke English in the home; and 15.8 percent had a maternal language that was neither French nor English, while 11.3 percent spoke neither French nor English most often in the home.[13] The population of the Montreal region in 1991 was 3,127,235.[14]

On the Island of Montreal,[15] for the same year, the 56.8 percent were of the French maternal language, while 58.4 percent most often spoke French at home; whereas, 20.6 percent had English for their maternal language and 25.7 percent most often spoke English at home; and 22.6 percent had neither French nor English for their maternal language, and 15.9 percent spoke neither French nor English most often in the home.[16] The population of

Montreal Island in 1991 was 1,775,870.[17] Finally, 83.8 percent of those from Montreal stated that they could carry on a conversation in French and 64.6 percent stated that they could speak English.[18]

The percentage of Quebecers whose maternal language is French has been increasing. Quebec's population grew approximately 782,000 or 13 percent from 1971 to 1991, whereas, those with French as their maternal language increased 14.7 percent[19]

One final element relates to 'linguistic transfer' in which one abandons one's maternal language in favour of another one as the one most often spoken in the home. The data suggests that by 1997, 36% of allophones underwent a linguistic transfer and tended to speak English more often by about 1.8 times.[20] However, since this figure does not include anglophones, it is difficult to compare with previous studies. In 1991, only 4.8 percent of Quebecers (317,000) persons stated that they had undergone a complete linguistic transfer in their lives in which the linguistic transfer of anglophones and allophones to the French language was well in excess of the numbers of francophones adopting the English language.[21]

Importance of Montreal

The region of Montreal, and particularly Montreal Island, is seen as important in the effort to preserve the French language in Quebec. In this area, the proportion of francophones diminish in comparison to the rest of Quebec, while still constituting a large majority. Furthermore, it is within this area that a vast majority of immigrants settle and where most anglophones reside. Contributing to this concentration is the "flight to the suburbs" phenomenon. Between 1986–91, 160,000 francophones departed the Island of Montreal, while 92,000 arrived, leaving a net loss of 68,000.[22] There was, during that time, a net loss of 84,000 people, 16,000 of which were anglophones and allophones.[23]

Quite clearly then, the French language in the province of Quebec outside the Montreal area is in a strong position and in no danger of being lost. The problem for most Quebecers is found within the Montreal area since the weight of francophones, while still remaining a substantial majority, is of a diminished proportion. Secondly, as a result of the concentration of immigrants and anglophones in this area, there is a fear that it will be more difficult to integrate allophones into francophone society, and who may, instead, adopt the English language to the detriment of the French language. Furthermore, It has been argued that due to federalism, contradictions such as bilingualism, multiculturalism, and cultural pluralism, on the one hand, create an ambiguity for immigrants in which they are torn between visions of a bilingual, multicultural Canada as opposed, on the other hand, to Quebec as a French province.[24] This contradiction is said to negatively affect their integration into and affinity for francophone Québécois society.

However, it is highly important to note that the proportion of the anglophone population diminished significantly in Quebec from 13.8 percent in 1951 to 9.7 percent in 1991,[25] while the anglophone birth rate was low at 1.5 percent for the time period 1981–1991.[26] By 1997, whereas the proportion of those with the French maternal language remained stable, the anglophone population diminished further to 8 percent in all of Quebec, 13 percent in the Region of Montreal and 17 percent on Montreal Island, and the percentage of people speaking English most often in the home decreased in all regions, especially Montreal.[27] Indeed, Quebec language legislation and growing Quebec nationalism served to increase the emigration of Quebec's anglophones and reduced further immigration from other provinces; those tending to migrate from other provinces to Quebec were francophones.[28]

Furthermore, the allophone population grew dramatically from 150,000 in 1951 to 559,872 in 1991.[29] By 1997, the allophone population constituted 9 percent of the Quebec population, 19 percent for the region of Montreal, and 26 percent on Montreal Island.[30] It is likely that under the demographic circumstances outlined, the allophone populations will be much easier to integrate into francophone society rather than anglophone society.

Care must be taken to bear in mind that the figures provided relate to maternal language and language most often spoken at home, not to the language most often used in public. Accordingly, these figures are missing an important element, which underestimates the strength of the French language in Quebec.

To address this deficiency, a study report was released on the public usage of the French language in Quebec, concerning the 1997 year. That report demonstrated the dominance of the public usage of the French language, including on Montreal Island.[31] Bearing in mind the present percentages regarding those of the French, English and other maternal languages, and languages spoken at home, the French language experiences the most dramatic gains as the province's public language in all regions. In all of Quebec, 87 percent used the French language in public, 11 percent the English language, and 1 percent spoke other languages.[32] In the region of Montreal, French was spoken by 78 percent of the population in public, English by 21 percent, and another language was used by 1 percent.[33] Even on Montreal Island, 71 percent spoke French in public, 28 percent English, and 2 percent another language.[34]

Therefore, even if the overall Québécois francophone population may lose some weight, that does not mean Quebec will be any less French. The changing face of Quebec society retains its French language and its dominant francophone culture. It is quite true that while, presently, the maternal language of many immigrants and the language most often spoken at home is not French, these same immigrants are very well integrated and participate using the French language in the public and collective life of Quebec. This fact exists despite no linguistic transfer to the French language occurring for many years, or even a transfer to the English language.

Given appropriate policies, the outlook for the survival and flourishing of the French language in Quebec is very positive. On the other hand, the struggle to retain a strong francophone presence in Canada outside of Quebec is far less certain. In 1991, 4.8 percent of the population had French for their maternal language outside Quebec; whereas, it was 6 percent in 1971.[35] Only 3.2 percent spoke French regularly at home compared to 4.4 percent in 1971.[36]

One final demographic concern of Quebecers relates to their relative weight in Canada, which has been diminishing. Linked with this concern is that if Quebec's relative weight declines, so too will its influence in Canada; an observation that helped to strengthen the nationalist cause in Quebec. Quebec's population as a percentage of the Canadian population dropped from 27.9 percent in 1971 to 25.3 percent in 1991, and finally to 24.8 percent in 1995.[37] The declining rate is due to several factors, including the province's low population growth, decreased immigration into Quebec, and outmigration from that province.

The Transformation of Quebec Society

Quebec society has undergone great changes such that its contemporary society resembles little its traditional roots. Traditional Quebec society was rural and religious, largely leaving business to anglophones, immigrants and foreigners, especially in the Montreal area. Government was anti-statist leaving much of education, welfare and health to Church institutions. Government protected the Church's role in society. Provincial jurisdiction was defended and, therefore, indigenous institutions protected. There was a pan-Canadian dimension to Quebec society in the sense that French Canadians outside Quebec were viewed as sharing the same language and as co-members of the Roman Catholic Church, therefore, were seen as entitled to the same protections enjoyed in Quebec. Finally, society was homogeneous. Its rural, Roman Catholic and French Canadian character was largely undisturbed by non-French elements. The birth rate was very high and net population growth resulted in emigration.

However, transitional forces drastically changed Quebec society. First and foremost, Quebec society underwent industrialization and urbanization, as was occurring elsewhere in Canada and the Western World. The shortage of arable land drove francophones to cities and industry. French speaking universities played a major role in the modernization of Quebec. The University of Montreal and Laval University mixed professional faculties and research, as anglophone Canada did, to produce technically oriented citizens suitable for the public and private sector. Instantaneous communication and television also played its role in Quebec's transformation.

By the 1960's, a profound secularization of Quebec society occurred and Church institutions lost their role in education, hospitals and welfare. There was more emphasis on individual values and fewer persons were practising their religious faith. The most important actors were now the new middle class, possessing highly specific and specialized skills.

Contemporary Quebec society is an integrated one in which francophones are involved in all occupations and sectors, including the private sector. Quebec governments became more active in society and the economy. These French-Canadians came to define themselves within the boundaries of the province. Quebec society is now heterogeneous and integrated resembling other parts of Canada.

The major factor that distinguishes Quebecers and other Canadians is still language. Francophones constitute a majority in Quebec, but, a minority in Canada. The Québécois share a common history and identity, which bind them together in outlook and interest. Another characteristic distinguishing Quebec from other parts of Canada includes the fact that civil law in Quebec is dictated by the Civil Code, whereas, other provinces follow the common law tradition. However, Quebec society is less distinct, and so too are the views and preferences of francophones and Quebecers *vis-à-vis* those of other Canadians with respect to most areas of public policy, and even way of life.[38]

Furthermore, there has been a sharper convergence among provinces, including Quebec, in patterns of public expenditures.[39]

Given that, to a great extent, due to global forces, Quebec society became less distinct from the rest of Canadian society, essentially being differentiated by language, many Quebecers felt within themselves a crisis of identity and a fear of assimilation of Québécois life because of a declining feeling of separateness. Other forces such as a growing multicultural composition and the emergence of new political pluralistic identities worked to undermine ideas of dualism or biculturalism, which may have existed in the past reinforcing a distinctive feeling within Quebecers.

Several authors stress this crisis of identity in explaining the rise of separatism in Quebec.[40] Some Quebec writers fear that this homogenization or convergence due to modernization, industrialization, urbanization, democracy, social mobility and the expansion of communications diminishes the desire of individuals and peoples to be distinct. For Dufour, the integration of another's cultural values is not the determining factor in a culture's eventual assimilation since national or ethnic identity for him is defined by its borders (i.e. the psychological border between members of different groups), and not by the content of that identity.[41] The relevant frontier is seen to be Quebec as a territory and boundary. It is thought to validate notions of a "people" and "nation", both concepts being useful in Canada and at the international level. Dufour believes that the border concerning Quebec's identity is still well defined and growing clearer due to the homogenization of cultural values.[42] The fear for him is the loss of political power for Quebec. Such loss is seen to strengthen Quebec's structural integration within Canada, which attacks the frontier that a national identity needs to survive. Yet, in a book published two years later, Dufour argues that the Americanization of English-Canada accentuates the process of linguistic and cultural assimilation of francophones, and he even suggests that the real peril comes from the United States.[43] However, he also states:

> Quebec is engaged in an agonizing process of folklorisation and assimilation, incapable of maintaining its minimal psychological integrity. The Quebec identity will literally break under the assaults on its identity and under the Canadian constitution, as I attempted to demonstrate in *Le Défi québécois*; the process has already began.[44] (translation)

One might wonder what occurred within those two years to justify such a negative outlook, and, particularly, moving from a position of clearly defined borders to a situation in which Quebec is incapable of maintaining its minimal psychological integrity.

Successive Chapters will examine whether or not, and to what extent, the Québécois have been acting successfully to protect the French language and to promote the flourishing of its francophone Quebec society. These actions and efforts, along with the political activism of Quebec governments will shed light upon whether or not the Québécois have been and are capable of maintaining their minimal psychological integrity.

Chapter 3
Quebec–English Canadian History

Numerous events during the history of Quebec-English Canadian relations from the Conquest to the FLQ crisis were conflictual in nature, especially with respect to certain issues of language, race, religion, and the British empire. Most often, the Quebec view on those issues, which attained a level of national importance, did not prevail over the view of the English Canadian majority, except when such issues arose within the borders of Quebec itself.

Some Quebecers argue that the Québécois collective conscience and historical memory, being structured on various defeats, diminished their confidence in themselves and, perhaps, even led to the Québécois questioning the value of their language and culture, which, in turn, may also diminish their willingness for and chances of survival. Therefore, the first theme of differing visions as a ground in support of separatism or sovereignty and the second theme of assimilation are implicated in this context.

Pre-Confederation

It must be recalled that being rivals as major powers, particularly during the eighteenth century, Britain and France often came into conflict with one another in Europe. Since these Powers were also imperialistic and trading rivals, their conflicts spread the world over and included North America. Not only had North America become part of several wars as a by-product of the conflicts between Britain and France, it also experienced conflicts specific to that territory, especially regarding the fur trade. The wars included the war of 1627 between England and France, the War of Devolution (1667), the Dutch War of 1672–78, the War of Spanish Succession (1702–1713), the War of

Austrian Succession (1744–1748), and the Seven Years War (1754–63) in which the outbreak of hostilities occurred two years earlier in North America than in Europe.

In the course of the Seven Years War, major forces were sent to North America. Although heavily outnumbered by almost twenty to one, New France did very well and even held the upper hand for a time. By 1758, the British, under Prime Minister Pitt, came to see North America as a primary theatre of war and sent substantial forces.[1] The French, on the other hand, would not commit a large army and, indeed, sent few reinforcements. In 1759, as part of a massive three pronged attack by the British, the Battle of the Plains of Abraham took place. The British under Wolfe succeeded in overcoming the French under Montcalm. Finally, in 1760, when Montreal fell to the British, so too did New France.

It should be noted that during this period, and particularly in April, when the French defeated a British army under Murray outside Quebec and were prepared to retake the city, the French were expecting reinforcements from France, but few arrived. France decided that New France was lost and abandoned it. When only British reinforcements arrived and being heavily outnumbered, the French had no alternative but to surrender. On February 10, 1763, the Treaty of Paris was signed. During the conquest discussions, England had to decide whether or not it would retain New France or the French West Indian sugar island of Guadeloupe. The French wanted the fisheries and so were able to retain the "French shore" of Newfoundland and recovered St. Pierre and Miquelon. France received Guadeloupe for Minorca and lost New France.[2]

Nonetheless, some writers from Quebec refer to the fall of New France as surviving in the psyche of many present day Quebecers; a term referred to as *conqêtisme*. Somehow, despite this interesting history, 1763 survives to the present as a reminder that the French are a conquered and not an equal people.

Since the Conquest, French and English identities became intertwined. Indeed, writers like Laforest and Dufour believe that English-French relations are structured on the Conquest, which implies that francophones are a conquered people even today, at least on a symbolic level, as manifested by certain historical events and recently by the refusal to recognize Quebec as a political community and a national collectivity in the Constitution. Laforest writes:

For Quebec to have a renaissance, it must learn to go beyond the conquest; this is the challenge and the opportunity that presents itself to us at the end of the twentieth century.[3] (translation)

By the time of the Conquest, New France established an order and way of life primarily centred on agriculture and the fur trade. After the Conquest, it does not appear that the Habitants manifested either opposition or great enthusiasm for the new regime.

It is not unfair to say that the British treated the French with tolerance, at least from the perspective that they did not try to destroy that colony, nor were forced assimilation or deportations undertaken.[4] The Royal Proclamation of 1763 could be seen as an attempt at assimilation, for example through denying public employment to Catholics, or through the use of immigration policy. Yet, Governor Murray put aside the Act's most unjust features. The *Quebec Act* of 1774 protected French civil law, and it reinforced seigneurial tenure, the system of land tenure then existing in New France. A degree of official status was conferred on the Roman Catholic Church and the borders of Quebec were enlarged.

The *Constitution Act, 1791* separated Upper Canada (now, Ontario) and Lower Canada (now, Quebec), each with a system of government headed by a Governor, Executive Council, elected assembly and a judiciary. This period experienced tensions between the British and French. The British often accusing the Habitants of using outmoded farming techniques and advocated their assimilation. The French naturally reacted to such comments and even defended French loyalty to the British.

Both Upper and Lower Canada experienced Rebellions in 1837–38. In Lower Canada, the Rebellion was more nationalistic. However, each Rebellion was basically a movement against a system of government. The Rebellion in Lower Canada was more nationalistic in the sense that the system of government was dominated by the English, therefore, the Rebellion was against such domination.

Other causes of the Rebellion in Lower Canada were identified[5] and include the economic crisis arising from the decline of the fur trade, an agricultural crisis and a general fall in prices. The seigneurial system was becoming an increasingly heavy burden, and by the 1820's the seigneuries became overpopulated and outmigration occurred. The mercantile middle class wanted to dissolve or reform the traditional way of life, including the seigneurial system. Finally, there was a fear of assimilation of the Habitants' lifestyle.

These political, economic and social issues contributing to the Rebellion of Lower Canada tended to coincide with racial delineations and class boundaries and were transposed to the political level as, for example, by demanding an elected legislative council. Finally, personalities such as Papineau were important to bring about the Rebellion. The Rebellion in Lower Canada was a more serious affair than that of Upper Canada with bloodier skirmishes, but, in the end, did not amount to a general and widespread rebellion.

The Rebellions led to investigations on the matter and the well known Lord Durham's Report. In that report, Lord Durham cited several problems such as government not being responsible to the elected assembly and that of racial conflict between the French and English of Lower Canada. The Report itself created controversy in maintaining that the French were less progressive and inferior as a result of their institutions, namely, the seigneurial system, the Church and due to the lack of proper education, which in turn repressed freedom, governmental involvement and intelligence. Lord Durham stated that the Rebellion in Lower Canada was also a result of the French possessing a separate settlement and, therefore, an intercolonial union was advocated, as was the assimilation of the French.

The *Act of Union, 1840* did not provide for the assimilation contemplated in Lord Durham's Report. Indeed, in the term of Governor Elgin, the first case of the acceptance of responsible government arose. Responsible government originated in Lord Elgin giving his approval to the Rebellion Losses Bill, which would compensate land owners whose property was destroyed during the Rebellion. Such acceptance was based on the advice of his executive council, composed of the leaders of the majority from the Assembly called upon to form a government, despite the fact that Lord Elgin was himself personally opposed to the Bill's contents.

Confederation

Confederation was brought about in response to circumstances faced by the British North American colonies that were beyond the capability of a divided colony to deal with adequately. Reciprocity was cancelled between the Colony and the United States, and changes in the British economy created commerce and trade problems for the Colony. Confederation was intended to improve the economic outlook of Canada through a national economy, which was to relieve dependence upon a few industries, lessen exposure to the effects of British and American economic policies and to deal with the problem of public debt.[6]

The American threat of annexation was manifested, in the past, by the Thirteen Colonies' attack on Quebec and the American invasion during the War of 1812. The Civil War, having itself created tensions between Canadians and Americans, left the Americans with a huge fighting force, and, coupled with the Fenian raids, encouraged a desire for a consolidated defence. Britain further encouraged Confederation by offering some trade benefits and by withdrawing its troops from the Colony, which meant that it would have to consolidate its own defence.

Perhaps, most importantly, there was political and sectional deadlock that arose from the *Act of Union* between Upper Canada, with its English majority, and Lower Canada, with its French majority. The deadlock, in effect, frustrated effective government and stability due to the requirement of double majority as the elected members of Upper Canada could rarely agree with those of Lower Canada.

Entering Confederation under the circumstances would necessarily entail compromise. The French wanted to protect their nationality and religion by protecting rights in Quebec. Provincial autonomy was sought in the Constitution to safeguard these interests and to free Quebec from English influence. The French rejected the need for a strong central government to provide for stability and feared the antagonization of localities.

The Fathers of Confederation knew the French Canadians would reject complete centralization as would the Maritimes. However, the Quebec Resolutions did not create a real system of federalism either. Rather, it provided the closest thing possible to a legislative union, but, provided guarantees for the French language, nationality and religion. The power to promote national life in Quebec was guaranteed through provincial control over education, civil and religious institutions, and the ownership and control of land and municipal affairs.

Despite the wording of the *Constitution Act, 1867*, including the lack of global recognition of Quebec's distinctiveness, Confederation was interpreted by many French Canadians to be an alliance or association of autonomous provinces, whose co-operation for common welfare would be regulated by a treaty drawn up among them. This exaggeration of an interprovincial compact was central for many French Canadians to accept Confederation and, again, despite the wording in the document itself, the federal Parliament was believed to have jurisdiction only on issues of general concern, like defence.[7]

In support of this compact view, it was true that section 94 of the

Constitution Act, 1867 did allow for uniformity of civil laws in provinces other than Quebec. Section 133 affirmed the official status of the French language in Quebec, in federal Parliament and in the courts. On the other hand, section 93 limited provincial powers to deprive the separate school system once they officially existed before Confederation.

More important, however, was the centralized nature of the Confederation document. There were, as we will see, unitary features of the Confederation settlement, which made it quasi-federal and central in nature, and not truly federal. Secondly, the bulk of the taxation powers, at that time, were transferred to the federal government as it assumed most of the financial burdens.[8] The indirect taxes, particularly customs and excise, constituting eighty percent of provincial revenues were transferred to the federal government.[9] The less costly functions of the provinces were matched with the less extensive taxation powers of direct taxation and licensing fees, and it was expected that provincial burdens would not grow dramatically.[10] Furthermore, federal statutory subsidies to the provinces were also contemplated under section 118 of the 1867 *Constitution Act.*

Post-Confederation

A series of conflicts developed between the English and French in Canada before and during the beginning of the twentieth century such that the French Canadians in Quebec began to identify more and more with Quebec.

The *Constitution Act, 1867* was itself a source of conflict. The Protestant minority of Lower Canada influenced the making of that Act. As a result, due to section 133 of the Act, English became entrenched in Quebec. One had the right to use the English language in the legislature and judicial institutions of Quebec, making it the only province entering Confederation with two official languages. The English position in Quebec was further enhanced through the Galt proposals of 1866, which protected English constituency ridings.

Such concessions created bitterness at the prominence of this Anglo-Protestant minority in a French-Catholic province. Meanwhile, these concessions were not reciprocated as French and Catholic minorities were losing rights and privileges in other provinces.

Further divisions with respect to ethnic and religious elements in Canadian life resulted in assertions by both the French and English of their particular traditional and opposing interests. Such interests related to religion, race and nationalism, which at times created and reinforced mutual resentment and reinforced the lack of homogeneity in Canada.

The previous interest of Quebec as a bastion of French-Canadian nationality was later combined with a concern for French minorities in other provinces. Quebec sympathy for franco-minorities resisting assimilation reflected a concern for the French Fact, which even became a conviction that the very existence of Confederation was based on such minority rights.[11] Quebec's identification with francophone minorities in the course of conflicts with "Ontario fanatics" and co-Confederationists convinced French Canadians that they would lose to the English majority on religious matters, or questions of national importance. It was believed by some that the losses sustained by franco-minorities constituted not only symbolic defeats for Quebec, but, indicated the eventual defeat of Quebec itself.

Confederation was also intended to facilitate expansion into the Northwest. Originally, Quebec did not look at this area as part of their country, nor did they see the French-Catholic Métis as part of their nationality. In fact, Quebec viewed the Red River uprising as a defence of local self-determination and saw the rebels' defeat as desirable.

Ontario papers interpreted the uprising in a perverse manner, accusing the Catholic clergy of encouraging the Catholic Métis 'barbarians'.[12] William McDougall, the appointed Lieutenant-Governor, spread notions that the insurrection was designed to overthrow British institutions and to create a French-Catholic province.[13] The execution by the Provisional Métis government of the Orangeman Scott, who attempted to lead a counter-Riel movement, was used by expansionist minded Canada Firsters in Ontario to arouse violent agitation by exploiting ethnic and religious hatred.

Quebec attributed these unjust attacks to fanaticism, which obsessed people like the Canada Firsters. Initially being against the killing of Scott, Quebec was drawn to the side of those responsible for Scott's killing. It was as a result of Quebec's view that Ontario wanted to repress the Métis because they were French and Catholic, and not just rebels, that Quebec began to favour the Métis. The Northwest was beginning to be seen as a second French-Canadian province and an ally of Quebec to balance Ontario's power.

When the uprising fell, Canadian rule was established. There were persecutions of French Métis that culminated in the killing of Goullet by Ontarians. Of course, no demands were made by Ontario for a trial arising out of that killing. An Orange lodge was set up in the area, which further alienated the Métis.

Bishop Taché of Quebec carried assurances of amnesty from Parliament and was confident that it covered all eventualities. Due to Ontario agitation over the Scott affair, Prime Minister Macdonald postponed the official application of amnesty and later denied the existence of it altogether. This was so despite the fact that Lépine and Riel both aided Canada during the Fenian Crisis. The question must surely have been asked in Quebec whether Ontario conclusively dominated Canadian politics.

After the arrest of Lépine in September of 1873, Quebec demanded a general amnesty to prevent further harassment of the Métis by Ontarians. Lépine's death sentence was commuted, but, Riel was still expelled from the House of Commons and banished. The accusation was made that Riel was betrayed to satisfy Anglo-Protestant fanaticism. Later, ordinances and press campaigns were launched both against separate schools and the official use of French in the West.

With further settlement, the Métis and Riel rebelled again in 1885. Again, Quebec and the Catholic Church were ambivalent toward the rebellion and desired its hasty suppression. French battalions were even sent to quell the rebellion. However, there was some sympathy towards the Métis, especially since some of the Ontario francophobe fanaticism seemed to be directed at Quebec.

Once the rebellion was put down, Quebec urged moderation in dealing with its participants. The hanging of Riel seemed to signify the defeat of French influence in favour of the demands of Orangemen. Some elements of the French view even went so far as to say that the execution was part of an attempt to eliminate French Catholics in the Northwest. The Riel affair was the first incidence of Quebec directing its attention beyond the borders of the province to protect bilingualism as part of the Confederation idea. It also served as a comparison with the privileged position of the Anglo-Protestants of Quebec.

In 1871, New Brunswick passed a common school act preventing local Boards from raising tax support for denominational schools. Only when J. Costigan went to the House of Commons to petition for the Act's disallowance in 1873, did Quebec become fully aware and concerned about the situation. In effect, the law deprived the right to send one's children to the school of choice.

In the House of Commons, the Bleu Party of Quebec was concerned not to anger the Protestant majority, or other minority Catholics might suffer. A further concern was that a precedent of federal intervention in education might be applied in Quebec. The courts, when faced with the issue, ruled that these denominational schools did not exist "by law"; that is, they were not established by provincial law, therefore, section 93 of the *Constitution Act, 1867* could not be used to aid the minority Catholics.[14]

In the end, the federal government did not encroach on provincial powers to reinstate Catholic school rights in New Brunswick. The arrest of Acadians, who refused to pay school taxes, and the violence at the Acadian village of Caraquet made Quebec think that these measures signified an attack on Catholicism and the French in New Brunswick. Franco-Ontarians would also face declining cultural privileges.

In 1890, D'Alton McCarthy, an Anglo-Saxon supremacist and imperialist, began to attack French language rights in the Northwest while the Manitoba schools controversy was beginning.[15] Manitoba had a common school system, but, certain privileges in practice were granted in favour of Catholicism and the French language in districts with large French or Catholic enrolment. The Manitoba school question became the French-Canadian national question in a political atmosphere in which there were other attacks against the French language. Such events led to an unprecedented involvement of Quebec politics and opinion. Due to the recent push from Quebec for more autonomy and assertion of their language and religion, many English Canadians made a concerted effort towards Canadian unification, criticizing the French language and separate schools as constituting sowers of separatism.

The Manitoba School Act and the McCarthy Bill were seen as war on the French race. The French Canadians interpreted the measure to be aimed against the protected rights contained in the Constitution and outside of provincial jurisdiction to disturb. The Judicial Committee of the Privy Council, however, found the Act constitutional.[16] The ruling angered many and led to the questioning of rights guaranteed to minorities. Quebec began to postulate that biculturalism and bilingualism were the basis of Confederation as an agreement of two nations.

The Liberals under Prime Minister Laurier were elected to power due largely to Conservative inaction on the issue. Laurier did not protect minority educational rights through the remedial legislation section 93(4) of the *Constitution Act, 1867*. The reason was that Laurier, instead, wished to affirm provincial autonomy.

By this time, the French Canadians could only be certain of equality in Quebec despite constitutional guarantees. It was thought that the only way to alleviate the problem, even if only temporarily, would be through English acceptance of cultural duality.

The Mercier, Parti National Party in Quebec arose out of the Riel Affair and their platform of nationality further divided French and English Canadians. English Canadians worried that Mercier was trying to set up a French-Catholic state. Indeed, Mercier did come to power with the aid of the conservative Ultramontane Castors, who believed that the Church should play a dominant role in preserving the French-Canadian nationality. Curé Labelle was appointed Deputy Minister of Agriculture and Colonization. The English did not like the appointment as it did not coincide with their notion of a separate church and state. In the end, perhaps, this alliance was more apparent than real since the rest of the ministers were liberals.

In June of 1890, Mercier began to travel in Europe for commercial and diplomatic reasons to strengthen Quebec. In fact, Mercier came back with a loan of four million dollars from Paris. The English thought this act to be one of disloyalty as it was not compatible with British Imperialism.

At the Catholic Congress of Baltimore, Mercier stated:

> We have returned to the Church, through the Jesuits the possessions of which they were despoiled by the same George III who wished to despoil you of your rights and liberties.[17]

With this speech, the Jesuit Estate controversy began. Quebec conservatives themselves were afraid of what appeared to be the beginning of a war of race and religion.

After the Conquest, Jesuit lands were confiscated and used for public education in Lower Canada and then Quebec. When the Jesuits returned to Canada, their campaign to get back the land previously taken created a division within the Church.

The University of Laval, in Quebec, possessed a monopoly on higher Catholic education at the time. Monseigneur Bourget wished to change this situation with a Jesuit university located in Montreal from Jesuit Estate lands. This division was, of course, a stumbling block to the settlement of the Jesuit Estates problem. The result of the battle itself was, however, indecisive as it was waged on two fronts — in Rome and in Quebec.

The Protestants began to worry that this situation was the beginning of Catholic efforts to control the province and usurp public funds for their own use. In 1886, Mercier incorporated the Jesuits and attempted to solve the conflict through the *Jesuits Estates Act*. Compensation was given to those Pope Leo XIII thought were entitled. In total, $400,000 was apportioned to the Church and $60,000 to the Protestants.[18]

The Protestants were suspicious of Catholics trying to maintain absolute control and to extend the Church's civil and ecclesiastical power. They viewed the Jesuits as a political, Catholic movement attempting to attain Papal control of the world. From this perspective, the Catholics were seen as a threat, especially when combined with French-Canadian nationalism and ultramontane religious nationalism. The Protestants of Quebec saw the Estates Act as part of a general campaign to push them out of the province, and it was a symbol of the erosion of their influence. Ontarians saw this event as an attempt at French domination.

Thus, it seemed as if there was no way to settle matters of race or religion uncontroversially. Ontario was always ready to contest their rival, Quebec, who they believed was the source of Ontario's grievances of French domination, Catholic aggression and as representing anti-progress. A petition was issued that the rights of the minority in Quebec should be upheld through disallowance of the Act. The Equal Rights Association was a very influential pressure group on this matter. McCarthy argued that the Estates Act was *ultra vires* the province because it violated the rule of separation of Church and State. Further, since it depended on the Pope and ignored the Queen, it was a danger to the country. In the end, the then Minister of Justice, Sir Thompson, defended the position not to use the disallowance power and the Act survived.

The Boer War introduced new ideas of imperialism and nationalism to national strife in Canada. The split occurred between supporters of French-Canadian nationalism and those in favour of British Imperialism. Quebec was unanimously against participation in the war, or to yielding to Ontario sentiment and British pressure on the matter. The view was that Quebec was far removed from European quarrels and that such conflicts were invariably waged in the British interest alone. Furthermore, it was thought that Canada did not owe the British anything.

Indeed, Britain would not make a sacrifice for Canadian interests as evidenced by the Alaska Boundary Award of 1903 dealing with the dispute over the interpretation of the Anglo-Russian Treaty of 1825 regarding the boundary of Alaska. The tribunal was comprised of three Americans, two Canadians and one British. The tribunal divided on national lines until the British member gave way to American pressure and sided with the Americans over the Canadians.

Ontario accused Quebec of disloyalty and maintained that English Canada was living under inferior French domination. When volunteers were sent,

Prime Minister Laurier maintained and the Order-in-Council affirmed that sending volunteers to participate in the Boer War did not create a precedent for future Imperial wars and that the Canadian Parliament was sovereign and independent of Britain.

Therefore, English-French relations in Canada up to the dawn of the twentieth century demonstrated that Confederation did not always ensure social unity or harmony through political union. Sensitive areas like religion and nationality continued to sever French-English relations. Anglo-Protestant minority rights in Quebec granted under the Constitution made French Canadians interested in preserving French and Catholic rights inside and outside of Quebec. Such minority rights lost out to English interests outside of Quebec and made Quebec more interested in a bilingual and bicultural view of Confederation. However, such loses, and the fact that the French seemed to be posited as inferior, led Quebec to attempt to consolidate its own interests, which in turn provoked the English to crusade for unity, leading to further problems in their relations.

The twentieth century again featured conflicts between English and French. In 1905, when Saskatchewan and Alberta were created, there was some controversy regarding whether the French language and Roman Catholic schools would be provided for in the constitution of the new provinces. English Canada wanted a public school system and only English to be used. The Liberal government then in power in Ottawa was divided regarding bilingualism and biculturalism. In the end, Prime Minister Laurier had to back down to a position of guaranteed language and religious rights, but on a watered down version.

Such a position antagonized French Canadians, such as Henri Bourassa and other Quebecers, who saw Confederation as an agreement of two nations on the basis of equality of status throughout Canada. Laurier rejected this view in favour of the view that each province must create its own identity.

Other imperialistic questions would divide British and French Canadians. In the early, twentieth century, the British became increasingly nervous about the growing power of Germany and its navy. In 1909, Britain asked for Canadian contributions to meet the German challenge. English Canada wanted to aid Britain and French Canada was antagonized over the matter.

In 1910, there were calls to create a Canadian navy which could be put under British command should there be war. The Imperialists viewed this idea as a "tin pot" navy scheme that would leave Britain weak and, instead, favoured direct contributions to Britain. French Canadian nationalists saw this idea as a loss of Canadian autonomy and as pressure from Britain for imperialist wars. The Liberal Prime Minister Laurier opted for the Canadian Navy option and the *Naval Act* was passed. One year later, the Laurier government was defeated in a general election.

In 1912, the Conservative Prime Minister Borden elected for direct contributions, causing French resignations in his party. Borden was, thereafter, shut out of Quebec. Laurier rejected the idea of an immediate need for contributions. The Borden government proposed an emergency contribution of $35 million to Britain for navy purposes to build three dreadnoughts. The Bill was forced through the House of Commons by May 15, 1912. Five Quebec conservatives voted against the Bill. The Senate, however, did not pass the Conservative Naval Bill and the Bill died.

Initially, it was thought that the First World War would be a short one. As time went on, it became apparent that the War was really a struggle of endurance. In 1914, most Canadians agreed with the government's decision to support Britain. Anti-imperialists like Henri Bourassa were in agreement as long as conscription was not introduced:

> It was Canada's natural duty to contribute, within the bounds of her strength and by the means which are proper to herself to the triumph, and especially to the endurance, of the combined efforts of France and England.[19]

Canadians from every province enlisted. But, as the war dragged on, volunteer enlistments and enthusiasm for Canadian involvement declined.

In 1917, Prime Minister Borden attended the Imperial War Cabinet summoned by British Prime Minister David Lloyd George. The main issue was that the British Army was running out of men to continue the war effort. This period was seen as critical for the War's outcome.

The volunteers were largely British born Canadians from cities that joined the war effort and not as many from Quebec were joining, particularly, outside of Montreal, nor were there many from rural Canada enlisting. In the rural areas, there was the least contact with military traditions and the organized social pressure for enlistment was not felt to the same extent as in the cities. Quebec was still a very rural society at this time. Another part of the explanation of why Quebecers were not joining as much was that there was a sense that French Canada and Europe were very different and that the war was really a European fight. French-Canadian soldiers were being commanded in English. There was a distrust of Britain. In addition, Ontario and Manitoba eliminated publically supported French language schools, which antagonized the French of Quebec.

On May 17, 1917, three days after Borden's return to Canada, the intention to introduce conscription was announced. The *Military Voters Act* and the *War Elections Act* were passed, which denied the franchise to conscientious objectors, those of enemy birth, or those of European birth speaking an enemy language. The franchise was given to all on active service and their wives, or widows of dead servicemen, and female relatives of servicemen overseas. Masson Wade writes that given the temper of English-speaking Canada, these measures were hardly necessary as an election winning device and constituted gratuitous affronts to many naturalized Canadians.[20] The *Conscription Act* was introduced on June 11, 1917 and passed on the 28th of August. The election of December 17, 1917 produced, as expected, a pro-Conscription union government.

In Quebec, resistance was strongest and the proposal met with general opposition, which culminated in mass demonstrations in Montreal. There was, also, resistance to conscription emanating outside of Quebec by organized labour, agriculture and liberal pacifists like the Social Gospel Movement, and by other groups who opposed the war based on religious beliefs.

Between the Wars, in 1926, a territorial dispute over Labrador took place between Quebec and Newfoundland, which was decided in favour of the latter. Many Quebecers did not accept this decision and termed this episode *La Perte du Labrador* (the loss of Labrador).

During the latter stages of World War II, the combined impact of Normandy and the offensive in southern Italy brought Mackenzie King to face again the question of conscription, even though the war was nearing its end. In November of 1944, a partial conscription was instituted in which approximately 13,000 conscripts were sent from the home service forces, the NRMA. English Canada tended to be in favour, while Quebec tended to oppose. Again there was some outcry from Quebec with the conscription crisis of World War I relatively fresh in their minds. However, in 1944, it was less violent and its aftermath much milder and shorter than anticipated. Not only did France fall, the Second World War could hardly be called a British Imperialist war.

Although the Quiet Revolution in Quebec was not an event of conflict between Quebecers and other Canadians, it did result in a new nationalism and assertiveness, which brought Quebec and Canada into conflict with respect to differing visions of what the new role of the Quebec government should be in this new modernized Quebec. Such conflicts arose especially in the context of constitutional reform, and with respect to the battles over citizen conceptions of community. Quiet Revolution reforms, improvements and impacts have been and will continue to be examined in this study. It bears noting that prior to these reforms, francophone Quebecers trailed anglophones within and outside of Quebec with respect to education and the economy. The same would not be true after the reforms.

Finally, among the issues that likely least affected division between Quebecers and other Canadians was the FLQ crisis. The FLQ was a loosely organized body with little overall co-ordination, numbering 133 active members in 22 cells and 2000 sympathizers.[21] In an attempt to gain recognition for their cause, the FLQ used terrorist bombings, kidnappings and even murder. There was little disagreement among Canadians that such activities were not to be tolerated within Canada. All the major separatist parties denounced the FLQ. With the declaration of the War Measures Act, civil liberties were suspended in Quebec, and with the FLQ killing of the kidnapped Quebec Labour Minister Laporte, two hundred and forty-two people were arrested without probable cause of any crime having been committed.[22] There was criticism on the part of some Quebecers regarding whether such measures were too extreme in view of the fact that detainees may have been innocent of any wrongdoing. However, at the same time, there was a genuine fear of further terrorist activities and killings if action was not taken. In the end, after the release of the kidnapped British Trade Commissioner Cross, seven FLQ kidnappers were flown to Cuba and there was no further evidence of FLQ terrorist activities.

Chapter 4
Historical Background: Constitutional

The written Constitution has been of considerable concern to Quebecers. It is seen as important because it provides a quasi-permanent framework for the governance of society. All three themes underlying arguments in favour of Quebec separatism or sovereignty are present at this level.

First, the Constitutional issue is said to demonstrate that Quebecers and other Canadians have visions of Canada that are too fundamentally different and irreconcilable. The Constitution is seen as highly important, not only regarding the terms of its legal text, but, perhaps, more so, regarding what vision it reflects of the country. Quebec's constitutional search for more powers and the long, arduous and ultimately unsuccessful process of constitutional accommodation and recognition as a distinct society is a case in point. The essential view is that given Quebec's distinctive situation, of a majority francophone population contained within an anglophone dominated Canada and North America, Quebec should have or requires powers that distinguish it from other provinces. In addition, given that it was a founding nation of Canada, it should be treated on an equal plane within Canada with respect to the rest of Canada, or at least with special status within a decentralized Canada. Such explicit recognition that Canada is composed of two peoples/nations, or more recently framed in terms of distinct society recognition in the Constitution, has been unsuccessfully sought. Also, especially since the Quiet Revolution, Quebec governments have been asserting an increasing desire to control the principle aspects of Quebec's economic, social and political life, along with the political tools to accomplish that task.[1]

Far from accommodating this two nation theory and respect for diversity, the Constitution after 1982, is said to undermine it.[2] The Charter aims to elucidate values citizens hold as members of the national community. It represents a centralization of power, reinforced by the importance of federal institutions.

Again, contrary to a vision of a decentralized Canada, the use of the federal spending power in areas of exclusive provincial jurisdiction is thought to allow the federal government to influence provincial priorities and to constrain provincial autonomy through the mere existence of federal spending, or through conditions attached to those transfers.

For some authors, what underlies the argument in favour of separatism or sovereignty arising from the unsuccessful search for constitutional accommodation by Quebec governments is the inability to obtain powers it needs to protect the French language and to provide for the flourishing of francophone society. In short, the second theme is implicated and there is a real danger of assimilation and a decline in the quality of francophone life in Quebec.

Furthermore, far from Canadian federalism facilitating these goals, it is argued that federalism further hindered their achievement after 1982 with the Charter. For example, in terms of the protection of the French language, Quebec's power was weakened as the Charter imposes restrictions upon it by guaranteeing English minority language education rights in Quebec on terms that are broader than those which were otherwise desired. The second fear generated by the Charter is far less apparent. The true purpose of the Charter is said to restructure the conceptions of loyalties of all Canadians, including Quebecers, in favour of Canada to the detriment of the provinces. Accordingly, the psychological barriers thought necessary for the preservation of the French language and the distinctiveness of francophone society are under assault given the entrenchment of new values and rights shared by all Canadians equally on the same terms, and, indeed, enforced by central institutions.[3]

The final theme reflected in the constitutional arena is that of illegitimacy. There are several possible strands to this argument. The most extreme form is that the French-Canadians (Quebecers) are a conquered nation, and, as such, Canada is illegitimate. Of course, this argument ignores the facts that France and Britain were warring rivals, the French-Canadians democratically entered Confederation and have not been treated as a conquered people, nor does Quebec's condition support any such "conquered" view.

Secondly, aside from its dubious validity as a matter of international law, the mere argument that a "nation" or "people" may always constitute its own political entity without question, as Premier Bouchard apparently maintains, is really, from a philosophical perspective, with little credence. In virtually all state entities, there will always be members of different "nations" or distinct "peoples", and to reorder the world on the basis of nations or peoples would not only be practically impossible to bring about, it would cause an inexorable, unsustainable and likely permanent amount of conflict, uncertainty and unrest. Therefore, such a proposition is too internally and fundamentally contradictory to serve as a basis for an absolute principle. The integrity of state units within the international order must be given great weight in the balance with self-determination. At a minimum, therefore, it would appear that any principle of national self-determination, aside from the legal requirements which must be satisfied, ought to be qualified by the "people" clearly and explicitly choosing this route in a context where it cannot, due to fundamental systemic aspects, reasonably exist within that state entity.[4] Thus, that the people of the relevant nation are prevented or excessively hindered from expressing or living according to their beliefs, or are prevented or practically obstructed from gaining a livelihood by persons of another group or "nation" within the entity, or are denied access and participation to the apparatus of government would satisfy this criteria. At the same time, such expression, life or livelihood thereby impeded, for example as a result of oppression or assimilation, should otherwise be consistent with the fundamental human rights of other people within that state entity.

Another illegitimacy argument, and one which is vigorously maintained by some separatists or sovereignists, is that the Constitution of Canada, as amended in 1982, is illegitimate given that not only was it not assented to by Quebec, Quebec was actually betrayed and stabbed in the back by the other Canadian governments in the process. Furthermore, it is said the ratification process was flawed from a legitimacy perspective.

The final strand of the illegitimacy argument is that the federal government illegitimately usurped for itself the federal spending power and began spending in areas of exclusive provincial jurisdiction. Not only is it said that such a power was not provided for in the Constitution, it has been used as a tremendous centralizing device. As a result, its use has subverted the entire Confederation agreement.

The balance of this Chapter outlines the long and arduous process of amending the written constitution. It is clear that differences still remain among Canadians regarding the visions they hold for the Canadian Constitution. Indeed, Kenneth McRoberts maintains that this debate has been sustained without hearing, let alone understanding what the other side is saying; a kind of "dialogue of the deaf."[5] Demands with respect to duality and distinct status for Quebec were resisted, especially during and after the time of Prime Minister Trudeau. On the other hand, many believe that Quebec can exist very well and even better within Canada than outside of it. Canada is intended, especially according to Trudeau, to reflect certain values like official bilingualism, a common set of entrenched rights (including language rights) and multiculturalism.

The Road to Patriation

The *Constitution Act, 1867* was a British statue by nature. Although agreed to by the parties entering Confederation, it was required to be enacted by Britain. The Act was itself incomplete, lacking essential features characteristic of a fully independent state. Among the lacking features were the existence of a constitutional amending formula, and the fact that Canada did not have true control over its foreign relations. With the Balfour declaration of 1926, recognizing Canada as an equal of the United Kingdom, a new domestic amending procedure would have to be established.

The Conference of 1929–30 produced no agreement regarding an amending formula. However, the *Statute of Westminster* was enacted in 1931 giving to Canada legal independence from Britain. In part, this independence meant that Canada could now pass a law even if it conflicted with British law. Prior to this statue, such an act would have been struck down by a court as being repugnant to the British statute.

Furthermore, Canada would have power over foreign relations. Now, for all practical purposes, Canada appeared to have all the trappings of an independent state except for a domestic constitutional amending formula. Accordingly, the only permissible amendments continued to be ones passed by the British Parliament.

The British Parliament passed several amendments to the Canadian Constitution. The most significant amendments affecting the division of jurisdiction after 1931 received the unanimous consent of the provinces directly involved. An interesting example arose in this respect, in 1949, when Newfoundland was admitted into Canada on the basis of consent of those provinces directly involved and despite the fact that other provinces did not agree or were not consulted. Other examples of significant amendments passed include the creation of various provinces under the *Constitution Act, 1871*. Another major amendment to the Constitution arose as a consequence of the Great Depression and a Judicial Committee of the Privy Council decision holding the federal Unemployment Insurance scheme to be unconstitutional. The provinces later agreed to transfer jurisdiction to the federal government. In 1951 and 1964, jurisdiction over old age pensions was transferred to the federal government on a concurrent basis with provincial paramountcy under section 94A of the *Constitution Act*.

Finally, in 1949, section 91(1) of the *Constitution Act, 1867* was added to permit the federal government to amend national elements of the Constitution, which paralleled the provincial amendment power contained in section 92(1) of that Act. Both amendment powers were of limited scope. Pursuant to this power, the provincial government could abolish its upper house, as done in Quebec. The same would not, however, be true of the federal government when it attempted to abolish the Senate under its amendment power.[6]

In fact, the inability to agree upon a constitutional amendment, although an irritant, did not prove to be a pressing matter until the 1960's. As D.V. Smiley stated:

> Prior to the 1960's there was an underlying consensus in Canada that the constitution itself did not stand in the way of any legitimate purposes that individuals and groups might want to pursue ... Thus the increasing disposition of Canadians toward explicit constitutional reform is a relatively new development, with few roots in our earlier history.[7]

The Quiet Revolution marked a turning point in the views of Quebecers regarding their future. Quebec, under Premier Lesage, sought an expansion of provincial powers to protect its distinct culture and language. With Daniel Johnson, there was a change in tone and perspective. Now, the assertion of the urgency for radical constitutional reform was backed by the threat of independence. A series of constitutional conferences were held, which featured the themes of a domestic amendment formula, Quebec seeking more jurisdiction, and, later, the idea of a Charter of rights and freedoms emerged.

In 1965, the Fulton-Favreau formula was discussed requiring unanimous consent of the provinces and federal government on most amendments. The amendment was rejected by Quebec, even though it would have given Quebec a constitutional veto, because it wanted a transfer of power before any agreement on amendments would be reached. The fear was that such agreement would not be forthcoming later.

In that same year, a federal government White Paper was released relating to the principles concerning amendment. Four principles were outlined in total. First, Canada must request an amendment. Second, the amendment must be requested by Parliament and not simply by Cabinet to allow for debate. Third, a request for amendment would not be acted upon at the request of a province since the national government represents Canada. Finally, provincial consent was required for an amendment that affected federal-provincial relations. The last criteria was a vague one and was left undefined.

A second attempt was made in 1971 with the Victoria Charter. It was agreed to by all the provinces at the Conference. That amending formula would require the agreement of the House of Commons and Senate, together with a majority of provinces comprising every province with at least 25 percent of the population (at that time, Ontario and Quebec), and at least two Western provinces and two Atlantic provinces, with 50 percent of the population of those four provinces. The Victoria Charter also contained a Charter of rights, which would have given fewer protections than the 1982 version that exists today. However, upon returning to Quebec, Premier Bourassa experienced intense pressure to reject the deal as Quebec did not receive its transfer of power. Accordingly, the deal died.

In 1976, when René Lévesque swept to power in Quebec with the Parti Québécois, there was a sense of constitutional crisis in Canada. Other provinces, especially in the West, were also beginning to demand more power.

The result was Bill C-60, a comprehensive amendment package involving an amending formula, a Charter of rights and freedoms, and the appointment of Senators. Certain elements the federal government tried to amend alone under s. 91(1) of the *Constitution Act, 1867*, like the Senate. The Supreme Court held that the federal government possessed no such power since the Senate was seen as a vital institution in the federal system created by the *Constitution Act, 1867*, to protect local interests and prevent sectional (regional) jealousies.[8] With the election of the Progressive Conservatives under Clark, no constitutional proposals were pursued.

In 1980, with the re-election of the Liberals under Trudeau, and the defeat of the sovereignty-association referendum in Quebec, there was an expectation by some Quebecers of a renewed and decentralized federalism. Alan Cairns argues that the Quebec sovereignty referendum defeat transformed Quebec's definition of the rest of Canada by seeing provinces as brothers and not irrelevant subdivisions of an English-Canada led by Ottawa.[9] Furthermore, the

P.Q. Party was not dedicated to renew federalism, on the one hand, but the people had rejected sovereignty, on the other. The federal government was most interested, at this time, to counteract the centrifugal forces threatening to rip apart the country.[10] Finally, some charge that the lost referendum allowed the federal government to control the constitutional process and its objective was not Quebec's objective.[11]

Intensive negotiations were undertaken, which featured the provinces demanding more power. Finally, Trudeau stated that if there was no agreement, the federal government would move unilaterally with its own "People's Package" of Patriating the Constitution to terminate British authority in Canada. The package contained three major provisions including a domestic amending formula, a Charter of rights and freedoms, and a recognition of the principle of fiscal equalization.

Only Ontario and New Brunswick were in favour of the move, while the other eight provinces opposed. Quebec maintained it had a veto that was not recognized by the formula.

Court challenges were initiated in Manitoba, Quebec and Newfoundland. Finally, the Supreme Court of Canada made a great compromise on the matter by giving something to both sides. The Court held, by a majority of seven to two, that if the Resolution was proceeded with, it would have force of law. The Court could have, and many say should have, stopped there. Instead, it went on to hold that a Constitutional convention existed requiring substantial provincial consent. The basis of this convention was not legal, but political in nature.

In the aftermath of the decision, a First Minister's Conference was held in November of 1981. No agreement was being reached at the Conference, and all were working under the shadow of an eminent unilateral move by the federal government, on the one hand, and, in doing so, the unsavouriness of breaking constitutional convention, on the other. It became clear that if the conference failed, the federal government would submit the question to the people of Canada in a national referendum; a position which all the provinces opposed with the exception of Quebec. At the eleventh hour, the nine provinces were able to come to agreement. This last ditch session occurred while René Lévesque was on his way back to Quebec for an overnight stay. The next day, the federal government and nine provinces agreed to the amendment leaving Quebec as the sole dissenting province.

Upon hearing news of the agreement, the Quebec Legislative Assembly denounced the agreement. The matter was referred to court regarding whether the process violated constitutional convention by not including Quebec. The Supreme Court of Canada held that Quebec did not possess a veto in constitutional convention and that constitutional convention only required substantial consent, which the agreement received.[12] The Amendment was legally binding on Quebec, as it was passed by the British Parliament.

Constitutional Life After Patriation

Some Quebec politicians maintained that even though the court battle was lost and Quebec was legally bound by the *Constitution Act, 1982*, it was not morally bound. On the whole, during the years after the Amendment, there was not too much hysteria and the people of Quebec went on as before without any real need to readjust. By the mid-80's, Quebec's nationalism and sovereignty movement were at a low ebb. Some concluded that the nationalist rhetoric lost credibility with the defeat of the referendum.[13] Indeed, prior to Bourassa's liberal electoral victory, the *péquistes*, led by Lévesque, wished to take the *beau risque* of negotiating Quebec's adhesion to the Constitution.

One point of tension that did arise was that certain provisions of Bill 101, particularly with respect to the language of education, were declared unconstitutional. This angered many Quebec politicians as they never agreed to the Charter.

Some argued that due to the bitter feelings in Quebec arising out of 1982, had English Canadian politicians rejected the first modest proposals from Quebec for a renewal of Confederation, the 1990–91 crisis (arising from the failed Meech Lake Accord) would have come five years earlier. However, this view fails to recognize that the dynamics were quite different in 1985 than in 1990. The argument appears to overvalue the extent to which the separatist movement could successfully revive itself on an instantaneous basis without some major crisis and resentment arising due to some external impetus. The mere search for and rejection of special status and further accommodation would not have produced, at that time, the necessary major crisis and resentment. Secondly, and relatedly, the argument underestimates the extent to which the situation in Quebec calmed down and life returned to normal. Finally, the argument underestimates the sheer sense of crisis and resentment in Quebec of a failed attempt to obtain "reasonable" accommodation, in a context where promises were being made by Quebec and other Canadian politicians, and in the context of hysteria surrounding constitutional conferences and a ratification process going down to the wire. Add to this situation another unsuccessful round of constitutional conferences, public consultations and a national referendum. Only this type of environment could provide the external impetus of major crisis and resentment necessary to revive the separatist movement in Quebec.

However, the leader of the Progressive Conservatives of the day, seeking to strengthen his popularity, had to come up with new bases of support. Brian Mulroney found that support in Quebec. By recruiting candidates of the Quebec nationalist persuasion and by offering accommodation, he was promising to bring Quebec back into the constitutional fold and to reverse the apparent 'humiliation' inflicted on Quebec. By suggesting that Quebec was not in the constitutional fold, which it clearly was, his election prospects as Prime Minister were greatly enhanced. Mulroney was gambling that accommodation could be successfully made at a first minister's meeting if done in private to prevent the participation of public interest groups and public debate. It may or should have been well known, that there was a potential for the issue to explode and, perhaps, result in the breakup of the country. As we shall see later, by 1985, constitutional reform became practically impossible. As a result, the slumbering separatist giant in Quebec was reawaken.

Nevertheless, the year 1986 seemed to the Prime Minister and Quebec Premier Bourassa to be right. Bourassa outlined the five minimum conditions for Quebec's acceptance of the patriated Canadian Constitution. First, the Constitution would have to state that Quebec is a distinct society. Second, Quebec must have a constitutional veto, which was seen as its traditional veto. Third, limits on the federal spending power in areas of exclusive provincial jurisdiction were required. Fourth, Quebec must have a greater role concerning immigration. Fifth, Quebec must have a role in determining Supreme Court appointments. Later, further additions were made regarding Senate reform and the requirements of an annual first ministers' meeting on the state of the Canadian economy and on constitutional affairs to gain provincial consent for the Accord. Understandably, there was surprise when Mulroney announced that the Meech Lake Agreement was reached when the people of Canada did not even know there had been negotiations!

Then, things began to unravel. Perhaps, proper consideration was not given to the hinge on which Meech Lake would pass or fail. Each legislature of the province and the federal government would have to ratify the Accord within a three year period, or even change its mind about ratification within that time. Parliamentary government is essentially party government, which features eleven Parliamentary assemblies, with eleven different party configurations at eleven different stages in the electoral cycle.[14] All of these elements provide for a built in dynamism and uncertainty in the process. For example, there could be a change in government during that time, which, in turn, factors in interest groups, political parties and the electorate.

Under the Constitutional Amending formula, some of the matters required unanimity among the federal government and the provinces, while others fell under the general amending formula. The Accord would not be proceeded with unless the whole package was incorporated into an amendment. In the end, in 1990, Manitoba and Newfoundland did not ratify the Accord. Thus, Quebecers saw the non-ratification of the Accord as a slap on the face by the other governments in Canada not meeting Quebec's minimum demands. If there would have been a referendum in Quebec on whether it should or should not become sovereign during the days following the death of Meech Lake, a vote in favour of sovereignty may very well have been the outcome. The death of the Meech Lake Accord inflamed passions in Quebec, seeing its modest demands refused by Canada.[15]

In the wake of the Accord's death, Canada became subject to a deluge of commissions, reports and position papers. Most of Quebec's final public consultations were carried out, between the fall of 1990 and the spring of 1991, before the other Canadian governments really began. There seemed to be a consensus within the Quebec committees or commissions that a high degree of autonomy for Quebec in a restructured Canada was required, or outright independence was in order. The Allaire Report advocated massive decentralization, while the Bélanger-Campeau Commission could not agree on substance, but, only process. The latter expressed a commitment for a sovereignty referendum in 1992. The Allaire Report called for a referendum before the end of 1992 to ratify any constitutional reforms proposed by Canada.

In November of 1990, A Citizens' Forum on Canada's Future, chaired by Keith Spicer, provided an opportunity for Canadians to speak about the future of their country. In December of that same year, a Parliamentary Committee to review the constitutional amendment process was established. Other committees and task forces were created, as well as a parallel process for aboriginals was instituted.

The process leading up to the Charlottetown Accord was sensitive to the criticism aimed at the Meech Lake process of secret negotiation between government elites to the exclusion of all others. Other concerns would have to be addressed in addition to that of federal and provincial governments. Under the so termed Canada Round, the federal government tabled a set of proposals, in September of 1991, for the constitutional renewal of the Canadian federation. The proposals were then referred to a Special Joint Committee of the House of Commons and Senate, which held meetings across Canada to elicit the views of the public. The provinces, also, sought public consultation. Aboriginal peoples were consulted by national and regional Aboriginal organizations. Between January and March of 1992, six televised national conferences took place involving experts, advocacy groups and citizens. Finally, beginning on March 12, 1992, representatives of the provinces, territories and Aboriginal leaders met with the federal Minister of Constitutional Affairs to discuss the report.

The final text of the consensus report was completed on August 28, 1992. When the question of whether or not the amendment should be accepted by their respective governments was put to the people of Canada in a national referendum, the people rejected it, not least because they had had enough of constitutional talks. As such, the Charlottetown Accord died. Separatists and sovereignists of Quebec would now say that not only did the governments outside Quebec reject Quebec's minimum demands, so too did the people living in the rest of Canada. It is important to bear in mind, however, that the results were not uniform from province to province. For example, Ontario, Prince Edward Island and New Brunswick were in favour of the Accord. Furthermore, and significantly, a majority of Quebecers did not vote in favour of the Accord.[16]

With the Parti Québécois back in power, a referendum on the future of Quebec was promised. Previously, the Liberals were not in favour of calling a referendum, at least, in the near future, and took no such action.

It seemed that the date for calling the referendum was being put off by the Parti Québécois until the polls were more favourable in support of sovereignty. Initially, it was thought that, and some confusion arose as to whether, the P.Q. would hold the referendum within eight to ten months of entering into office, but, that was not to be the case. Later, the then leader of the Bloc Québécois, Lucien Bouchard, suggested that there should not be a referendum until the sovereignty side was sure of winning.[17] Furthermore, it was reported that Premier Parizeau waited for the last minute to release the referendum question and that such additional time permitted the various versions of the question to be market tested.[18] Such actions could be regarded as a blatant attempt to manipulate the public.

When it may have appeared that no further delays would be acceptable, the referendum was set for October 30, 1995 and the date would not thereafter be postponed. Throughout most of the referendum campaign, it appeared that the sovereignists had little momentum under Premier Parizeau. It was not until Lucien Bouchard took the helm that the popularity of the sovereignist campaign exploded. The federalist forces, under Prime Minister Chrétien and Quebec Liberal leader Johnson, were slow to act on behalf of Canada and were thereafter criticised in not acting earlier and with more vigour. In the final days before the referendum, in a show of solidarity, Canadians from all over Canada attended a unity rally in Montreal to demonstrate that Quebec is a valued member of the Canadian community.

On the 30th of October, 1995, Quebecers voted on their future with respect to the Canadian federation in a somewhat convoluted question of whether or not Quebec should become sovereign in the event that a formal offer from Quebec for a political and economic association with the rest of Canada was made and rejected by the rest of Canada such that no agreement was achieved. Quebecers voted against such a proposition by a narrow margin of 50.6% to 49.4%.

That same night when the referendum for sovereignty was lost, Premier Parizeau, on public television, blamed the defeat on 'money' and the 'ethnic vote' and resigned as leader of the Parti Québécois the next day. Bouchard then stepped into the shoes of leader of that Party, and as Premier of Quebec. In that capacity, Bouchard indicated that he will call another referendum within short order and will keep calling them until Quebec becomes sovereign. He even indicated a willingness to call a 'snap' referendum.

The referendum gave rise to several controversial issues and events. Among the issues were: what percentage of Quebecers must be in agreement before Quebec may become sovereign and what would be the impact of a Canadian national referendum on the matter?

The unity rally sparked controversy in Quebec, with some Quebecers alleging that other Canadians were interfering in the internal politics of Quebec. Charges were laid under Quebec law against passenger carriers providing discounts to those who attended that rally. Furthermore, and of great concern is the fact that an investigation was undertaken pertaining to sovereignist ballot counters who may have, in effect, attempted to steal the votes of Quebec federalists by not counting perfectly valid ballots.

Guy Bertrand, an ex-sovereignist, successfully sued in Quebec Superior Court to obtain a ruling declaring it illegal for Quebec to separate unilaterally, but, no injunction was granted to stop the October 30th referendum. After the referendum, Bertrand asked the Court to make several declarations and injunctions, including an order to prevent Quebec from separating, unless it does so according to the amending formula contained in the 1982 Constitution. The federal government also intervened in that appeal. The province of Quebec declined to participate and a representative was appointed by the Court. Three questions were put and argued before the Supreme Court of Canada in 1998 concerning the issues of whether, as a matter of domestic and/or international law, Quebec may legally unilaterally separate from Canada, and if there is a conflict between domestic and international law, which would take priority in the circumstances. The Supreme Court answered that although there was no right of unilateral secession under Canadian law, its view of constitutional principles led it to the conclusion that federalism and democracy dictate that if the people of Quebec voted for secession in a referendum, there would be a reciprocal obligation on the parties to Confederation to negotiate constitutional changes in good faith to respect that desire, and that the secession must respect the rights of others.[19] However, Canadian law requires a "clear" majority *and* the referendum question itself must be free of ambiguity. Otherwise, secession would be contrary to domestic (Constitutional) law. By and large, the rest must be determined by the political process. The Court also held that there was no right of unilateral secession under international law in the case of Quebec, particularly as Quebecers are not oppressed, or denied access to or participation in government. Interestingly, although initially all the major political actors appeared to have accepted the decision, it was not until over one year later that it was publically challenged by the Party Québécois in asserting that it alone would set its own rules for a referendum. Perhaps, it was thought that a referendum on sovereignty could not be won if a "clear" majority was to vote in favour of a "clear" question.

Another unresolved question relates to how would the massive federal debt be divided for which Quebec will be responsible, in addition to its own rather large debt and deficit. Finally, the issue of the divisibility of Canada gave rise to questions concerning the divisibility of Quebec, particularly in respect of Montreal and due to the fact that the Cree overwhelmingly voted to separate from a sovereign Quebec.

It appears that Prime Minister Chrétien and other Premiers have since been and will continue to be more active in the defence of Canada. First, it appears that only a clear referendum question on sovereignty will be accepted as valid; that is, does the Quebec voter wish to separate, yes or no? No pretensions for partnership or any such thing will be seen as acceptable in any future referendum question. Secondly, something more than a bare majority of 50 percent plus one voter will be required. Indeed, these two positions were explicitly incorporated into federal legislation. Third, the rest of Canada seems to be taking a position of "yes means yes". In other words, once Quebec is a sovereign entity, it will be treated as such and not as part of Canada, including with respect to economic and trade matters. Accordingly, Canada will be uninhibited in considering and pursuing its own interest in its relations with Quebec. Issues were raised regarding Canadian citizenship, the necessity of Quebecers being required to show passports or visas when entering Canada, and that Quebec would have no further say on any matters concerning Canada, or be entitled to Canadian currency not in its possession. Thus, the aftermath of the referendum reflects uncertainty with respect to the future of Canada.

Finally, there have been more recent efforts on the part of the federal government and the English provinces to recognize Quebec's distinctiveness. For example, the federal government, under Chrétien, stated that it will not pass constitutional amendments without the consent of Quebec. An interesting question arises as to whether such a constitutional convention will arise. The premiers of the English speaking provinces met to discuss what kind of distinct society recognition they could agree to, which led to the Calgary Declaration on national unity. That Declaration recognizes that all provinces are equal, but Quebec is unique. Most of the Legislatures of the English speaking provinces since ratified the Declaration, but, as with Meech, ratification can be recinded. Quebec, under the Parti Québécois, undertook its own hearings on the Declaration. Thus, in any event, despite the recent referendum in Quebec, the constitutional differences between many Quebecers and other Canadians remain.

Chapter 5
The History of Economic and Business Control in Quebec

Prior to the late 1970's, Quebec's economy was largely controlled by the minority anglophone population centred primarily in Montreal, and by American capital. A number of studies provide considerable evidence regarding British and American dominance of the economy of Quebec, and the fact that the French worked almost exclusively at the operative level.[1] This situation could very well produce serious assimilatory pressures with respect to the survival of the French language and certainly would prevent the flourishing of francophone society. As such, the second theme underlying justifications for separatism and sovereignty, namely assimilation, is most intimately implicated.

The Report of the Royal Commission on Bilingualism and Biculturalism observed noticeable income disparities between Canadians of British and French origin in all provinces, including Quebec.[2] Those of British origin always earned higher average incomes, above all in Quebec. The same pattern emerged when English and French language groups were analysed, except that whereas in the rest of Canada where bilingual Canadians tended to earn higher incomes, in Quebec unilingual anglophones of British origin tended to earn more, followed by bilingual anglophones and then bilingual French.[3]

In terms of ethnicity and occupations in Quebec, one study published in 1957 by Yves de Jocas and Guy Rocher examined two generations and the following results were obtained.[4] Of the first generation examined, the British were concentrated at the white collar level and the French at the working level. During the next generation, the British proportions at the worker level fell and French increases at the white collar level were not as great as for the British. The proportion of the younger generation French in the workers' class scarcely changed. The British increased their representation in three areas: as

Professionals, proprietors and managers; as Semi-professionals and lower administrators; and, in Clerical and sales. Whereas, the British decreased in the skilled and semi-skilled category, the French would increase their proportion of its male labour force in these areas.[5]

Certainly, the British in Quebec enjoyed greater control over and social mobility in developing industry than the French. John Porter wrote about the period from 1931 to 1961 in Quebec in these terms:

> ... by and large the British run the industrial life of Quebec. The higher up the authority structure of industry that one proceeds the greater is the proportion of British personnel. The French are predominately workers at the lower end of the class system with, on the average, lower levels of skill than the British.[6]

Taken as a percentage of the male labour force broken down by race, the British were increasingly overrepresented as a proportion of their population at the professional and financial level moving from +5.0% in 1931 to +7.1% in 1961.[7] The French were becoming increasingly underrepresented at those levels moving from -0.9% in 1931 to -1.5% in 1961.[8] In the clerical field, the British overrepresentation dropped from +7.1% in 1931 to +5.2% in 1961, but was still significant.[9] On the other hand, French underrepresentation decreased from -1.4% in 1931 to -0.7% in 1961.[10] Finally, the French were overrepresented in the primary and unskilled area increasing from +0.3% in 1931 to +1.1% in 1961.[11]

The importance of the English language in the workplace and in business may be further appreciated in the context where Quebec society, as elsewhere in Canada and the World, was rapidly becoming more and more urbanized and industrialized after World War II and, therefore, giving rise to assimilatory tendencies. This situation is so as the industrialization of Quebec set the stage for ethnic interaction in Quebec given that anglophone controlled industry existed in a society with surplus francophone populations, often of the unskilled variety, looking for work.

Furthermore, the scale of urbanization was truly startling. In this way, a large and significant proportion of the population was subject to the assimilatory pressures associated with an anglophone dominated business world. Porter stated of out-farm migration that the old rural life was completely broken, which is supported by the figures presented in the Trembley Report.[12] Agriculture, as a percentage of the total Quebec labour force, dropped from 27.4% in 1931 to 9.1% in 1961, which displays a tremendous shift reflecting the urbanization and industrialization of Quebec.[13]

Furthermore, French overrepresentation in the area of agriculture dropped from +4.8% in 1931 to +1.6% in 1961.[14]

Families began to outgrow the land on which they farmed and changes in the farming business, especially since 1951, such as increasing farm sizes, increased mechanization and the combining of farm and non-farm work made farming more of a business, and an increasingly concentrated activity. There were other economic factors at work. A 1959 study of 1460 French wage-earning families in Quebec showed that the farther away from urban centres the family resided, the more it was affected by unemployment during the year before the survey.[15]

Francophone Canadian ownership of Quebec industry tended in 1961 to be concentrated in agriculture, services, retail and to a lesser extent construction; whereas, in the manufacturing sector, francophones accounted for a low proportion of the province's value added production, tended to be less productive, had fewer and lower paid employees, produced essentially for the Quebec market, and were based in the traditional industries.[16] Foreign owned establishments stood in complete contrast in terms of productivity, number of employees, salary and wage levels, market orientation, and produced in industries that had developed recently in which the then modern technology played a key role as in primary retail products, chemical products and the petroleum industry. Anglophone Canadian interests shared characteristics with francophone and foreign owners. The real advantage lay in working for these anglophone Canadian and foreign interests.

The Bilingualism and Biculturalism Commission tended to conclude that the closely related factors of education and occupation were most important in explaining income disparities between Canadians of British and French origin, with age of the labour force, relative unemployment levels, the characteristics of industries in which those of British and French origin tended to participate, and region of inhabitance playing a lessor role.[17]

Education in Quebec before the Quiet Revolution was not in keeping with the changes occurring in Quebec society. In particular, French-Canadian education was not geared to the provision of industrial skills at the managerial or technical level. Quebecers of French and Catholic origins ranked consistently below those of British and Protestant origins with respect to several educational measures such as the number of years spent in school, the proportion of students aged 15–24 still in school, school attendance and retention rates, as well as teacher qualifications.[18] Proportionally, fewer completed secondary or university education, which was by then vital for entry into most professional and administrative careers in large organizations. Francophones tended to obtain degrees in arts and social sciences, with much lower proportions in natural sciences, engineering, commerce and administration. Links between French language universities and industry were more tenuous than for the English-language institutions. It was not until the province of Quebec began to exercise its power over education and to take on a more active role that education would become more appropriate to the needs of Quebec's society. Furthermore, anglophones tended towards the private sector, while higher proportions of francophones worked in the public sector; the service industry, such as law and accountancy; or, tended towards small enterprises where they could work primarily in their own language.

Undoubtedly, working in a second language, lack of kinship ties or similar backgrounds with anglophone managers, differing cultures, geographic mobility, and discrimination also posed barriers to French speaking Quebecers in attaining management positions in anglophone controlled businesses. Indeed, some francophones felt that working for anglophone corporations meant the risk of foregoing their individual and collective identities.

Several authors modelled explanations for anglophone dominance.[19] Given the significant off-farm migration, these workers were often unskilled and less educated, not being well suited for management positions. As a result, they filled lower level jobs. French ascendancy in the business world would generally be more step by step in the sense that off-farm migrants to urban centres took unskilled labour positions and then they, or future generations, progressed to skilled work, then to work as clerks, salesmen or entering the public service and, finally, were in a position to ascend to the top occupations. The British possessed a distinct advantage as earlier generations were better placed to benefit from the increasing growth of industry by being more industrial and commercial in their occupations. Consequently, they experienced greater social mobility during this period.

One highly significant implication for anglophone dominance of Quebec's business world was that it threatened to pose the most serious challenge to the survival of the French language and to the flourishing of francophone society. For the most part, management and the technical levels in the private sector were controlled by anglophones, while francophones tended to concentrate at the labour and lower management levels. The language of the workplace was French, but, with a significant amount of English.

The Bilingualism and Biculturalism Commission found that in the larger manufacturing corporations, bilingualism was demanded of most francophones, but not of most anglophones, for most higher level positions in the early 1960's, particularly as one began to earn more income.[20] At the middle to top levels, English was a prerequisite. A substantial degree of bilingualism or English was required or used for positions or matters involving internal communications between anglophones and francophones, employee relations, plant operations and internal technical documents. Of course, smaller firms in Quebec outside of Montreal displayed a relatively high degree of internal communications in French. In terms of external communications regarding the larger manufacturing concerns, purchasing was mostly conducted in the language of suppliers, usually English. In terms of marketing, French tended to predominate with respect to consumer goods, but not industrial ones. Even francophones at lower levels may have been required to use English at meetings, in conferences, telephone conversations and written reports.

Furthermore, as the language of management and of ascendancy was English, there were greater incentives to learn that language and to learn American or English-Canadian norms of business, particularly by allophones, if one wished to progress through the ranks of the business world. The pressures were most acute in the Montreal area, which contained the largest concentrations of anglophones and allophones in Quebec.

This cultural division of labour and anglophone dominance of the business world were part of the everyday experience of French speaking Quebecers, and became a "social justice" concern. Indeed, Québécois *joual* (slang) grew out of the context of English in the workplace and loosely speaking constitutes a mixture of English and French. In many ways, *joual* was a protest to the predominance of the English language in the business world and workplace of Quebec.

Perceptions and the Making of Illusion

From the demographic situation and the fundamental changes occurring in Quebec society, as well as the brief historical outline provided, including its constitutional, historical and business/economic aspects, it may very well appear that nothing seemed to work well with the Canadian federation insofar as Quebecers are concerned. Without considering many important facts, the non-workability of Canadian federalism might appear to be a compelling argument.

Significant differences respecting political-historical matters were illustrated in Chapter 3. From the outline of events, it appeared that it was historically almost impossible to avoid conflict between Quebec and the rest of Canada, at least on matters of race, language, culture or the British Empire. Quebec's view always seemed to loose out to the majority English Canadian view on issues that achieved a level of "national" importance, except, perhaps, where such issues arose within the confines of Quebec itself. Although transformations in Quebec and Canadian society have rendered these traditional conflicts largely obsolete, new tensions arose with or out of the Quiet Revolution and its aftermath.

Canada's constitutional history, especially during and after the 1960's, might indicate that the Constitution was not serving the people of Canada well and, particularly, the people of Quebec. The three themes underlying arguments in favour of separatism and sovereignty are implicated. Successive Quebec governments in seeking further transfers of power and special status were unsuccessful. This lack of success was used by some to maintain that Quebec's vision of Canada is vastly different from the views held outside of Quebec and that the differences are irreconcilable. Secondly, especially with the Charter, it is argued that the threat of Québécois assimilation is greatly enhanced. Finally, some argue that Canada is, or parts of its Constitution are, illegitimate.

One may add the fact that Quebec's business world was historically dominated by anglophones and the language of business, ascendancy and, to an extent, the workplace involved a significant amount of English. Anglophone domination along with the urbanization, industrialization and modernization of Quebec, the low francophone birth rate, and immigration posed a threat to the survival of the French language and to the flourishing of francophone society in Quebec since the preferred language of business and the language necessary to further one's career was English. Furthermore, and, not surprisingly, this state of affairs of anglophone dominance engendered much discontent among francophone Quebecers who could claim that they, as the majority population in the province, were not masters in their own house.

PART III
Canadian Federalism

Part III of this book examines whether or not the apparent differences in views and interests between Quebec and the rest of Canada, particularly on historical and constitutional issues, logically compels a re-ordering of their relationship, and whether or not federalism is working well to protect the needs and concerns of Quebecers. At its core, one of the greatest criticisms of Canada by separatists and sovereignists is that Quebec does not have enough of the powers thought necessary to protect the French language and to provide for the flourishing of francophone society. This assertion will be tested to determine its validity.

In the course of the analysis that follows, one must not forget the legitimate preoccupation of Quebecers to protect and promote the French language and francophone society in the context of a North America dominated by the English language. The survival of the French language and the flourishing of francophone society is a worthy and necessary goal to be pursued within the boundaries of Canada.

Finally, and perhaps most importantly for the survival of the French language and the flourishing of Quebec francophone society is the fact that Quebec francophones were required by necessity to take greater control of and participate more fully in Quebec's economy and business world. Although Chapter 5 stressed that Quebec's world of business had been dominated by anglophones and the language of business was English, that state of affairs no longer exists in the Quebec of the 1990's, and can no longer be the basis of any criticism of Canadian federalism.

Chapter 6
Does Quebec Have Enough Power?

The Business World of Quebec in the Post-1980's

As stated earlier, perhaps, the greatest challenge facing the survival of the French language and the flourishing of francophone Quebec society was anglophone dominance of the business world. As such, the second theme of assimilation is most intimately implicated. From an economic perspective, it is necessary to have jobs and income for survival and quality of life. Quality of life also includes the ability to work in one's language. A predominance of English in the world of business, and the necessity and desirability of learning English would also have likely lead to the linguistic assimilation of a considerable percentage of francophones and allophones, most significantly in the Montreal area. This eventuality was structured because the population of Quebec became urbanized, industrialized and integrated in which there were and are francophones in all occupations and sectors. Quebec society was no longer the homogeneous community largely undisturbed by non-French elements. Furthermore, the birth rate of Quebec fell dramatically and immigration would play an increasing role in the linguistic composition of Quebec society. However, such anglophone domination with the result of significant assimilation of francophones and allophones did not occur.

The reason for this state of affairs is linked to the overall theme of federalism in which while federalism does not protect all cleavages, it does give salience to territorially based ones. The province of Quebec possesses ample powers to address the most fundamental interests arising within its territory, like the creation of a comprehensive system of measures and initiatives to facilitate and secure the survival of the French language and to facilitate the assertion of francophone business in Quebec. It was stated that:

... expansionist state strategy enacted largely at the behest of this new middle class has served to cultivate and bring to maturity an indigenous francophone bourgeoisie which had long been subordinate to English-Canada and American capital.[1]

Structural Dominance

During the final years of the Duplessis era, progressive economists and Quebec businessmen working through the local Chamber of Commerce advocated increased state participation in the economy. The Lesage Liberals, in 1960, initiated an experiment by creating the Conseil d'orientation économique (COEQ). The COEQ would go on to produce blueprints for state strategy to expand and entrench the role of francophone Quebec capital in an "economy dominated by monopoly capital in a process of concentration."[2] The means would require a reorientation of savings held by "national" financial institutions.

An alliance developed in the COEQ between representatives from Mouvement Desjardins, financial institutions and institutional capital. This alliance was important to the creation of the Société Général de Financement (SGF) in 1963, which later gave way to the successes of the Caisse de dépôt et de placement, created in 1965.[3] The Caisse, which administers the Quebec Pension Plan, became instrumental to the formation and consolidation of the "new business class" of francophone Quebec. The business-government collaboration was aimed at the partial rationalization of the economic structure and the promotion of capital accumulation.

Important governmental factors facilitating the rise of the new business class included the Caisse de dépôt et de placement; educational reforms; public sector procurement practices; the nationalization of hydro resources and the asbestos industry; government sponsored megaprojects in Northern Quebec; and, the creation of provincial Crown corporations in the metallurgical, mining and resource exploration industries. All of these initiatives have had significant indirect benefits for Quebec capital.[4] Furthermore, and, more importantly, it was the first time francophone Quebecers could aspire to a range of senior management positions denied to them in an anglophone dominated private sector.

Gagnon and Paltiel argue that Quebec's language law, Bill 101, completed the environmental transformation necessary for the *épanouissement* (flourishing) of a new business elite.[5] Bill 101 caused the famous Route 401 migration south of angolphones and discouraged immigration of young anglophones from the rest of the country into Quebec. This outmigration and the vacuum left by the postwar decline of Quebec in the North American economy created important opportunities for the young, well educated and experienced Quebecers, and a revitalized Quebec business class was able to capitalize on the opportunities opened by these developments.[6]

Bill 101 with its *Charte de la langue française* (*"Charté"*)[7] was a clear rejection of bilingualism. It was thought that bilingualism allowed francophones to acquire fluency in English to function in industry and commerce. Bill 101 instituted the French language in the workplace and included conditions of employment and promotions based on the French language. In essence, it was linguistic affirmative action.

There are two major provisions in Bill 101 dealing with the workplace. The first requires employers to speak French to employees and publish in French offers of employment or promotions. The second forbids requiring the knowledge of any other language for a position of employment other than French. However, there is a discretion in the Office de la langue française to allow exceptions based on necessity.

Although the Bill was not received well by many within and outside of the province, it was quite within the jurisdiction of Quebec to enact, which it did. This episode is a prime example of the fact that while federalism does not protect all cleavages, it does give salience to territorially based ones. It, furthermore, demonstrates that the Quebec government had enough power to take steps thought necessary to protect the French language and to provide for the flourishing of its majority francophone society. On the other hand, while federalism is a compromise which seeks to protect territorially based interests, other principles such as democracy, the rule of law, the Charter, constitutionalism, and the activism of groups and communities serve to temper the actions of the majority in the national, territorial or local level of government with respect to minorities.

In order that Quebec successfully develop its new business class, changes in values and ideology on a social and political level were necessary. At the level of party and electoral politics in Quebec, this ideological shift was most dramatic in the Parti Québécois after political independence failed in 1980. There was a renewed effort to achieve economic independence. It was clear, by 1979, with the release of the government's economic strategy *Challenges for Quebec (Bâtir le Quebec)*, that the private sector would be the primary avenue of economic development.

In this context, the Régime d'épargne - action du Québec (REAQ), or the Quebec Stock Savings Plan (QSSP), was created in 1979, by the then Finance Minister of the Parti Québécois, Jacques Parizeau, as a generous tax shelter for residents of the province to invest in Quebec companies. By offering a generous income tax deduction, the QSSP was an enormously successful means to stimulate investment in Quebec companies and was even described as one of the principal motors of the contemporary business boom in Quebec.[8] As one could deduct up to $10,000, it was primarily in the interests of upper income residents. There was a growth in the value of stocks and an increase in the number of listings and shares. The percentage of adult Quebec shareholders in Quebec companies more than doubled within a relatively short time.

Subsequent Quebec governments undertook measures that continued Quebec's move to the right, such as restricting public sector spending, more restrictive labour legislation, and enhanced incentives to Quebec businesses. For example, Quebec companies may also establish a trusted profit-sharing plan so that employees can deduct an extra 25% when buying their company's shares under the QSSP. Task forces on privatization, deregulation and state reorganization were business dominated. There were recommendations for a turn to the right in Quebec state and society, including selling state owned companies, a 25% cut at the senior levels of the public service, an addition to taxable income of the first $2000 worth of health care, and a reversion to the private sector of certain health care institutions and practices.[9] All of such measures were, not surprisingly, well received by the province's business community.

In terms of the changes in values and ideology on a social level, the École des Hautes Études Commerciales produced high power graduates such as Jacques Parizeau, who challenged the cultural division of labour view of Quebec. In fact, by the mid-1970's, business leaders were even developing an analysis of business in Quebec that provided a counter-ideology to nationalist consensus.[10]

Finally, there were social forces at work. The new generation of Quebecers faced with no opportunities in the public sector, which already absorbed a disproportionate number of their parents, turned to commerce, administration and computer science in the private sector. Educational reforms simultaneously played a key role by providing the type of education that was needed to better serve the needs of Quebec's economy. Between 1962 and 1965, Quebec business schools accounted for slightly under one-third of the Canadian total of bachelor and master degrees in commerce, and by early 1978 these schools graduated one out of three of Canada's MBA's.[11] Many graduates go on to small and medium sized retail and manufacturing enterprises or become entrepreneurs. In 1985, the share of jobs created by small business in Quebec was 14.9%, exceeding all provinces except Alberta.[12] These are jobs created by francophones in which French is used on the job and in management.

However, transitional forces in Quebec by themselves did not produce the fundamental alteration of the Quebec economic structure. Not only was government action key, but appropriate government policies were necessary. For example, between 1962–72, the SGF encountered considerable start up problems when it concentrated the bulk of its resources on buying up nearly bankrupt family run enterprises in the province. From 1973 onward, when the Movement Desjardins and caisses populaires networks were no longer required by Lesage to finance the SGF, the SGF began acting as a wholly owned government holding company with its stated purpose "to create Quebec industrial complexes and to participate in management and financing of medium sized and large Quebec firms."[13]

The Caisse de dépôt et de placement only achieved mixed results in its initial years because of its tendency to invest in major banks and in large English-Canadian financial institutions instead of distinctly francophone Quebec enterprises. Once its purpose was clarified, the Caisse played a fundamental role in conjunction with the savings co-operatives, state subsidies and private capital in stimulating Quebec's new and old bourgeoisie.

From the late 1980's, the Caisse has been the largest single shareholder and penetrated the boards of directors of some of Quebec's leading industrial companies. Its power sparked controversy and uneasiness with a government pension fund that takes control of private companies. Given this control, much influence can be generated in terms of French in the workplace, or by blocking any mergers that might adversely affect the French language.

State intervention in Quebec is declining as it cannot be justified on the grounds of entrepreneurial shortcomings. In 1985, in a speech given by Premier Bourassa, he stated:

> The presence of a strong, dynamic and well established Quebec enterprises means that economic power will stay in Quebec hands. But, instead of resting with the state, it will be in the hands of Quebec businessmen.[14]

Now fluency in French is necessary in the business world of Quebec.

With the establishment of the new middle class, the major building blocks are in place to facilitate the survival of the French language. Naturally, government measures were not the only factors in promoting French in the workplace. The private sector was necessary to create initiatives, business and jobs. Reforms in education were a necessary prerequisite before government measures could be successful. State expansionist strategies facilitated the creation of an economic and social environment in which Quebec capital would flourish and the French language would become the language of business in Quebec. It is, also, interesting to note the relatively high degree of collaboration exhibited between the Quebec government, business and labour in planning the Quebec economy. The 'super summit' of 1996, initiated by the Parti Québécois, to reduce the deficit and to revive the sluggish Quebec economy is a case in point.

It should be noted that federal government policies, also, contributed indirectly to the rise of the middle class. Policies like French language policy (the *Official Languages Act*) expanded the career options of francophone Quebecers and regional development policies aided in strengthening local business interests and promoted both growth and expansion.

The question, at this juncture, is whether these structural changes have in fact produced the desired changes. The following discussion reveals francophone dominance of the public sector and the business world of Quebec, and the language of work and the language of welcome and service in the public and the commercial private sectors are, by and large, French. These structural changes and the desired results all occurred within the context of Canadian federalism.

Francophone Economic Dominance of Quebec

Chapter 5 discussed anglophone dominance at the higher ends of the private sector, whereas, francophones were overrepresented at the lower levels. This situation of anglophone dominance, in turn, created assimilatory pressures on francophones and provided a greater incentive for immigrants to learn English. However, by the 1990's, the Interministerial Committee on the situation of the French language in Quebec (1996) agreed that this problem has been rectified:

> In the last twenty years the question of "social justice" or equality of linguistic groups has been practically resolved.[15] (translation)

Francophone dominance of Quebec's business and working world and the rectification of the "social justice" question outlined in Chapter 5 may be illustrated by referring to statistics accepted by the Interministerial Committee related to occupations by language group, linguistic breakdowns regarding management in Quebec businesses and the "profitability" of learning English,

French, or both, in Quebec.

Francophones substantially dominate the business world outside of the Montreal area, including with respect to the major occupations within the private sector. In terms of representation within occupations in the private sector of Metropolitan Montreal, persons of the French maternal language have increased to a position of dominance, whereas the proportion of those of the English maternal language decreased substantially. As administrators, francophones increased their representation from 41 percent in 1971 to 67 percent in 1991; whereas, the anglophones decreased from 47 percent to 20 percent.[16] The ranks of francophone professionals increased from 45 percent in 1971 to 67 percent in 1991, and anglophones dropped from 43 percent to 19 percent.[17] Finally, as technicians, francophones increased their representation from 53 percent to 69 percent, during the same time period, while the anglophone proportion decreased from 30 percent to 15 percent.[18] Allophones in these categories comprise between 12 and 15 percent.

If one is to include the financial sector, services to enterprise, and various industries such as machinery, material, plastic, electric, electronic, chemical, telephone and audiovisual, francophones progressed from 55 percent to 68 percent between 1971 and 1991; whereas, anglophones diminished from 34 percent to 18 percent during that time.[19] Allophones, also, increased their proportion from 11 percent to 14 percent.[20]

The increases of francophones in management positions are similarly remarkable. Francophones are occupying greater posts of decision-making and management and in bigger industries. Despite the fact that francophones still do not play a large role in large anglophone or foreign corporations, francophones have made great strides and are generally the dominant force. Between 1977 and 1988, francophone corporate directors and officers increased from 38 percent to 58 percent, whereas, anglophones diminished substantially from 45 percent to 26 percent.[21] In terms of the largest corporations, between 1976 and 1993, in enterprises with one thousand or more personnel, francophone directors increased from 19 percent to 35 percent in which 43% of those boards of directors were dominated by francophones.[22] The majority of these directors manage francophone corporations.

As a result of these changes, by 1990, it was no longer more profitable for those thirty-five years of age or younger to be unilingually English, than to be unilingually French, even in Montreal.[23] Rather, the opposite is true. However, it is still more profitable for one to be bilingual in Montreal.

Bilingual francophones will generally earn more than bilingual anglophones, which was not the case before the early 1980's, when the opposite was true.[24]

Perhaps, the most significant effect of these structural changes for the flourishing of the French language relates to the gains that the French language has made in the workplace of Quebec. Outside Montreal, the percentage of workers working generally in French (i.e. 90 percent or more of the time) increased from 84 percent to 88 percent between 1971 and 1989.[25] In the region of Montreal, during that time period, workers working generally in French rose from 42 percent to 56 percent.[26] Workers using French between 50 percent and 89 percent of the time on the job increased from 27 percent to 29 percent.[27] Perhaps more striking is the fact that the percentage of workers usually using English in the workplace diminished from 31 percent to 15 percent.[28] Given that francophones control the vast majority of smaller enterprises in Quebec, it is not surprising that French is more often used in the smaller enterprises. In its Report released in August 1999, the Conseil de la langue française indicated that it will later be specifically tackling again the issue of French in the workplace and that the figures contained in the 1999 study cannot be relied upon on that issue.[29]

Similarly, breaking the figures down according to maternal language in the region of Montreal between 1971 and 1989, one discovers that, in 1971, 52 percent of francophones used French over 90 percent of the time in the workplace, and by 1989 that figure was 63 percent.[30] If one were to consider the percentage of those working in the French language more than half the time, then 93 percent of francophone workers worked in French.[31] Conversely, francophones working most of the time in English dropped from 12 percent to 6 percent.[32]

On the other hand, the percentage of anglophones working in the English language dropped significantly. Whereas 86 percent of anglophones worked in the English language in 1971, that figure dropped to 55 percent by 1989.[33]

The situation practically reversed itself in respect of the usage of French by allophone workers in the workplace. Since 1971, allophone workers have been using significantly more French on the job. In 1971, 17 percent of allophone workers were using French 90 percent of the time or more, 25 percent used French between 50 and 89 percent of the time, and the majority (58 percent) used English usually.[34] By 1989, 24 percent of allophone workers were using French 90 percent or more at work, while 39 per cent were using French between 50 and 89 percent of the time, and only 37 percent were using English most of the time.[35] Again, a future study is promised by the Conseil to accurately update these figures. It is very likely that the late 1990's and beyond will bear out the conclusion that even greater percentages of allophone workers will be working in the French language.

Despite the fact that French is generally the language of the workplace, francophones still have a tendency to communicate in English with anglophone superiors, co-workers and subordinates. However, more and more francophones are using French when communicating with superiors. Furthermore, it is estimated that the use of French only is necessary for work in Quebec seventy-five percent of the time.

The language used to welcome people in stores in all regions and in different types of commerce is for the most part French, including on Montreal Island. However, on Montreal Island, the language of welcome in French was weaker in stores in the Montreal West area (where 66 percent were greeted in French), and in the Côtes-des-Neiges, which has a strong allophone population, where French was the language of welcome 53 percent of the time in stores and 62 percent of the time in commercial centres.[36] Otherwise, in all other areas of Montreal, customers were greeted at least 80 percent of the time in the French language.[37]

The language of service is predominately in the French language, including in Montreal and this situation reflects significant change. One 1979 telephone survey indicated that 16 percent could not be served in French in Montreal in the six months prior to the survey.[38] In 1995, when service in French was demanded, it was received between 95 and 100 percent of the time, except for the Côtes-des-Neiges where it was received 89 percent of the time.[39]

Government in Quebec

The Quebec government and its organisms are dominated by francophones, especially, at the higher ranks. Therefore, another substantial proportion of Quebec society, the public sector, works in the French language.

Furthermore, governmental measures in relation to the French language are applicable to the public sector in Quebec. First, under the *Charte de la langue française*, public sector bodies must receive certification that the French language has achieved the desired degree of generalization within that particular body. The public sector is already to a great extent francophone dominated and the language of work is French. Most ministries and government bodies received their certifications relatively quickly. Secondly, government bodies are obligated to create a linguistic policy in consultation with the Office de la langue française regarding communications with individuals and regarding other matters not dealt with by the *Charte* to further the generalization of the French language. Third, there is a purchasing policy of the Quebec government that documents must be in French or translated into French (*Politique d'achat du government du Québec*). *La politique d'utilisation du français dans les technologies de l'information*, adopted in 1992, requires government bodies to elaborate a plan of 'francification' of information technologies within five years. Of the one hundred and fifty-two government bodies concerned, in 1995, forty-three submitted an acceptable plan and sixty-three transmitted the required information.[40]

Although the language of work within the public sector is predominately French, there is nevertheless the use of other languages in communications with Quebecers. One study indicated that relating to several services, in 1994, citizens corresponded with government bodies in French 89 percent of the time in all of Quebec, 79 percent in Metropolitan Montreal and 70 percent on Montreal Island.[41] These conversations were at a percentage greater than the proportion of Quebecers who most often spoke French at home. In another study of a large ministry in which telephone information was sought between April 1, 1994 and March 31, 1995, out of 1,051,635 calls, only 14.9 percent (156,839 calls) were in the English language.[42] Therefore, in the great majority of cases regarding government bodies and regarding a wide range of matters, French is the dominant language of communication even without imposing a legal obligation on citizens to address government in the French language.

An indication of the generalization of French may, also, be provided by examining the certification of health and social services bodies, Municipalities, and school boards under the *Charte*. In 1995, 97 percent of those bodies received certifications in all of Quebec.[43] However, the percentages differ according to whether or not services are provided to those in an area that is not majority francophone. In March of 1995, there were 19 school boards, 110 municipal organizations and 84 health and social service bodies providing services in areas where the majority of people were not francophones.[44] By 1995, 83 percent of those organisms that operated in non-francophone areas were certified, which included 98.8 percent of health and social service bodies, 77.3 percent of municipal bodies and 47.3 percent of school boards.[45] Otherwise, 98 percent of bodies in a majority francophone area were certified.[46] Given the relatively small amount of bodies operating in a majority non-francophone area and given the amount of certifications, a good indication is provided regarding the dominant use of French within those organizations, as compared to the use of other languages.

Demographic Policy

Policies aimed at demography are primarily in relation to influencing the birth rate in and immigration into Quebec.

Birth Rate

The complete overhaul of Family Allowance policy and taxation in 1974 resulted in increased monthly payments and made it possible for provinces to configure the amount of federal family allowance to age and rank in the family. These configurations would still be paid for by the federal government at a specified average per month, per child under the age of eighteen years.

In 1989, the amount of family allowance paid for by the federal government would be an average of $32.74 per child, per month.[47] Quebec chose to configure as follows: for children up to the age of 11, $20.93 for the first child, $31.21 for the second child, and $78.76 for the third through sixth children.[48] For children between the ages of 12 and 17 years, $29.97 was payable for the first child, $39.25 for the second, and $86.60 for third and subsequent children.[49]

During that year, Quebec chose to augment federal Family Allowance with a Dependent Children's Credit as follows: $9.31, per month, for the first child under the age of 18 years; $12.41 for the second child; $15.51 for the third child; and $18.58 for subsequent children.[50]

In 1992, the federal allowance amounted to $34.88 per month, per child. Quebec chose to configure as follows: for children under the age of 11 years, $22.30 for the first child, $32.25 for the second and $83.02 for the third through sixth children.[51] For children between the ages of 12 and 17 years, $30.86 was paid for the first child; $41.81 for the second; and $91.58 for the third through sixth children.[52]

Quebec again augmented that amount by a payment of $10.70 per month for the first child, $14.25 for the second child, $17.82 for the third child, and $21.35 for every other child.[53] Quebec provided additional monthly allowances for children under the age of six years to the amount of $9.58 for the first child; $19.16 for the second child, and $47.87 for the third and subsequent children.[54] Finally, there was also be a lump sum allowance for newborns of $500 for the first child; for the second child, $1000 was payable in two instalments; and $7500 was payable in quarterly instalments of $375 for the third and subsequent children.[55]

In 1993, family allowance comprising the non-refundable income tax credit for dependent children and the refundable child tax credit were consolidated into one unified child tax benefit of $1020 per child per year under eighteen years of age rising to $1095 for the third and subsequent children.[56] A payment of $213 per child is made for children under 7 years of age where no child care expenses are claimed.[57] The system is structured to most benefit lower and middle income families.

In 1994, Quebec, not surprisingly, again, configured Family Allowance: for children under the age of 11 years, $868.92 for the first child, $999.96 for the second and $1596.96 for the third and subsequent children. For children between the ages of 12 and 17 years, $971.88 for the first child, $1102.92 for the second, and $1699.92 for third and subsequent children.[58] Quebec similarly configured in 1995.[59]

It is clear that Quebec developed a demographic policy that is sensitive to the low francophone birth rate in Quebec. Configuring Family Allowance, and the addition of a provincial incentive are attempts to financially entice Quebec families to have more children. There is, however, no real evidence, as of yet, that the policy is working as the birth rate in Quebec remains low. It is open to the Quebec government to further augment its Dependent Children's Tax Credit, subject to fiscal considerations and considerations regarding whether or not any such measures would have any likelihood of success.

Indeed, with the transformation of Quebec society, there are powerful sociological factors keeping the birth rate down. In contemporary Quebec society, there is less influence promoting larger families. More importantly, modernized Quebecers are career orientated and less inclined to have larger families. Creating a financial incentive large enough to reverse those factors would likely be prohibitive even in the context of relative stability that exists in the province of Quebec within Canada.

Immigration

The Cullen-Couture agreement of 1978 was a result of negotiations between the federal government and the Quebec government, and reflected the gradual process of an increasing Quebec role in immigration from the time of Premier Johnson. The McDougall-Gagnon-Trembley Accord, 1991, prolonged the Cullen-Couture Agreement. Pursuant to these agreements, Quebec is given powers in the selection of independent immigrants, which make up approximately 40 percent of the immigrant population. Quebec immigration selection officers may staff consulates and embassies, most importantly, in French speaking countries. As a result, Quebec possesses a greater measure of control in ensuring that immigrants will be predominately francophone or francophile. The ability of Quebec to so attract and retain francophone or francophile immigrants might be severely limited in the context of an independent Quebec where immigrants may not wish to live in such an entity, and instead tie their fortunes to a perceived more prosperous and stable Canada.

Furthermore, Quebec maintains full responsibility over the receiving and linguistic integration of these immigrants with federal financial compensation. Le Ministère de l'Immigration et des Communautés culturelles enlarged and diversified its French instructional services to immigrants. In 1994–95, for example, 6195 full-time and 20,751 part-time immigrants availed themselves of these services.[60] The evidence strongly suggests that Quebec governments have successfully employed these immigration and integration provisions to promote the dominant use of French in the public domaine.[61]

In the past, there was a strong tendency for the children of foreign immigrants in Quebec to be educated in English rather than French and to join the English speaking community. The declining francophone birth rate in Quebec also occasioned the passing of legislation to promote the French language.

Other Language Policy

Other major language policies in Quebec are aimed at the language of work, education and the French face of outdoor advertising.

The Language of Work

As we have seen, the language of work is at the heart of linguistic policies and legislation in Quebec. The first aspect of the *Charte* in relation to the language of work, is to make French the normal and usual language of work. The second aspect relates to the francification of enterprises themselves. A certificate is granted when the French language attains the desired degree of generalization within the enterprise. The requirements for the private sector are more stringent than for the public sector. The matters to be considered regarding private enterprises are outlined under Article 141 of the *Charte,* and Law 86 since 1993.[62] These factors include: the degree of knowledge of French by the Directors and other personnel; the number of Directors on the Board with a good knowledge of French; utilization of French at work in internal communications, with suppliers, clients and the public; the use of French terminology; French public advertising; maintaining a linguistic policy; and the use of French in information technologies. By

1995, 73.5 percent of enterprises with one hundred or more employees and 81.5 percent of enterprises with 50 to 99 employees obtained their certificate.[63] Fewer enterprises obtain certificates where their head office is located in Montreal or outside Quebec, being 71 percent and 64 percent respectively in 1995; whereas, 86 percent of enterprises in other Quebec regions were certified.[64]

Although certificates do not necessarily mean or guarantee that the enterprise will generally function in French or continue to do so, on the whole, certified enterprises tend to use more French than non-certified ones. Even though the certification process does not apply to small enterprises with fewer than 50 persons, of the 3700 small enterprises solicited in 1990, 3277 accepted a visit from counsellors from the Office de la langue française for advice.[65]

As discussed, other measures apply to the Quebec government and its bodies to provide for generalized communication in French and to ensure that Quebecers are informed and served in French as consumers of goods and services. Furthermore, in the area of consumer protection, Article 51 of the *Charte* requires packaging to be in French. The Report of the Quebec Interministerial Committee on the Situation of the French language in Quebec stated that some difficulties are encountered in applying that provision to imported products due to the wording of that section.[66]

Education

Section 23(1)(b) of the Charter of Rights and Freedoms guarantees minority language education rights, and was enacted as a compromise to Quebec in that it is more limited in protection than the first language clause of s. 23(1)(a). Neither subsection is subject to the legislative override contained in s. 33 of the Charter. The first language clause provides citizens of Canada whose first language learned and still understood is of the English or French linguistic minority population of the province in which they reside, the right to have their children receive primary and secondary school instruction in that language in that province. The narrower protection applicable within Quebec allows minority anglophone residents of Quebec, who received their primary school instruction in Canada in English, to have their children receive a primary and secondary school instruction in English.

Section 59 of the Charter states that s. 23(1)(a) does not apply in Quebec until the Quebec National Assembly says it does, and that is not very likely. This compromise is an example of constitutional asymmetry in which the Constitution treats Quebec more favourably in light of its concerns and distinctiveness.

However, the Canada clause, s. 23(1)(b), clashed with Quebec's Bill 101 instructional clause, which stated that English language education is guaranteed only to children of Quebec residents whose parents received an English education in Quebec. The Supreme Court of Canada ruled, in *Attorney-General of Quebec v. Quebec Protestant School Boards*,[67] that s. 23 of the Charter prevailed over Bill 101. The Court looked to the intent of the Charter provision to demonstrate the fundamental Canadian compromise that the section entailed. The measure was struck down as the clause was not seen as a reasonable limit of the right; it was a total denial of the Charter protection.

As a result of the decision, René Lévesque charged that the Supreme Court was dictating language policy in Quebec and that the Supreme Court was biased. Furthermore, he protested that Quebec must live by an illegitimate 1982 *Constitution Act*, which was imposed on Quebec. However, the Charter has not operated, especially with respect to the allophones, to prevent the establishment of a heavily dominated French-speaking public educational system. What is furthermore ironic is that prior to the Charter and prior to the provincial government taking a more active role in education, the Church controlled system and policies resulted in many non-Roman Catholic students attending Protestant English schools, which played an important role in the anglicization of certain groups.[68]

This Constitutional restriction, also, works the other way around. That is, the only way French speaking students may receive an English education is by enrolling in private schools. Therefore, the Constitutional restriction encourages and provides a dominant place for the teaching of French in Quebec public schools.[69]

Since the 1970's, the dominance of French language public school education at the primary and secondary school levels increased significantly. At the same time, the overall number of students in Quebec schools dropped appreciably, particularly due to the declining birth rate in Quebec, emigration from the province, and changes in the school system. The decline was most dramatic in terms of English language education.

In all of Quebec, during the 1971–72 school year, the number of students receiving an English language education was 256,251, or 15.67 percent of the overall number of Quebec students.[70] By the 1994–95 school year, that number dropped 57 percent to 111,466 students or 9.7 percent of the total number of Quebec students.[71]

The number of students receiving a French language education remained stable due to allophone enrolment. In 1971–72, 1,378,788 students (84.22 percent of all the students of Quebec) received a French language education.[72] In 1994–95, 1,036,202 students received a French language education.[73] Now 90.3 percent of Quebec students receive a French language education at the primary and secondary school levels in Quebec.

The same trend is evident on Montreal Island. In 1971–72, 36.2 percent of students, or 154,338, received an English language education.[74] By 1994–95, that number dropped 61 percent to 60,832 students.[75] On the other hand, in 1971–72, 271,753 students (63.8 percent) received a French language education.[76] By the 1994–95 school year, 74 percent of students on Montreal Island, or 176,074 in total, received a French language education.[77]

This growing predominance of French language public education has occurred despite the right of some Quebec students to receive an English language education. First, Law 86 integrates the essential dispositions of sections 23(1)(b) and 23(2) of the Charter into the Quebec *Charte de la langue française* (Article 73). Other students permitted to receive an English language education include those students attending English schools before the enactment of the *Charte*; where special permission is given, for example, due to familial or humanitarian reasons; or, students illegally attending English language schools who received amnesty under Law 58 passed in 1986. Despite the fact that there are students permitted to attend English language schools, many opted for French language instruction. That number rose from 4164 students in 1977–78 to 10,255 in 1994–95.[78]

What is similarly striking, as the numbers of students receiving French language public primary and secondary school education, are the numbers of anglophone and allophone Quebecers attending French language educational institutions. Since 1976–77, the year proceeding the *Charte*, 92 percent of students with a maternal language of English and 80 percent of allophone students received an English language education.[79] Since that time, English language education diminished 53 percent in gross numbers and, in 1994–95, 83 percent of students with a maternal language of English and *only* 21 percent of allophones received an English language education.[80] The rest attended schools that taught in the French language.

The numbers according to maternal language, with respect to Montreal Island, are once again striking. In the 1976–77 year, 93 percent of anglophones, 87 percent of allophones, and 4 percent of francophones received an English language education on Montreal Island.[81] In the 1994–95 year, only 3 percent of francophones, 84 percent of anglophones and 21 percent of allophone students received an English language education.[82] Between the 1976–77 and 1994-95 school years, anglophone attendance at French language schools rose from 7 percent to 16 percent.[83] French language education has, therefore, risen dramatically for students with English as their maternal language, and most dramatically with respect to students whose maternal language is neither French nor English.

The shift in terms of allophones was truly remarkable. Clearly, in terms of the language of education, French language predominance has been growing. The integration of allophones into the French language school system and, hence, into the francophone linguistic society of Quebec underwent tremendous progress. In terms of vocational, occupational and professional training in 1994–95 in Quebec, only 7.6 percent received an English language education.[84] Clearly, the great majority of such training is in the French language.

The French Face of Outdoor and Commercial Advertising

Bill 178 was a response to the Supreme Court of Canada overturning certain features of Bill 101 prohibiting outdoor signs and posters and commercial advertising in any language other than French. In 1988, the Supreme Court of Canada decided the case *Quebec v. Ford et.al.* (the Quebec Sign's Case).[85] In an unanimous decision, the Supreme Court held that freedom of expression protected commercial speech such as advertising. Furthermore, although *l'image linguistique française*, or maintaining a "French face" of outdoor advertising, was a valid objective under the Charter as it addressed the vulnerable position of the French language in Quebec and Canada, protecting the French language did not mean excluding all other languages. Such policy could be used to reflect the demography of Quebec by making the French language dominant; however, exclusivity of the French language was held not to reflect the reality of Quebec as a distinct society.

It was significant that the Supreme Court of Canada was taking into account the distinctiveness of Quebec without there actually being a distinct society clause in the Constitution! In *Reference re Quebec Secession*, the Supreme Court of Canada explicitly acknowledged that in Quebec the majority of the population is French-speaking, possesses a distinct culture, and furthermore the principle of federalism facilitates the pursuit of collective goals by cultural and linguistic minorities, which form the majority within a particular province.[86] Finally, it is important to note that the Supreme Court in *Ford* also relied extensively on Quebec's own Charter of rights and freedoms, as had Quebec's lower courts.

Quebec's Charter alone would have been sufficient and indeed was a necessary and integral part in striking down the offending provisions.

As a result of those parts of Bill 101 being struck down by the Court as unconstitutional, the Quebec legislature invoked s. 33 of the Charter so that Bill 178 could override Charter protections. Given the grass roots movement in support of the *visage français*, the use of s. 33 to override the Supreme Court of Canada's decision appeared to be politically necessary at that time. Furthermore, the use of s. 33 showed just how effective a tool the *Constitution Act, 1982* was for instituting measures thought necessary to protect the French language.

Subsequently, the s. 33 override was not to be re-enacted. In its place, Law 86 was passed to conform with the requirements of the Charter and was, hence, not accompanied by the non-derogation clause.[87] Outdoor signs and posters and commercial advertising are required to be predominately French, but, exceptions are outlined in Articles 15–25 in the *Règlement sur la langue du commerce et des affaires*.[88] Such exceptions may allow for signage without French predominance, or require French only signage, or permit the use of another language. Article 15 requires unilingual French signage of billboards 16 square metres or larger that are visible to public streets and not on the same place as the enterprise. Commercial advertising on or in areas of public transport must be in the French language.

The public outdoor advertisement issue sparked controversy among the anglophone minority. For example, some take exception to the fact that some stores advertise unilingually in French. That group took steps to boycott those stores that do not also advertise in the English language, even if in a less predominate manner. Some also wished to make Quebec's language troubles known to Wall Street investors, which may, in turn, make those investors more hesitant about investing in Quebec and/or may result in Quebec having to pay more to borrow money due to uneasiness. It was also argued that the Quebec Liberals, during the mid-80's were enforcing language legislation more vigorously than the P.Q. previously did because the P.Q. were thought to be more interested in promoting an image of linguistic peace, even though it was they who devised that legislation.[89] This argument also tends to raise questions regarding whether independence would really increase the protection of the French language, when the *péquistes* were not even enforcing their own laws within Canada.

Recently, provisions in the *Charte de la langue française* requiring the predominance of the French language in bilingual commercial advertising were challenged. The significance of this case is difficult to assess since the Quebec government chose to present absolutely *no evidence*, unlike in the *Ford* case, upon which the court could consider and conclude that the limitation on expression was reasonably justified.[90] Accordingly, the law was struck down. Perhaps, it was thought that it could not be proven that the French language in Quebec is threatened at this time, although the Supreme Court in *Ford* appeared to show deference to the material presented by the government of Quebec. It will be interesting to see whether or not the Quebec government will pursue avenues to protect the law requiring predominance, aside from the use of the Charter s. 33, or require equality of the French language with another. Even with linguistic parity, any changes will likely be only marginal.

To date, few figures are available regarding the language of advertising. One sample conducted on Montreal Island involved 3000 businesses and 26,000 commercial messages. The sample showed that 71 percent of businesses on Montreal Island displayed a predominate French face in the sense that at least 66 percent of its messages were uniquely in French, which was more accentuated in the Eastern Zone (84 percent of the businesses), than in the Western Zone (55 percent).[91] The Quebec Interministerial Committee on the situation of the French language estimated that a stranger walking on the streets of Montreal would see an *image linguistique* of a place occupied by a francophone majority.[92]

Another study showed that looking at the language of each commercial message on Montreal Island, one finds 80 percent are exclusively in French, 7 percent are bilingual and 4 percent have indeterminate names like VISA or Mastercard, totalling 91 percent of the signs.[93] Again, the language of the signage is predominately French, although some areas like the East and North display more French than the West and Central areas. One should not forget that Quebecers are extremely vigilant in reporting signs to the Office de la langue française that are thought not to be in conformity with the law.

The Language of Culture and Media

There might be some concern that in Quebec there is more English used in cultural mediums than French in other provinces. A concern, however, over possible assimilatory effects due to the presence of the English language in the cultural life of Quebec is not realistic though. The French language in Quebec culture is alive and well and, indeed, very much dominant in that province, as a survey of the subject-matters of books, newspapers, cinema and videocassettes, and radio and television demonstrate. It is interesting to note at the outset that allophones generally watch/listen to/read the media in their own language and then in French.[94]

Broadcasting, be it radio or television, is under the jurisdiction of the federal government. Federal regulatory authority over radio was first established in the *Radio Reference* case in 1930.[95] Its primacy over cable T.V. was established in *In re Capital Cities Communications Inc. v. Canadian Radio-Television Commission*, relying on the *Radio Reference* precedent.[96] For the most part, the regulation of the print media industry is largely the regulation of a particular industry and, therefore, a matter of provincial regulation, subject to the rights and freedoms set out in the Charter and the willingness to use section 33.

The existence of federal regulatory authority over radio and television did not prevent the predominance of the French language in these areas. French language AM/FM radio stations multiplied from fifty to one hundred and three since 1970.[97] There are presently eleven English language radio stations, and the number of stations broadcasting in other languages increased from two to ten.[98] French radio is generally listened to outside of Montreal by francophones (approximately 95 percent of the time) and by anglophones 34 percent of the time.[99] In Montreal itself, the francophones and anglophones generally listen to radio stations broadcasting in their own language. As for television, francophones and anglophones generally watch shows in their own language.

A study conducted by the Quebec Interministerial Committee illustrates the following situation. Two-thirds of Quebecers read books at least occasionally.[100] Of the population fifteen years of age or older, francophones and anglophones read generally in their own language. For example, in 1994, 86 percent of francophones were reading, for the most part, in French; whereas, 82 percent of anglophones were reading above all in English.[101] However, more anglophones read in French than in the past. As for the allophones, in 1994, 43 percent read above all in French, 23 percent in both languages and 34 percent particularly in English.[102] Clearly, then, in gross numbers, the vast majority of books are being read in French, which include growing numbers of anglophones and a majority of allophones.

Newspapers in the French language have made much progress. Since 1970, the printing of newspapers in French increased over 24 percent from 770,000 to 962,000 printed dailies in 1990.[103] The printing of English newspapers, on the other hand, diminished a substantial 45 per cent from 330,000 to 184,000 printed dailies.[104] In terms of papers printed in Quebec, in 1960, 69 percent of printing was in French while in 1990, the figure was 84 percent.[105] In 1997, francophones, anglophones and allophones generally read in their own language.

Although there is not a substantial amount of data regarding magazines, the evidence appears to point to a very strong and stable presence of the French language. A 1989 survey revealed that nineteen of the twenty-five magazines preferred by those in Montreal were published in the French language and made in Quebec.[106] Of the 284 magazines found in Quebec in 1995, 70 percent were in French.[107] However, it is accepted that in Quebec there remains an important market for American and European magazines.

Since 1987, greater numbers of movie goers in Quebec want to see films in the French language, including dubbed ones. French films accounted for two-thirds of all showings and two-thirds of all spectators.[108] In 1997, 59 percent of movie goers watched films at least 90 percent of the time in French.[109] Since 1987, the proportion of those watching videocassettes exclusively in French rose from 45 percent to 61 percent in 1994.[110]

Given the dominant amount of the French language in the cultural field in Quebec and given the dominance of francophones in the public and private sectors of Quebec, as well as controlling the provincial level of government, which resulted in the various government initiatives that facilitated the survival of the French language and promoted the flourishing of francophone society, the existence of the levels of English presently in the cultural arena can pose no reasonable threat to the language and society of francophone Quebec.

Protecting Culture

Quebec governments possess adequate jurisdiction to protect and promote cultural life in Quebec. What protects and promotes culture in Quebec are democracy, federalism, the Québécois desire to protect and promote culture, and the marketplace. Francophones, constituting a majority in Quebec, also comprise the largest market. As a result, cultural outputs reflecting francophone Quebec culture, for example, through theatre and film, will be in demand in that province.

The Francophone majority in Quebec may chose the government best thought to forward their interests. Governments can provide for a variety of measures such as incentives and grants to provincial cultural bodies and institutions in support of cultural endeavours. In terms of government initiatives, both federal and provincial governments have attempted to play a role in the promotion of culture. The Quebec government possesses extremely wide scope of authority for the promotion of culture in Quebec. However, the end of the Duplessis era left Quebec with a poor legacy for such promotion. Lacroix notes that presently, the Quebec Ministry of Culture is provided modest means in support of its mandate, reflecting a quasi-secular approach and tradition.[111]

Exclusivity of federal jurisdiction over broadcasting was criticized by several provinces including Quebec, while federal officials defended their jurisdiction "primarily on nation-building grounds, expressing a suspicion regarding the motives of Quebec and other provinces wishing to develop broadcasting systems."[112] Secondly, an exclusively provincial system may very well have produced an American dominated system in most provinces.

The federal government sought to promote national unity by extending CBC network services in both official languages throughout the country. The strong national focus provided an important counter-balance to the predominately local focus of the press and private broadcasting. It is argued that there existed federal intentions to provide a counterbalance to the Quebec government, which was thought to be encouraging separatism in the way it portrayed Quebec news and events.[113]

Failed attempts to control mass communications were seen by many in Quebec as a rejection of their aims to freely define their new culture. In 1969, with growing pressure from Quebec, Ontario and Alberta, the federal government issued an Order-in-Council directing the CRTC to issue licences for educational broadcasting to arm's length provincial agencies.[114]

The experience of Quebec illustrates the potential of regionally-focused broadcasting:

> ... the existence of a distinctive French service has contributed substantially to community-building in Quebec. Though formally controlled by Ottawa, the French radio and television networks, especially the latter, were major contributors of the development of a strong distinctive and politically significant popular culture in Quebec.[115]

It is further said that attempts to control 'separatists' in Radio Canada probably contributed to the growth of Quebec nationalism throughout the 1960's and 1970's.[116] This concern reflected a recognition of the province-building role that the French service played in Quebec, and may have been responsible for the federal government's determination to include in the 1968 *Broadcasting Act* the requirement that the CBC promote Canadian national unity and identity.

During the mid-80's, ententes were reached between the federal and Quebec governments relating to funds for research, the development of Quebec communications enterprises, and with respect to harmonization for the development of francophone television.[117]

The regulation of the newspaper industry is largely a matter of provincial jurisdiction and, since 1982, enjoys considerable Charter protection. French language newspapers have played an important role in articulating the French viewpoint and providing a self-image for French-Canadian and Québécois society. It also helped to provide for a national and indigenous ideology. Such leading papers included, among others, *La Presse*, *Le Devoir* and *Le Soleil*.

Promoting cultural endeavours does not take place solely at the domestic level. Although the area of international relations is, at least insofar as treaty making is concerned, one of federal jurisdiction, the Quebec government attended the Francophonie conferences and signed, with federal government approval, several important cultural agreements with the French government. To this end, the Quebec Department of Cultural Affairs was created and there was a strengthening of ties with France.

Indeed, it bears noting that Quebec's involvement in the domain of international relations goes beyond merely cultural endeavours, appearing more to reflect its nationalism and the aspirations for Quebec autonomy. France has played a significant role in welcoming Quebec as an international actor and even inviting and/or instigating Quebec to act, including by inviting Quebec to conferences to the exclusion of Canada.[118] Conferences attended included education, culture and technology, and since the 1980's there has been a shift towards economic matters and immigration.

Another aspect regarding the preservation and promotion of the distinctiveness of Quebec society is education, which is a matter of provincial jurisdiction. There can be no danger that French-Canadian and Québécois history and culture will not be taught in public school, especially if insisted upon by the Quebec provincial government. A second aspect with respect to education is that given the transformation of Quebec society, contemporary education more reflected the needs of a modernized and secularized society than previously. One commentator noted that in public education there was an assumption that Quebec was the national collectivity.[119] Accordingly, education became a vehicle for Québécois nationalism.

On the other hand, some social groups, including those among organized labour and middle class nationalists, fearing an erosion of distinctiveness, believed that not enough emphasis was being placed on distinctive values and culture, which, in turn, helped to foster alienation and disillusion, and provided a greater impetus for those groups to support political independence.[120] Such a position is somewhat ironic in that, as we have seen, the change to a more secularized and modernized education was precisely the necessary ingredient to protect the French language and francophone society, through the rise of the technically oriented new middle class and to establish francophone dominance in the Quebec business world.

To the extent to which culture survives as a result of the activities of people and not government action, there is nothing in Canada preventing the legitimate, non-violent expression of that culture, be it the teaching of Quebec's history or in pursuing artistic or cultural endeavours. Indeed, the Charter guarantees such expression against the enactments of federal, provincial or municipal governments, unless limits imposed are reasonable and demonstrably justified in a free and democratic society.

Some Further Issues

Global Forces

It is suggested by some Quebec writers that separatism is required because although there is francophone dominance in the business world of Quebec, when Quebecers do business outside of Quebec they must learn and use English. It is thought that through the bilingualization of francophones who are directly responsible for dealing with others outside of Quebec, Quebec francophones will become bilingual and eventually assimilated. It is difficult to imagine how, under the circumstances, all but a small percentage of the francophone population in Quebec would be directly involved in such bilingual networks. Secondly, it is difficult to see how this relatively small percentage of bilingual Quebecers will lead to the assimilation of francophones in a Quebec dominated by francophones. In the context that exists, there is no real danger of the loss of the French language in Quebec.

On the other hand, far from being in a better position to protect the French language, there would be a greater potential for francophone assimilation in a sovereign Quebec. The reason is that, due to Quebec's small domestic economy, the only chance a sovereign Quebec would have to survive and flourish economically and as a people would be to enhance its exports. To do so would require far more Quebecers to learn English, particularly in a context where there would be less incentive or willingness from the rest of Canada or elsewhere to speak French. In short, the creation of a sovereign Quebec would on a systemic level produce greater pressures towards bilingualism, which, ironically enough, is exactly what the separatists or sovereignists say is part of the reason for separatism or sovereignty! The position is, therefore, untenable.

All of the foregoing is not to say that the globalized economy and informational technologies do not create pressures to learn more English or American technical norms. With the global economy, there is a tendency to move towards the harmonization of norms and to adopt international and usually American norms. This trend is most commonly occurring regarding the processes of production and of quality control. Also, automation processes and information technologies are mostly in English. On the other hand, a great majority of the major software packages are *already* available in French versions, generally, at the same price as the English version; however, the French versions are not being used on a widespread basis even by a majority of francophone enterprises.[121] The Quebec government developed French terminology for the workplace so that such terminology will be more accessible to francophone workers.

The problem, in essence, is not one arising as a result of Canadian federalism at all, but, rather, is part of a global phenomenon. It is likely that the Quebec government possesses jurisdiction to create and implement many policies aimed at addressing many of those problems, such as creating a French terminology for new technology, without requiring any substantial decentralization in the Canadian federal system. More stringent restrictions could be examined with respect to packaging, or, regarding the production or translation of technical manuals in the French language. Finally, international business plays a role in satisfying the demands of the domestic market, for example, in offering French versions of important software packages.

The nature of the emerging technological norms and informational technologies do not, to a great extent, require any generalized bilingualism. However, these trends do create more pressures for some Quebecers to learn more English or foreign technical norms, unless French speaking countries and provinces can develop and use French norms and informational technologies that will actually be used by the private sector. Nevertheless, it is practically inconceivable to imagine how technological norms and informational technologies could work to assimilate the people of a non-English speaking country, or, francophones in the context of a Quebec society dominated by francophones. To cite these issues in support of separatism or sovereignty is not logical and amounts to a red herring.

The Left and the Move to the Right

Another fact that appears to be somewhat ironic and self-deceptive is that many powerful unions in Quebec support separatism. However, what those unions do not appear to appreciate is that, as we have already seen, Quebec governments are moving more and more to the right politically in terms of economic values given the realization that their survival as a province and people depends on enhancing Quebec's economy. Nowhere is Quebec's movement to right of centre politics more pronounced then in 1996, with the separatist leader of the Parti Québécois, Lucien Bouchard, being sworn in as premier of Quebec. Premier Bouchard made it abundantly clear in word and deed that Quebec would be cutting government spending, fighting the deficit and attempting to enhance Quebec's business and economy.[122] Furthermore, an independent Quebec would likely become even more pro-business if it is to survive successfully.

Conclusion

The real issue regarding the preservation of the French language in Quebec is francophone dominance in Quebec, and not whether on the part of some francophones there may be a feeling of being less distinct from the rest of Canada than in the 1950's. The forces of modernization, communications, urbanization and industrialization made Quebec less distinct. The changes in ethnic composition, the rise of new political identities and the politicization of these groups served to undermine the notion of French-English dualism in Canada, which has been a sore point for many Quebecers. It is this feeling of having grown to be less distinct that fuels many separatists/sovereignists to pursue a massive acquisition of power or independence for Quebec. It is, however, the reality and not feeling that illuminates the true situation in Quebec. In fact, had Quebecers remained in their 1950's pre-modernized and pre-Quiet Revolution mould, there is little doubt that there would have been significant linguistic assimilation of francophones and allophones, and the flourishing of francophone society would be impeded due to anglophone dominance of Quebec's business world.

Therefore, it is clear that the structural changes that occurred in Quebec society, especially after the mid-70's, produced, and continue to produce, the desired results of ensuring the flourishing of francophone society within the province of Quebec and of securing the present and future use of the French language in Quebec. These changes and results occurred within the constitutional context and structures of Canadian federalism. It is clear that Canadian federalism has not prevented and indeed has provided or allowed for the realization of these goals.

It is also interesting to note the perceptions of anglophones, allophones and francophones on the question of whether or not English will inevitably remain the language of business and finance of Quebec. In 1979, 46 percent of anglophones and 53 percent of allophones of Montreal surveyed agreed that it would; but, in 1989, those numbers dropped to 32 percent and 41 percent respectively, and 70 percent of francophones disagreed.[123] Thus, even the perceptions of Quebecers have been changing. A recent study of ethnic groups demonstrates the acceptance of the French language in education and the business world, which reflects the contemporary reality in Quebec.[124]

Together with a business world and workplace dominated to a large extent by francophones and the French language, one may add the fact that the government and public sector of Quebec is dominated by francophones. Therefore, in two large segments of Quebec society, the French language flourishes.

The third major pillar supporting the survival of the French language relates to the language of public education. Within the context of the Charter of Rights and Freedoms, students of immigrant parents are required to attend francophone schools and so become integrated into the francophone linguistic community. Finally, the treatment of immigration under the Cullen-Couture and McDougall-Gagnon-Trembley Accords successfully provide Quebec with greater control over the selection and integration of immigrants than might otherwise be the case.

With ever increasing numbers and proportions of allophones becoming integrated into the francophone, as opposed to anglophone, society, Quebec will continue to be French even if the Québécois francophone proportion of the population declines somewhat. This fact might also be considered in the context of the decline of anglophone numbers and proportions in all aspects of francophone society such as overall population, business and education. Clearly, the greater incentive is for allophones to become integrated into francophone society, including on Montreal Island, even with its concentration of allophones and anglophones. The fact that some allophones may speak a language other than French at home or may also wish to retain their culture does not mean that they do not fully participate in francophone public life. Indeed, quite the opposite is true. Although the retention of a vibrant anglophone minority in Quebec is a positive goal, one cannot say that francophones have not taken control over their destinies and successfully promoted the flourishing of their French language and francophone society in Quebec. One Québécois writer who supports separatism correctly states:

The presence of a strong anglophone community in Quebec today and long into the future is not a source of concern for us. Quite the contrary, we believe that all the conditions are in place to make Montréal a centre of cultural, economic and intellectual creativity in the 21st century.[125] (translation)

All of these accomplishments have occurred within the context of the Canadian Constitution and the Canadian federation. It is clear from the foregoing that the fact that many Quebecers may feel themselves less distinct today from the other parts of Canada in no way impedes their desire or ability to secure these accomplishments. By constituting a majority in their province and controlling the major levers of powers of provincial jurisdiction, all evidence shows that as assertive as francophone Quebecers were in the past, such efforts will continue to successfully promote the flourishing of francophone society and to preserve the French language in Quebec.

Furthermore, such efforts clearly demonstrate that, contrary to what some writers believe or may suggest, the cultural, societal and public policy preference convergences between francophone Quebecers and other Canadians have not undermined the 'psychological integrity' of Quebecers. Rather, this convergence served to accentuate differences between the two, particularly on a political and nationalistic level. Stéphan Dion argues that this paradox of cultural convergence and the reinforcing of nationalism can be explained by several factors such as the evolution towards greater social mobility, the greater equality of conditions of individuals, democratic political liberty, and the increasing uniformity or homogenization occurring in the world.[126] As a result, the similarity of peoples stimulate their rivalries through emphasizing their distinctiveness.[127] These manifestations of Quebec nationalism although occurring in many areas, are most acute when the Constitution comes under discussion.

Thus, the argument that as Quebec increasingly becomes a province *not* unlike the others, the "justification" for sovereignty, being rooted in republican thought, paradoxically, is stronger than forty years ago, due to the fact that support for separatism has grown is simply untenable. To be rationally justified, reasonable and substantial grounds must be demonstrated justifying separatism/sovereignty. A referendum on a clear question in favour of separatism by a clear majority might be a procedural "justification" for secession in the sense that democratic legitimacy follows from the result of a referendum. Anything short will not do and any other level of support for separatism is no "justification" at all. Even a successful referendum does not necessarily mean in Quebec's case that independence would be achievable as a matter of law, or would be recognized. Yet, the component which gave rise to the increased support for secession since the 1960's in Quebec is nationalism. Nationalism is inherently emotional, not rational, although may have a rational basis for its existence. It may also be irrational, destructive and even hateful. The central question therefore is whether or not secession is rationally justified. If it is not, then Quebecers should not vote in any referendum to separate. Once it is shown, as it has, that the Quebec government and francophone Quebecers possess the ability to protect the French language and to promote the flourishing of Quebec francophone society within the present state of Canadian federalism, there leaves little or nothing else in support of the proposition that Quebec should separate or become sovereign. All other justifications remain an empty shell.

Chapter 7
The Constitutional Aspects of Federalism

As we witnessed in the last Chapter, the province of Quebec and Quebecers, within the Canadian federation as it exists today, have enough power and the ability to protect and promote the French language, francophone society and Québécois culture. The reason is that although Canadian federalism does not protect all interests, it does effectively protect territorially based ones. On a simple level, the Constitution provides provincial governments with power over matters that are of local or provincial concern. Yet, the federal level of government also plays an important part in building provincial and national societies and economies. Reality would, therefore, dictate that rational and reasonable grounds for separatism and sovereignty in the Canadian context do not exist when federalism has operated to protect and promote the most fundamental needs and concerns of francophone Quebecers. Logic would dictate, then, that any shortcomings faced by the Quebec government or Quebecers in protecting the French language, or in promoting the flourishing of its francophone economy and society are largely inadequacies with a basis other than in Canadian federalism. Indeed, to a great extent, anglophone dominance of the Quebec business world was allowed to continue unchallenged because Quebec governments previously refused to take greater responsibility in managing the economy and society of Quebec. Nevertheless, Quebec governments often focus on symbolic matters, particularly within the constitutional domain. As a result, separatists and sovereignists state to the Quebec public that Quebec and Canada cannot live together; in essence, their visions of the country are too dissimilar.

This Chapter will consider the constitutional aspects of Canadian federalism in more detail. The first part considers the nature of demands made by Quebec governments, and whether or not further constitutional accommodation is necessary with respect to Quebec. Interestingly enough, one will discover that Quebec's distinct society is already reflected and provided for in the Constitution, in the workings of Canadian federalism, and within government structures themselves. Although the constitution of Canada serves the needs of Quebecers well in reality, it is not always portrayed as such, primarily at the symbolic level.

The second part of this Chapter answers the symbolic indictments made against the *Constitution Act, 1982*, and whether the other provinces and the federal government can now gang up on Quebec and pass amendments harmful to that province.

Finally, it cannot be said that significant accommodation within Canada is not possible. Indeed, Canadian federalism is continually evolving and accommodating the needs and concerns of the participants and citizens in the federal system, including those of Quebec. The next Chapter examines the constitutional evolution of Canada in becoming truly federal and decentralized in nature.

Is Further Accommodation Necessary?

An overarching question that is being asked in various contexts is whether further Constitutional accommodation is necessary. The sub-question is to identify what accommodation is "necessary" to what end.

The question then arises how to recognize the symbolic species in the Canadian federalism wilderness when one sees it. A symbolic demand is one that is status seeking, unnecessary, or not proportional in nature. It can be distinguished from functional demands or considerations, which are based on necessity or efficiency in dealing with specific concrete problems or issues. Symbolic demands, thus, exhibit certain characteristics. A demand, or package of demands, may not be a solution to a problem at all either because, as stated, the demand is not addressing a concrete problem or issue, or, a solution has already been achieved. It may be that the government demanding more power possesses sufficient powers to deal adequately with the problem. Additionally, a symbolic demand may be one that goes well beyond what is necessary to solve the problem. In other words, the solution must be proportional to the problem encountered and having regard to its impact on the workings of the federation as a whole.

Many constitutional demands made by Quebec are symbolic in the sense that Quebec already possesses the powers necessary to deal with the problem or issue underlying the demand, or, that a successful solution to the problem or issue is already implemented. Often demands from Quebec are made of the wholesale variety and are, as a result, not proportional to the problem, or, regarding its effects on the workings of the federal system. Questions such as what should Quebec's proper role in Confederation be given its distinctive qualities and demanding that this role be explicitly reflected in the Constitution lead to symbolic demands being made. In essence, it has status seeking elements and involves Quebec governments attempting to distinguish itself from the other provinces. Such status seeking elements have little or nothing to do with analysing a problem or issue affecting Quebecers, arising, perhaps, due to one of its distinctive features, and surveying and analysing various solutions in order to implement the best one in the circumstances.

The choice of policy instrument itself provides a good indication about whether a demand is symbolic or functional. An emphasis on constitutional change involves a greater likelihood of reflecting the symbolic approach since constitutions are thought of as supreme law and have the ability to fundamentally reshape the political order of a polity, or the underlying vision or philosophy of that state entity. Constitutional solutions can be distinguished in this way from technical or administrative solutions. The later can also be of fundamental importance or can involve much symbolism. Yet, it is the high politics and symbolism of a Constitution that can make its creation or modification far more prone to symbolic demands and pressures. In this way, choosing a constitutional (or high politics) solution when another one is available that is effective and more conducive to achieving an effective solution is an indicator of symbolism.

It is quite possible that, in a given case, a constitutional amendment is necessary because no other solution may effectively deal with the problem or issue. In such a case, pursuing this option would reflect functionalism. However, the cumbersome amendment process, the passions that it tends to provoke, and the relative permanence of Constitutional amendments, as well as the types of actors tending to be involved make it a difficult process in which to achieve agreement and, thus, should be used only as a last resort when there is no other effective and feasible solution available. Other possible solutions may involve one or a combination of: government suasion, the use of a constitutional power already existing, constitutional convention, intergovernmental agreement, or, resorting to the courts to better define the constitutional framework of the area in dispute, if there is one. The tool of intergovernmental agreement generally provides for a highly flexible method of solving problems, it may be backed by an expert infrastructure, it has the advantage of being subject to readjustment, and can effectively integrate citizen or group participation. On the other hand, the quasi-permanence of a provision or taking an issue out of the political arena may be desirable, such as with respect to an entrenched bill of rights. However, these types of matters tend to be relatively few.

Although not all present and future issues can be analysed or predicted in this study, the major areas will be discussed. Two overall themes emerge underlying the symbolic search by Quebec governments for more constitutional accommodation. Either more constitutional power is sought to protect the French language or to promote the flourishing of francophone society; or, more broadly, further accommodation is necessary to recognize Quebec's distinct nature within Confederation. The reality within the Canadian federation presently supports neither basis as a necessity compelling further accommodation through Constitutional amendment and accommodation, at least on a fundamental scale.

Clearly, as demonstrated in detail, Quebec needs no new powers to protect its French language and to provide for the flourishing of francophone society within the Canadian federation as it exists. Nothing in the workings of Canadian federalism or in the Constitution itself, including the Charter, prevents Quebec and Quebecers from achieving these goals.

One example of the symbolism of constitutional demands relates to the policy area of immigration. The constitutional demand made by Quebec in the Meech Lake Accord consistent with the theme of the protection of language included provisions relating to immigration. Under the Meech Lake Accord, Quebec sought essentially to constitutionalize agreements between the federal and Quebec government with respect to immigration. This point was certainly the least criticized aspect of the Accord. In effect, it would have constitutionalized the Cullen-Couture Agreement. That agreement has been working well and constitutionalizing it is not necessary. Given that type of agreement, being sensitive to Quebec's demographic anxieties, there is little fear that it will not be continued, as the McDougall-Gagnon-Trembley Accord demonstrates.

Secondly, to the extent that the survival and flourishing of culture comes from the people and not government initiatives, it cannot be said that Canada, in any way, inhibits that survival and flourishing. Indeed, the Charter of Rights and Freedoms, an often criticized document by separatists and sovereignists, would itself protect against government intrusions, be they at the federal, provincial or municipal level, aimed at denying Quebecers their beliefs and expression of their culture.

In view of the facts and as we will continue to see, it is difficult to see what further accommodation in constitutional text is necessary to protect language and culture in Quebec. Not only does the provincial government's jurisdiction relate most intimately to culture, language and society, even to the exclusion of the federal level of government, but, the citizens of Quebec are constitutionally entitled to express their language and culture. Furthermore, nothing in the Constitution or the workings of Canadian federalism has prevented the accomplishment of these highly important goals.[1]

The second aspect of constitutional demands involves Quebec governments seeking greater accommodation to recognize Quebec's distinct nature within Confederation. A major aspect of distinctive nature is language and the existence of its francophone society, which does not support calls for constitutional amendment, at least, on a fundamental basis.

There are two basic ways in which distinctive nature may be explicitly recognized in the Constitution. First, the Constitution may say that Quebec is a distinct society. Secondly, Quebec might possess more powers than other provinces, thereby, distinguishing itself from the rest of Canada.

The argument for the necessity of such greater accommodation recognizing Quebec's distinctiveness is in error as it assumes that if a province reflects distinctive qualities, it must be treated differently in written constitutional text. That statement does not necessarily hold true. Furthermore, if true, Canada would have ten provinces and two territories being treated differently in constitutional text such that there would be multiple constitutions and no real Canadian or national constitution. Additionally, such a position is in error as it tends to focus upon symbolic differences of how one province is distinguishable from other provinces in the explicit provisions of the Constitution and not the reality of whether within the federation a province and its people already have the ability to ensure its most basic and fundamental values and interests. Furthermore, Quebecers already demonstrate a desire and ability to successfully promote these goals. There are various ways, both constitutional and non-constitutional, in which Quebec's distinctiveness has been recognized and accommodated in the context of Canadian federalism.

Constitutional Recognition

The Division of Jurisdiction

The fact of the matter is that Quebec does enjoy distinct society recognition in the Constitution along with constitutional powers adequate to preserve and allow for the flourishing of its distinctiveness. First and foremost, distinct society recognition is embedded in the division of jurisdiction. To illuminate this statement it is important to recall again that federalism, while not protecting all interests, does protect territorially based ones. In other words, Quebec can be as distinct as it likes, and federalism, far from inhibiting that distinctiveness, constitutionally protects it through the division of jurisdiction! Thus, every time the Quebec government acts or legislates within its jurisdiction in a way that is distinct or concerning one of its distinctive qualities, such action is constitutionally protected and can only be challenged if it violates the Charter.

Quebec and Quebecers possess adequate power and the ability to protect the French language and to promote the flourishing of francophone Quebec society and culture under the Constitution, including the Charter, and examples were provided of how Quebec governments acted in a distinctive manner. A prime example of such distinctive developments relates to the structural changes instituted in that province to facilitate francophone dominance of Quebec's business world, including Bill 101, the Caisse de dépôt, the caisses populaires, and so on. Quebec governments acted distinctively because they were dealing with specific problems faced in Quebec and due to distinctive aspects of its society, which were not faced by other Legislatures in Canada in the same sense, although those Legislatures may face similar challenges with respect to promoting provincial economies. Other provinces have the same types of powers as Quebec and, in fact, created their own innovations, or instituted similar initiatives. Provincial stock savings plans, or funds to invest in the economy like the Heritage Trust Fund in Alberta bear some similarities to certain Quebec initiatives. In other respects, innovations from Quebec made it less distinct from other Canadians both as a people and the manner in which some of those institutions operate. Some argue, for example, that the Mouvement Desjardins now operates more than ever in a technocratic fashion similar to other North American banks.[2] However, it is the scale of these initiatives in Quebec, their purpose of addressing the historical "social justice" concerns, and to facilitate the flourishing of francophone business that make these developments 'distinctive'. In other words, it is the distinguishing characteristics of Quebec society, particularly relating to language, history and demography that gave rise to the use of constitutional powers to create distinctive measures and initiatives. This distinctiveness arises irrespective of whether or not Quebec is provided with additional constitutional powers to place it apart from other provincial governments, or, whether or not a distinct society clause exists in the Constitution. Quebec is distinct in various ways because *it is* and not because everyone is told that it is. What is important is that the distinction exists in reality and Canadian federalism allows provincial and federal governments and citizens sufficient powers and the ability to protect and facilitate the flourishing of that distinctiveness. In this way, Quebec governments have used provincial powers in distinctive ways and may continue to do so, thereby reflecting its distinct society reality. Such reflection is also apparent within the federal government and through intergovernmental relations and agreements. This kind of real distinct society recognition is far more valuable than a symbolic distinct society clause.

The *Constitution Act, 1867*, itself, sets Quebec apart in recognition of its distinct society within Canada. Section 94 allows for three of the four provinces then entering Confederation, namely Ontario, Nova Scotia and New Brunswick, to transfer their power over property and civil rights and the procedure of provincial Courts to the federal government. Quebec, was not given such an option, particularly, due to its Civil Code as opposed to the other provinces who have a common law system. Therefore, s. 94 recognizes Quebec's distinct society, as did the *Quebec Act* of 1774.

The Constitution Act, 1982

Even in the context of the *Constitution Act, 1982*, there is distinct society potential. One example is the general amending formula, which gives the right of a province to opt out with compensation of amendments having the effect of transferring provincial jurisdiction in the fields of education and culture to the federal government.

As we already observed, the Charter recognizes and protects Quebec's distinct character through s. 23, dealing with minority language educational rights in which the more restrictive rights apply in Quebec unless the National Assembly adopts s. 23(1)(a), which applies throughout the rest of Canada. This provision is a protection of Quebec's distinct character, as well as providing a nation-wide recognition of the importance of the French Fact in Canada since the provision applies only to English and French minority language education rights. French minority language educational rights outside Quebec are protected by the first language clause, s. 23(1)(a) of the Charter, which gives wider protection than s. 23(1)(b) would. Francophones outside of Quebec who received a primary school education in Canada in French are guaranteed the right to see their children receive primary or secondary school education in the French language in areas of the province where numbers warrant and with support of public funds.

As will be discussed later, even when assessing whether or not the infringement of a Charter right or freedom is "demonstrably justified" under s. 1, regional/provincial circumstances will be taken into account and specifically when Quebec's laws are under scrutiny.

Under section 33 of the Charter, Parliament or any legislature of a province may expressly declare that its Act, or a provision thereof, shall continue to operate notwithstanding anything stated in the Charter's section 2 or sections 7 to 15. Thus, the fundamental freedoms, legal rights and equality rights contained in the Charter may be overridden.

There are, however, great political costs in overriding such important rights and freedoms, both in the eyes of other Canadians and even in the eyes of the international community. The federal government never invoked s. 33, and it was only used once by an English speaking province with respect to one piece of legislation. In that instance, Saskatchewan enacted strike ending legislation. Given that the Supreme Court of Canada held, on appeal, that freedom of assembly guaranteed by the Charter did not include the right to strike, not only was the override unnecessary, there does not appear to be many situations in which an English speaking province or the federal government will ever invoke s. 33, particularly, due to the political costs associated with doing so.[3] Alberta's Ralph Klein found this out when he attached the notwithstanding clause to a Bill limiting compensation payable to persons sterilized without their consent. The next day, the measure was withdrawn. It may even be a matter of constitutional convention or understanding that the English speaking provinces and the federal government each should allow s. 33 to fall to disuse. The same is not necessarily true for Quebec.

Between 1982 to 1986, Quebec invoked s. 33 for all legislation, until its universal invocation was suspended by Premier Bourassa due to the negotiations taking place leading to the Meech Lake Accord. The invoking of s. 33 was primarily a symbolic protest regarding the *Constitution Act, 1982*. As such, there is distinct society potential by the very use of s. 33 in view of the fact that other provinces and the federal government will not, or, cannot use that provision. Therefore, Quebec has a power the others do not.

More important than this symbolic indiscriminate use of s. 33 is the fact that, if necessary, it could be invoked to protect the French language in Quebec. Section 33 was attached to Bill 178 to protect the *visage linguistique* of

Quebec. Indeed, there was a tremendous grass roots pressure in support of invoking s. 33 at that time. In the end, the overriding legislation enacted under s. 33 must be re-enacted every five years. The political costs in overriding fundamental freedoms weighed heavily and the s. 33 declaration attached to Bill 178 was not re-enacted, most likely, because it was not seen as necessary in order to protect the French language in Quebec. Indeed, the evidence demonstrates its use not to be necessary. That is not to say should it become truly necessary to attach s. 33 to a piece of legislation, it could not be used and, hence, its invocation would reflect the realities of Quebec's distinct society and needs.

The French Fact in Canada

The protection of the French Fact in Canada includes the use of French and the participation of francophones in federal Parliament or federal institutions and in federally created courts. As a national symbol, it shows the equality of status between the English and French speaking members of Canadian society. To the extent that the French Fact exists within Quebec, the provision is a reflection and protection of its distinct character. Indeed, the number of Members of Parliament to which Quebec is entitled to send to the House of Commons, being seventy-five, is greater, as a percentage of the number of seats in the House, than its proportion of the Canadian population. The French Fact is also simultaneously recognized outside of Quebec.

The importance of the French and English languages in Canada is recognized in s. 16 of the Charter. Both are official languages of Canada sharing an equality of status. Sections 16–20 of the Charter guarantee the use of either language in all institutions of Parliament and government in Canada; statutes, records and journals of Parliament must be printed and published in English and French, and both language versions are equally authoritative. Furthermore, any member of the Canadian public has the right to communicate with and to receive services from Parliament or federal institutions in English or French where there is significant demand; or, due to the nature of the office, it is reasonable that communications be available in both English and French.

In addition to the protection of official language rights in the federal Parliament and government, either French or English may be used in any proceedings in a Court established by Parliament. Provincially created courts, with the exception of those in New Brunswick, are not required by the Charter to extend the same rights. However, the dictates of a fair hearing must be followed and an interpreter may be required. In Courts established by the federal government, the Supreme Court of Canada decided that, under the Charter, aside from natural fairness considerations and legislative requirements, one is guaranteed the right to be heard in one of the official languages, but, not necessarily to be understood in that language.[4] Mr Justice Beetz, speaking for the Court, held that in absence of a system of testing, judges must assess their own ability to determine whether they are competent in the relevant official language to hear the case.

These Charter rights are similar in nature to the rights guaranteed in section 133 of the *Constitution Act, 1867* regarding the use of the French and English languages. Sections 16 to 20 of the Charter extend recognition and protection of the French Fact in the Legislature, government, and courts of New Brunswick.

Non-Constitutional Recognition
Federal Government

Despite the fact that inherent in Canadian federalism is a dynamism for conflict between the federal and provincial governments, it does not mean that the federal government is not sensitive to regional interests.

For example, the federal government sought to recognize the French Fact in Canada through a policy of bilingualism. In the wake of the report of the Bilingualism and Biculturalism Commission, the federal government used its jurisdiction to enact the *Official Languages Act* to further promote bilingualism in federal institutions and government. The Act not only gives all Canadians the right to use either language in communications with government, and requires bilingualism in public documents and court decisions; but, it expands opportunities for francophones in the federal public service, especially at its higher levels. The proportions of francophones rose to between 28 and 29 percent by 1987, from 21 percent in 1965, and up to 26 percent from 17 percent regarding senior positions during that time.[5] In examining the composition of senior executives in the federal government, one would find an overrepresentation of Quebecers and francophones from all of Canada, while the overrepresentation is not as pronounced with respect to francophone Quebecers.[6]

Significant monies were allocated by the federal government to official language programs. Other initiatives in this respect included a major expansion of Radio-Canada services and facilitating organizational infrastructure of official language minorities. Although official bilingualism did not transform Canada into a *de facto* bilingual state where both languages are used interchangeably in daily life, it is clear that bilingualism increased substantially among English Canadians and opened up opportunities for francophones in the federal public service.

On the constitutional level, the federal government pressed for language rights in the Charter and insisted upon the Canada clause contained in s. 23(1)(b) applying to Quebec instead of the first language clause.

Furthermore, it cannot be said that francophones from Quebec are not well represented in Parliament through the number of seats it is guaranteed in the Constitution, or in the numbers or composition of the governing party's Cabinet and in policy-making structures at the federal level. Michel Sarra-Bournet noted that since 1945, Quebec francophone federal Members of Parliament were almost always overrepresented in ministerial caucus *vis-à-vis* their representation in the House of Commons, while this representation is generally reduced in Cabinet.[7] The time frame used in support of this observation insofar as the representation of Quebec francophone M.P.s in the federal Cabinet is concerned begins in 1945. It is clear that before the Quiet Revolution, before francophone Quebecers began to assert themselves, their position in Canada was less favourable, and indeed may have reflected a legitimate cause of grievance. That situation is not the case today. The appropriate time of reference is contemporary Canada and, particularly, with the onset of the Quiet Revolution. Since 1963, francophone Quebecers have always been, with few exceptions, overrepresented in the federal Cabinet.[8] Regional caucuses give an additional voice to Quebecers.

Quebec benefits extensively from federal policies and gained significant federal spending, for example in the area of regional economic development, at least on a per capita basis. According to Stats Canada, the contribution of Quebecers to federal revenue fluctuates between 21 percent and 22 percent, whereas, Quebec receives 24 percent to 25 percent of federal spending.[9] In terms of federal transfers respecting Equalization, and the major shared cost programs pursuant to Established Programs Finance and the Canada Assistance Plan (now called the Canada Health and Social Transfer—the "CHST"), Quebec certainly received its fair share on the basis of per capita and interprovincial equity.[10] Indeed, with respect to the social union, Quebec on a per capita basis benefited the most, even *vis-à-vis* less wealthy provinces such as Newfoundland. It is only now that the CHST is being restored to an equal footing. Nevertheless, in terms of the increase in new transfers to the provinces, one-third goes to Quebec, which only makes up one-quarter of the population.[11] All these facts disprove Premier Bouchard's allegations that Quebec is not being treated fairly.

Quebec federal politicians have played a significant role in the formation of federal policy, and federal policies are fair towards Quebec. Indeed, in the last half century, with few exceptions, Quebecers commanded a monopoly as Prime Ministers of Canada.

Supreme Court of Canada

Finally, and partly due to s. 94 of the *Constitution Act, 1867*, Quebecers are guaranteed three Supreme Court of Canada judges. Due to the fact that the Supreme Court of Canada might from time to time be called upon to adjudicate Civil Code matters, the *Supreme Court Act* states that three of the nine justices must be from Quebec. Those same three judges, of course, also, sit on other matters not concerning the Civil Code.

Intergovernmental Relations

It is incorrect to say that territorial interests are only protected through formal Constitutional provisions. Intergovernmental relations and the agreements they produce, also, allow for the recognition and accommodation of the distinctive interests of provincial governments and societies.

As outlined in Chapter 1, the structure of Canadian federalism naturally gives rise to relations between the two levels of government. Such relations reflect the need for a non-judicial mechanism of policy adjustment. Its proliferation reflects an attempt to manage the multifaced interdependencies of autonomous federal and provincial actors, arising, especially, from the growth of the modern administrative state. With almost deceiving simplicity, D.V. Smiley defined executive federalism as the "relations between elected and appointed officials of the two orders of government in federal-provincial interaction."[12] The relations can be bilateral (between the federal government and a province), or multilateral (between the federal government and more than one province). Relations can, also, be interprovincial (between provinces), and these relations can be bilateral or multilateral.

We have already seen an important example of how Quebec's distinct society is recognized through intergovernmental agreements. Due to Quebec's demographic anxieties, the Cullen-Couture and the McDougall-Gagnon-Trembley bilateral agreements were signed and, thereafter, used by Quebec governments in their attempt to promote greater francophone or francophile immigration into Quebec, and to better control the linguistic integration of immigrants. This agreement gives to Quebec greater control over immigration than what might otherwise be the case under the Constitution.

Quebec's distinctive interests, as well as the interests of other provinces, have been recognized in the context of shared cost programs, like Family Allowance. Greater detail will be provided in Chapter 9 regarding the changes that fiscal and other aspects of Canadian federalism underwent. There has been, in fact, accommodation of Quebec's interests in practice. This aspect of intergovernmental relations is highly significant and its positive aspects are often ignored or downplayed.

Conclusion

The broad scope of the inquiry conducted thus far demonstrates that federalism has worked to protect and promote the most fundamental needs and concerns of francophone Quebecers. It furthermore suggests that, at present, no further constitutional accommodations appear to be necessary with respect to accommodating Quebec's needs, especially on a fundamental scale. Quebec and Quebecers already possess the powers and the ability to protect their French language and society. Its distinct society characteristics are already reflected and provided for in the context of the Constitution or in the workings of Canadian federalism, primarily through the division of jurisdiction, its constitutional and nonconstitutional workings, the Charter, the composition of the federal government and federal courts, as well as through intergovernmental relations and agreements. The exercise of jurisdiction reflects Quebec's needs and concerns, as do the accommodations that continually occur with respect to Quebec and the other provinces in constitutional and non-constitutional manners. In this way, Quebec's distinctiveness is clearly recognized in the workings of the Canadian federation.

All of this is not to say that discrete matters could not be considered as candidates for some sort of constitutional adjustment between the federal and provincial levels of government; or, that the necessity of constitutional amendment may not arise in the future. Any such matters must be carefully considered on their own merits. Indeed, we will see in later Chapters that modifications in the workings of Canadian federalism continuously occur, including in the context of extremely important and complex matters. The truth, however, is that demanding large scale constitutional amendment or other change on the basis of protecting the French language in Quebec, or to provide for the flourishing of francophone Quebec society, or in otherwise recognizing its distinctive qualities is indefensible. No such justification exists.

Whenever a demand for constitutional amendment is made, one must determine whether it is necessary. One must identify, first, what is the precise problem sought to be remedied. Secondly, due to the difficulties associated with constitutional amendment, one must determine if there are no other effective means to deal with the problem. Rarely, will constitutional amendment be necessary. Finally, one must determine whether the particular constitutional demand is proportional to the problem sought to be corrected and regarding the impact of the proposed amendment on the workings of the federation as a whole. Only then can a demand for constitutional amendment be thought of as really justified within the context of the Canadian federation.[13]

Constitution Act, 1982: **The Indictment**

There are three major indictments preferred against the 1982 *Constitution Act* to support the argument that the Amendment is illegitimate, and the themes underlying the grounds for separatism or sovereignty are reflected in these indictments. The theme of legitimacy is implicated in that it is argued that Quebec was "stabbed in the back" and betrayed during that process, or that the Amendment suffers from a lack of democratic legitimacy. The second theme of assimilation with respect to the preservation of language and flourishing of Quebec society is also implicated. One concern was that if English Canada could gang up on Quebec to patriate the Constitution in 1982, then so too can it gang up on Quebec to pass constitutional amendments harmful to it in the future. The third indictment shares elements of two themes, namely, assimilation and competing visions. The essential argument is that the Charter has, or will have, negative implications for Quebec. The first negative implication is that the Charter weakens Quebec's power to preserve the French language. The second is that the Charter restructures citizen's conceptions of community in favour of the national government to the detriment of Quebec loyalties and therefore threatens assimilation.

Patriation and the November Conference

The Constitution of Canada, including the *Constitution Act, 1982*, serves the needs of Quebecers well in reality even if it is not always portrayed as such at the symbolic level. Therefore, there appears little need to go on discussing separatism or sovereignty. However, much is made at the symbolic level of the fact that Quebec was not a signatory to that constitutional amendment by separatists and sovereignists in their indictment of Canada. The event will be assessed to separate the illusions from reality. The illusion that English Canada stabbed Quebec in the back was created by focusing on one fact to the exclusion of all others.[14] The reality was far more complicated than that. An examination of the events leading up to agreement, which itself would later be subject to further modification and public consultation, will be made including assessing the dynamics then occurring from the perspective of the Quebec delegation.

The situation after the Supreme Court of Canada's decision in the *Patriation Reference*[15] was that the federal government possessed the legal authority to patriate the Constitution, but, a political or constitutional convention existed requiring substantial provincial consent. Therefore, there was great incentive on the part of both the federal and provincial levels of government to reach agreement. However, the negotiations were deadlocked with a block of eight provinces, including Quebec, forming a seemingly unbreakable common front in opposition to the federal proposal.

Even examining Claude Morin's own account, as a member of the Quebec delegation, there is little evidence to show that Quebec was betrayed or stabbed in the back. The Gang of Eight opposing the federal unilateral move were Quebec, Saskatchewan, Alberta, British Columbia, Manitoba, Nova Scotia, Newfoundland and Prince Edward Island. Morin points to the September 28th meeting between Jean Chrétien, Roy Romanow and Roy McMurtry after the Supreme Court of Canada's decision in the *Patriation Reference* as the first instance of the Common Front breaking apart. Secondly, in response to Trudeau's threat to move unilaterally if the provinces did not come up with some concrete proposals, Premier Bennett from British Columbia began acting as mediator between the Gang of Eight and the federal government. Thus, the betrayal, according to Morin, had its roots in Saskatchewan and British Columbia searching for a middle acceptable position between the federal project and the Gang of Eight's Accord, as an attempt to bring Trudeau to the table and avoid failure of the negotiations. Therefore, Quebec was believing, going into the November Conference, that the Common Front existed, but, its objectives were changing. Would other provinces go? Saskatchewan, British Columbia and Ontario would then attempt to arrive at a compromise position.

During that last ditch Conference, the Common Front had an air of solidity except for Saskatchewan and British Columbia, who were trying to come up with a new constitutional proposal. The positions were still too diametrically opposed to produce agreement. During the second day of the Conference,

B.C. announced a new common position, which Lévesque accepted. This accord was rejected by Trudeau, essentially due to the proposed truncated Charter. Blakeney of Saskatchewan announced that he would present his proposition the next day to get around the dead end. Quebec believed, at this time, that the Common Front no longer existed.[16]

The next day, the proposition was considered. Still, the Conference was looking like a failure and Trudeau was threatening to go the national referendum route to break the impasse.[17] Trudeau proposed that the outcome be determined by majorities within the four regions defined by the Victoria Charter. At this point, Lévesque placed his support behind the referendum option, much to the chagrin of the other provinces, who were in opposition to that position. Likely, thinking that time was on their side, and that they could win the proposed referendum, the Quebec delegation abandoned its allies to support the federal proposal.[18] Claude Charron wrote:

> It was the ideal solution for us. We put off the threat for two years and are sure of victory in the referendum.[19]

One writer from Quebec, Max Nemni, put the matter in this way:

> However, what matters most here is not the reason why Quebec abandoned her allies but, rather, the enthusiasm and the speed with which she did so. René Lévesque asserted that this was "a respectable and extraordinarily interesting way of getting out of this imbroglio" (La Presse 5 November 1981). Nor was Lévesque alone in his enthusiasm. The Quebec delegation was jubilating and, despite the risk of displeasing its partners of the Common Front, it did not hesitate one instant to climb aboard Ottawa's band wagon.[20]

Publically, Lévesque announced that to break the impasse, Quebec accepts the idea of a referendum. Trudeau stated that a new alliance between Ottawa and Quebec had been formed.[21] René Lévesque would later simply claim that on closer view the proposal was not what it seemed and tried to cover up the facts by saying that "all of a sudden everything has become a real mishmash."[22]

The provinces were astounded. Romanow, the Intergovernmental Affairs Minister of Saskatchewan, was angry and confronted Morin, the Quebec Intergovernmental Affairs Minister, asking him why his province took the position that it did. Morin replied:

> It's very simple ... the Common Front has disappeared and to a large extent by the actions of your own province. Why should Quebec not opt for something else in its turn.[23] (translation)

The Common Front then fell apart. By this time, Trudeau held little hope for the possibility of a successful outcome, but, later agreed to a further meeting the next day.[24] That night, after the Conference, Romanow, McMurtry and Chrétien met in a secluded room in the conference centre to attempt a last ditch effort to draft an entente to avoid immanent failure, which would result in Trudeau initiating a national referendum. That meeting, ending at 3:30 a.m., produced an agreement, which was presented to and accepted by most of the provinces, the remainder of which would join the next day. Thus, in the morning, with the Quebec delegation's return from Quebec city, the Accord was presented to them, in large part already accepted by the provinces. During the Conference that followed, the proposal was then discussed and adopted by the federal government and by all of the provinces except Quebec, claiming that it was abandoned.

Further modifications in favour of Quebec, rights advocates, womens' groups and Aboriginals were later made before the amendment passed in its final form.

A conspiracy theory against Quebec is simply not reasonable on the facts. It appears that for Morin any attempt at compromise signified a disintegration of the Common Front and was part of a larger betrayal of Quebec, which, under Lévesque, would not consider any further compromises, any Charter of rights, or any loss of power to the Quebec National Assembly. What the facts do show is a complex interaction among multiple parties in a context of immanent patriation by the federal government, on the one hand, and the undesirability of such a unilateral move, on the other. Without the last ditch effort, it appeared, by Morin's own account, that the Conference would have ended in failure and a national referendum called. The referendum route appeared to be the final option available where all else failed.

What would have, or would not have happened, if Quebec did not support Trudeau's referendum option, we will, perhaps, never know, but, to say that Quebec was stabbed in the back or betrayed is quite another thing altogether. What is known is that, Quebec, at the very least, contributed to its own isolation. Secondly, the evidence points more persuasively to a last ditch effort on the part of the provinces and the federal government to come up with an agreement, as opposed to a grand Machiavellian trap for Quebec. Neither is it maintained that the Quebec delegation did not feel intense pressure and uncertainty, or the result of Quebec not being a signatory to the Amendment was solely it own fault. It is simply that the language of "betrayal" does not accurately describe what transpired.

Some even argued that the P.Q. did not really bargain with a view to achieving a compromise solution.[25] What is of primary importance, in the circumstances, is not whether or not the Parti Québécois may or may not have been bargaining with a view to arrive at compromise and agreement, but that it was not betrayed in the process, which it was not. However, not only was the illusion of betrayal allowed to go unchallenged publically, it was, in fact, given seemingly greater credibility by the then Prime Minister, Brian Mulroney, who stated that "[a]bove all, we must never forget that in 1982, Quebec was left alone, isolated and humiliated."[26] Furthermore, he stated that Quebec must be brought back "with honour and enthusiasm" within Canada's constitutional family, as if it was not already so.[27]

The fact that there was no "betrayal" tends to support the conclusion that the negotiating process was not illegitimate. However, the fact that Quebec was not a signatory to the Amendment was nothing to rejoice about either. The ultimate test in terms of assessing justifications for separatism or sovereignty must be the effect of the Amendment upon the needs and concerns of the francophones of Quebec.

The Legality and Legitimacy of the *Constitution Act, 1982*

It must be recognized at the outset that a unique situation existed with respect to the incompleteness of the Canadian constitution. No clear legal procedure existed to patriate the Constitution. Indeed, it was Patriation itself that remedied this situation. A legal patriation, in the circumstances, meant a Resolution procedure. A legitimate constitution, taking into account constitutional convention, meant substantial consent by the provinces. If there be consolation to Quebec not being a signatory to the 1982 Amendment, legal procedure was observed and the constitutional convention of substantial provincial consent was obtained. Even those who criticize the 1982 *Constitution Act* admit the legality of Patriation, and that the constitutional amendments it contains can no longer be doubted.[28]

The legal procedure of Resolution was properly carried out and the *Canada Act* was passed by the U.K. Parliament. This section examines the prevailing constitutional values or principles existing at the time, which invokes the issue of constitutional convention.

In explaining the nature of a constitutional convention, the Supreme Court of Canada, in the *Patriation Reference* case stated that the main purpose of constitutional conventions is:

... to ensure that the legal framework of the constitution will be operated within the prevailing constitutional values or principles of the period.[29]

As such, conventions are not judge made, unlike the common law, and, as they are not derived from statute, constitutional convention is not enforceable by the courts. Such rules may themselves be in conflict with legal rules.

However, constitutional conventions constitute a fundamental part of our constitution, and in many ways can be more important than many of its written aspects. One might recall that responsible government in Canada, in which political power is to be exercised in accordance with the wishes of the people as expressed through the majority of the elected Members of Parliament or the Legislature, has its basis in constitutional convention. The representative of the British Crown in Canada may not, as a matter of constitutional convention, pass any law not passed by Parliament or the Legislature of a province. Furthermore, the relevant British representative may not refuse to give assent to any law passed by Parliament or a Legislature. Finally, government must hold the confidence of the elected legislative assembly. The Crown representative must in all cases act on the advice of the Prime Minister or Premier, as the case may be. There were only two exceptions in Canadian history when such advice was not followed, the 'King-Byng' and 'Tupper-Aberdeen' episodes.[30]

It is inconceivable from a political perspective that such fundamental constitutional conventions as responsible government could be breached, despite the fact that the courts could not enforce the convention if called upon to do so. The reason is that constitutional conventions constitute political practices accepted as binding. They are so important that they possess the status of being a part of the constitution, which, in turn, make them very difficult to ignore or violate.

Regarding the existence of a constitutional convention, the Supreme Court of Canada[31] accepted the formulation of Sir Ivor Jenning's three prong test:

1. What are the precedents supporting the existence of a convention;

2. Did the actors in those precedents believe that they were bound by a rule; and

3. Is there a reason for the rule.

Furthermore, "a single precedent with a good reason may be sufficient to establish a rule, while many precedents without such a reason is not sufficient unless it is certain that the persons concerned regarded themselves as being bound."[32]

The Supreme Court of Canada authoritatively decided in the *Patriation Reference* that substantial provincial consent was required for constitutional amendment, which was achieved, and that in the *Quebec Veto Reference*, Quebec did not possess its own special veto over constitutional change.

Given the nature of conventions, being unwritten rules coming into being due to the actions of relevant actors, the Supreme Court of Canada, in the *Quebec Veto* case, was quite correct, at least to the extent that it stated recognition by the actors in the precedents (the second prong of Jenning's formulation) is not only an essential element of conventions, it is the most important one since it is a "normative one, the formal one which enables one to distinguish it from a rule of convenience or political expediency."[33] The Supreme Court then stated that it knew of no convention being born while being completely unspoken and, indeed, none was cited.[34]

Some have criticized the formal recognition test as being too high.[35] Yet, practice alone is not enough, it must be normative. A situation of express recognition would certainly be determinative of the matter. However, if explicit recognition is not or should not be the only test, then any other circumstance of recognition, going beyond mere practice and attaining a normative dimension so as to distinguish a rule of convenience or political expediency from constitutional convention, must meet a high standard. For example, one persuasive test would be whether there is evidence of such recognition through the relevant actors changing their behaviour and acceding to the invocation of a norm. That is, was there a kind of detrimental reliance upon the rule, and was such reliance clearly referable to the rule. Otherwise, or, in addition, what may be required is such a long and unambiguous line of precedents that there could reasonably be no other conclusion except that the relevant actors thought themselves bound by constitutional convention. Therefore, even had Lord Elgin not given explicit recognition to the principle of responsible government, it was clear that he gave assent to the Rebellion Losses Bill of 1849 because he thought himself to be bound by the legislation proposed by the elected assembly, although he was personally opposed to such legislation. Even if this precedent may not have been enough to establish the rule, it is clear that no instance of a representative of the British Crown refusing royal assent has ever occurred thereafter; a very lengthy time indeed. Thus, in a case where there is no explicit recognition, the acts of the relevant actors must clearly support and be clearly referable to the particular rule of constitutional convention; nothing short will do.

In attempting to elucidate what the prevailing constitutional norms were respecting constitutional amendment, it is worth bearing in mind that the circumstances involved ill defined procedure and a variety of debatably acceptable rules. This period was one of muddling through in terms of the proper level of provincial consent. Furthermore, no one actor could ensure a favourable outcome and there was always the possibility of devastating defeat.[36] As Cairns points out, the circumstances produced a brutal power struggle, which undermined civility and trust.[37] Thus, the question arises, in this context of uncertainty and struggle, what was the norm that would finally emerge as constitutional convention at the relevant time. Even if there existed a view being more accepted as desirable at a given time, that is not sufficient. The rule must attain a status of constitutional convention, and, secondly, at the relevant time. Indeed, it is often in response to uncertainty that conventions do arise.

As for the first prong of the test, even the precedents themselves are not completely unequivocal in their support for provincial unanimity. There was a 1907 amendment to which only B.C. objected on the basis of the finality of the increased subsidy, but, in the end, did not refuse to agree to the Act being passed. Furthermore, the 1949 Amendment involving Newfoundland's entry into Confederation, and confirming the Quebec-Labrador Boundary as delineated in a 1927 JCPC report, was achieved without Quebec's consent. Neither the Quebec, nor the Nova Scotian premiers made any formal demand for consultation or protest regarding the Amendment.

The Supreme Court of Canada observed in the *Patriation Reference* that the unanimity rule was not accepted by all actors involving the relevant precedents, but, concluded that substantial provincial consent was recognized. Several statements of relevant political actors can be cited casting doubt on any unanimity principle, such as that of Prime Minister Mackenzie King avoiding the issue because prior agreement was obtained in that circumstance. Previously, Prime Minister Bennett expressed concern during the Dominion-Provincial Conference of 1931 as to any requirement of unanimity. The federal government's White Paper of 1965 cast doubt on unanimity by stating that the fourth general principle with respect to constitutional amendment involving provincial jurisdiction required provincial consent, but the nature and degree of provincial participation have not lent themselves to easy definition. Finally, fifty years of constitutional discussion of the quantification of provincial consent without arriving at consensus indicates that the principle of substantial provincial consent was required, not unanimity. Indeed, during the *Patriation Reference*, Ontario and New Brunswick argued the constitutional amendment process was not regulated by conventions concerning the province *at all.* [38]

The fact that the proposed amendments initially agreed to at the Constitutional Conferences, during and after the 1960's, were not proceeded with because one or more of the provinces did not finally ratify the same does not mean the relevant actors felt themselves bound by a rule of constitutional convention requiring unanimity, but, rather, may have felt it desirable to attempt to achieve unanimity. There must be clear evidence of recognition, which is not the case in these circumstances, and especially so in light of the considerations already discussed.

Quebec Veto

It is clear that the case of Quebec veto did not meet the test for constitutional convention. Donald Smiley, who was critical of the Supreme Court's judgement on this issue, admitted that up until 1971, the precedents were ambiguous. However, for him, what was more relevant was the Victoria Charter of 1971, which proposed significant changes to the division of jurisdiction:

> After the Quebec government had given notice of its dissent from those changes, there was no serious discussion to the effect that the Charter should be embodied in a Resolution of the Parliament of Canada requesting Westminster to amend the Canadian constitution in these terms. In this situation, ... the major *political actors showed at least tacit acceptance of the principle* that Quebec assent to amendments altering federal-provincial powers was by convention required.[39]

This one precedent, in the circumstances, cannot meet the rigorous test establishing the existence of constitutional convention. Clear recognition of a convention of a Quebec veto by the federal government and provinces is required to demonstrate convention. First, this precedent is highly ambiguous as to what the relevant actors thought. Did they not proceed with the amendment because they felt themselves bound by a rule of convention which had developed, evidently since 1965 requiring Quebec's consent, or was it really a matter of convenience or political expediency to achieve its consent to ensure harmony? Secondly, there was no evidence of detrimental reliance upon the rule, nor was there a long and unambiguous line of precedents that could reasonably lead to no other conclusion but the existence of a constitutional convention.

Indeed, the existence of a veto recognized in convention for one province but no other would have been curious in the Canadian context. Not only was there no evidence of explicit recognition by federal and provincial actors outside Quebec acknowledging the existence of a Quebec veto despite the fact that there was plenty of occasion to do so, the actions and statements of the relevant actors themselves indicate a rejection of such veto.

The White Paper of 1965 made no mention of such a veto, but spoke in terms of provincial consent. Secondly, even if Prime Minister Trudeau ever recognized a Quebec veto, by April of 1981, that was no longer the case:

> Unfortunately, Mr Lévesque exchanged the veto for a hill of beans by signing an agreement with seven other provinces in April 1981, providing for an amending formula without special consideration for Quebec.[40]

At least five provinces indicated a position that either directly or implicitly rejected the existence of a Quebec veto. In the *Patriation Reference*, Manitoba, Prince Edward Island and Alberta all pleaded in favour of the unanimity rule, which is compatible with the principle of equality among the provinces and not of a special Quebec veto; whereas, Ontario and New Brunswick stated the constitutional amendment process was not regulated by conventions concerning the provinces.[41] It would be highly incredible to believe, in the circumstances, that the federal government and the provinces recognized such a veto as a rule of constitutional convention.

Certainly, as stated earlier, the criticisms of the Supreme Court's decisions in the *Patriation Reference* and in the *Quebec Veto* decision notwithstanding, the authoritativeness of these decisions and of the *Constitution Act, 1982* are beyond question.

Democratic Legitimacy: The Legislative Role

However, some would argue that the force of this legally and conventionally valid procedure still suffers from a lack of democratic legitimacy insofar as Quebec is concerned. It is asserted that Quebecers were never consulted regarding the 1982 Amendment, nor did they give their consent. Yet, in terms of law, convention, and the direct and full participation of the Quebec government during those constitutional talks, it is clear that Quebec and Quebecers were consulted and such consultation occurred in a manner consistent with democracy and the prevailing constitutional norms.

Secondly, Trudeau argued that the *Constitution Act, 1982* was legal and possesses all attributes of legitimacy, particularly since a majority of democratically elected representatives by the people Quebec voted for Patriation. Seventy-one out of seventy-eight Quebec M.P.s in the federal House of Commons and thirty-eight of one hundred and thirty-eight in the

Quebec National Assembly approved. In total, therefore 109 representatives (or 61 percent) approved, while 70 rejected.

What the argument that Quebec was never consulted or never gave its consent furthermore ignores, of course, is the Parliamentary nature and procedures of Canadian government. It must never be forgotten that Quebecers, and particularly francophone Quebecers, were the driving force behind Patriation. First and foremost, it was the then Prime Minister of Canada, Pierre Trudeau, a Quebecer with deep francophone roots, who was the main proponent of Patriation, and without whom there could not have been Patriation in the manner or in the substance achieved.

Additionally, Quebecers were overrepresented in the governing party caucus at that time, demonstrating that the federal Liberals enjoyed the confidence of Quebecers. Indeed, while amounting to 26.6 % of M.P.s in the House of Commons in 1980, Quebecers comprised 50.3% of caucus and 37.5% of Cabinet, being significantly overrepresented in the governing party.[42] Furthermore, in 1982, Canadian francophones were the major force in the federal Liberal government's cabinet. Francophones comprised 46.9% of Cabinet, which reflected an overrepresentation by a ratio of 1.59 compared to their proportion of the population of approximately 29.5% or lower.[43]

What Guy Laforest, for example, disputes regarding Trudeau's argument is that the consent given by Members of the Quebec National Assembly does not really count and a problem of legitimacy remains.[44] In essence, he argues that the Quebec Liberals were really just voting against a *péquiste* motion denouncing Patriation and setting out conditions for its acceptance. Therefore, there was no clear 'yes' in favour of Trudeau as if the question was directly posed. However, what cannot be ignored is that the *péquistes* were in control of the Quebec National Assembly and posed the question themselves.

Secondly, he denounces the validity of Liberals voting against a Parti Québécois motion as it could be merely reflecting partisan rivalry. This argument ignores the fact that in a Parliamentary democracy, which is the accepted form of government in Canada, and due to the constitutional convention of the governing party being required to maintain the confidence of the elected assembly, as well as party solidarity (along with a party whip to enforce), all sorts of legislation is passed or opposed based on party stance, irrespective of whether an individual Parliamentarian, in a particular case, may have wished to vote in the manner in which he or she actually did. Indeed, rivalry within a party is common and the P.Q. Party is no exception; yet, Parties tend to vote uniformly. What counts is how a Parliamentarian actually votes and we recognize legislation properly passed as legitimate. Thus, in our system of government, the operative result is the number of votes cast in favour of a proposition and not the individual motivation of a Parliamentarian in casting the vote, absent corruption, conflict of interest, or any such thing. Therefore, while it may be open for Laforest to question the Canadian system of government, in favour of a more congressional approach in which individual members enjoy more individual freedom to cast their votes, he did not do so in the context of his argument. Thus, it is not open for him to otherwise impugn the legitimacy of the outcomes of Parliamentary votes, given Canada's democratic acceptance of that system of democratic government, let alone the legitimacy of a Constitution based on those terms.

In absence of a clear question posed by the *péquistes* in the Quebec National Assembly as to whether its members supported or rejected Patriation, the fact that the Liberals voted against the P.Q. motion tends more to support a consent for Patriation, than to a simplistic dismissing of the significance of those votes as merely partisan voting against a P.Q. motion denouncing Patriation and the conditions for Quebec's acceptance of the same.

Although the record may remain somewhat ambiguous as to the level of consent given for Patriation in the Quebec National Assembly, the support given by Quebecers and francophones for Patriation in the federal Parliament is unequivocal and francophone Quebecers played an important and driving role during that process.

Democratic Legitimacy: The Necessity of Referendum

Nevertheless, some like Laforest still maintain that the *Constitution Act, 1982* is illegitimate *vis-à-vis* Quebec since it was without the consent of the Quebec government, nor were Quebecers consulted. Citing Locke, he argues that the consent of the people is always necessary to establish the legitimacy of political authority, and reforming a constitution is equivalent to changing the social contract, especially when such change affects legislative powers considered crucial for Quebec.[45] Given Canada's monarchical foundations of government, Laforest incorrectly theorizes that the people delegated part of their power to the province and part to the federal government. In the Canadian Parliamentary system, it is the Crown that is theoretically sovereign, although as a matter of practice it may not be recognized or function as such. The only exception may be with the Charter, which works to "constitutionalize" Canadians. In any event, he concludes that the 1982 Amendment amounts to a breach of confidence. He goes on to say that although Quebec does not have a right of secession, it does possess an internationally recognized right of self-determination that can be exercised by referendum, or even a unilateral declaration of independence based on the illegitimacy of the *Constitution Act, 1982*.[46]

In essence, he argues that neither the 1867, nor the 1982 *Constitution Acts* satisfy the contemporary exigencies of democratic and liberal political theory, in which the active consent of the people is necessary for legitimacy.[47] In 1867, Confederation was not achieved by referendum, but, rather, through elected representatives. At least, for him, in 1867, such a procedure was in accordance with the elitist political culture of the time, but the same cannot be said for 1982. Interestingly, it may be noted that the separatist/sovereignist Parti Québécois under Lévesque initially agreed to the Gang of Eight's proposal for Constitutional amendment, which did not include referendum.

Notwithstanding what one may think about the desirability of popular referendum for the creation or reformation of a Constitution, Laforest's argument makes little sense when applied to the real world. Indeed, few regimes in the world today would be legitimate according to his theory as a great many came into being by conquest or unification movements and legitimacy developed thereafter. Not only have few countries come into being as a result of referendum, constitutional amendment is not usually a product of popular referendum. Could Laforest really, in any seriousness whatsoever, deny the legitimate existence of countries like Canada, the United States, Germany, France, Italy and Japan? Would citizens in those countries consider their country to be illegitimate, or would the international community conclude illegitimacy?— Of course, not.

However, notwithstanding the desirability of a referendum in the context of constitutional change, to insist on it as a condition of legitimacy in the circumstances existing in the real world at this time is simply untenable. All of this is not to say that popular referendum should not or will not be required or accepted in Canada for Constitutional amendment as a matter of law or convention in the future, but that is another question altogether.

Legitimacy, Trudeau and the 1980 Referendum

Finally, it is charged that Trudeau duped the Quebec people by promising that if they voted No in the 1980 sovereignty referendum, Canadian federalism would be renewed. Trudeau never himself hid his views in opposition to Quebec special status and never promised the kind of constitutional reform envisaged by Ontario Premier Robarts or Quebec's

Daniel Johnson. His views were well known. Furthermore, Trudeau argued that people like Claude Morin made people believe that what the Liberals actually promised since 1968, was not what was promised in 1980.

Nevertheless, some state that one must look to how the words were understood at the time and in the historical context to determine how the Québécois interpreted Trudeau's words. Laforest argues that during the 1980 referendum Trudeau was, for the first time, imprecise and ambiguous on the Quebec question, and the ideological activity surrounding renewed federalism in 1979–80 was the Task Force on Canadian Unity and the Quebec Beige Paper.[48] Yet, an important flaw occurs in his argument as he attempts to elucidate what Quebecers thought about what Trudeau meant, on May 14, 1980 in Montreal, about being committed to change, but admits:

> What proportion of the electorate was affected by these famous interventions? We will never really know, and, in the end, it is not of significance. What is essential lies elsewhere.[49] (translation)

One would have thought that to be the essential question. If one wishes to determine if Quebecers were duped, one must ask how Quebecers interpreted Trudeau's words. The reason why historians look to how words may have been interpreted at a given time and in the historical context is that direct evidence of how those words were actually interpreted is not available. It is a situation of obtaining the next best evidence when the best evidence is unavailable. This situation would not apply to the 1980 Quebec referendum. Other Quebec writers, like Nemni, dispute that any promise was ever made at all.

It is clear that Trudeau did not lie to the people of Quebec. It might be said is that Trudeau was not as clear and precise during the course of a speech as he might have been by defining precisely what the commitment to change meant. At most, he may have played on a vagueness. It is possible that although Trudeau never changed his opinion about what constitutional change meant for himself and for the Liberals, some Quebecers may have thought something else. Yet, we do not know what proportion of the electorate, in fact, misunderstood Trudeau's words.

Nevertheless, to put the burden of illegitimacy on an entire constitution based on one vague phrase spoken during the Quebec sovereignty referendum, without much more, and to use the same as a justification for separatism is a far stretch for reason or the imagination. The ultimate test is to examine the outcomes and realities of the Canadian federation, including whether Quebec has been negatively affected by the 1982 Amendment. Indeed, one does not hear separatists criticize Parizeau or Bouchard for being vague or silent on a whole host of issues leading up to the second separatism referendum, not to mention the referendum question itself. What is principle for one, must surely be principle for the other. Finally, Trudeau stated clearly in writing, at the time of the 1980 Referendum, that real reform was impossible with a P.Q. government bent on the destruction of the federation.[50] Such a view suggests that special status and decentralization of powers in favour of Quebec was not going to be pursued by him.

Thus, the argument with respect to the illegitimacy of the 1982 *Constitution Act* based on a vague phrase of renewed federalism is untenable. This argument is even more unreasonable when combined with the fact that Quebec was never "betrayed" during the constitutional conference leading up to that Amendment in which it fully participated, the process itself was legitimate, and the government and people of Quebec were consulted in a manner consistent with democracy and the prevailing constitutional norms of Canada. Indeed, in 1995, Quebecers voted against sovereignty in a second referendum when no indications of reformed federalism were made.

Changing the Rules of the Game

A second indictment by separatists and sovereignists relating to the passage of the *Constitution Act, 1982* is that if nine provinces and the federal government could conspire to gang up on Quebec, in 1982, then it can pass amendments that are harmful to Quebec today. As such, the French language and the promotion of the flourishing of francophone society may be imperilled. This concern is not a realistic one.

To begin with, as we have seen, the other provinces did not gang up on or betray Quebec. Secondly, constitutional patriation was necessary and perhaps inevitable in the early 1980's, with or without substantial provincial consent. Today, constitutional reform is neither necessary, nor inevitable, and is not even seen as desirable with good reason. There is little political will for constitutional changes, let alone ones that affect a single province as the defeat of the Meech Lake Accord demonstrates. Furthermore, far from being homogeneous in outlook, the English speaking provinces have their own interests. Constitutional agreement even among themselves is not necessarily an easy matter.

Admittedly, one should not underestimate within the Canadian federation the constitutional morality of respect for the citizens of Canada, be they represented by the federal or provincial government. Federalism respects both national and regional interests. Furthermore, the French Fact in Canada is recognized and protected in many ways such that it is ingrained within Canada's constitutional morality. Quebec, as a province, contains a majority of francophones, and through both provincial and federal powers, that fact is recognized and protected.

Finally, there are the legal aspects of constitutional amendment. There was a far different process to amend the Constitution in 1982, than exists under the present amending formula contained in the *Constitution Act, 1982.* Patriating the Constitution required only a Resolution of the federal Parliament, which incorporated an amendment to be signed by the British Parliament. Substantial provincial consent, although not strictly required, was achieved through a first ministers summit agreement. With such agreement and passage of the Resolution through the Parliamentary system, Britain would then sign the Amendment.

However, in contrast, after 1982, the general amending formula requires a Resolution of the Senate and House of Commons, and Resolutions of the legislative assemblies of at least two-thirds of the provinces that contain at least fifty per cent of the population of all the provinces. Thereafter, the Governor General is required by constitutional convention to issue a proclamation bringing into effect the amendment.

Where an amendment derogates from legislative powers, propriety rights, or any other rights or privileges of the Legislature or government of a province, it must be supported by a majority in the House of Commons and legislative assemblies of two-thirds of the provinces under the general amending formula. Furthermore, and, significantly, such an amendment *shall not have effect* in a province in which the majority of the legislative assembly expresses its dissent prior to the proclamation of the Governor General. That legislative assembly may, thereafter, choose to revoke its dissent and authorize the amendment, in which case the amendment will apply to it.

Some constitutional amendments require the unanimous consent of the federal Parliament and each province, for example, regarding the right of a province to a number of Members of Parliament in the House of Commons to be not less than the number of Senators to which that province is entitled. Also, unanimous consent is required regarding amendments to the use of the English or French language.

However, where an amendment does not apply to all the provinces, it requires a Resolution of the Senate and House of Commons and legislative assembly of each province affected by the amendment. Similarly, while Quebec or any other province remains in Canada, its present borders cannot be altered in the Constitution without a resolution of the legislative assembly of each province to which the amendment applies.

Therefore, the constitutional amendment sections, as well as the prevailing circumstances demonstrate that the provinces and federal government cannot gang up on Quebec to force an amendment upon Quebec to its detriment that would derogate from its powers and to which it does not consent.

Negative Effects of the Charter?

Although the passage of the 1982 Amendment was not illegitimate given that Quebec was not stabbed in the back and the process itself was not illegitimate, it certainly suffered somewhat, especially related to the Charter, in terms of perceived legitimacy in the eyes of many Quebecers given that Quebec was not a signatory. Yet, if the process and outcome were truly flawed and the 1982 Amendment, therefore, suffers a corresponding loss of political or legal legitimacy, one critical indication and measure would be to consider the extent to which, if any, it has been or is detrimental to Quebecers. A just procedure is instituted to facilitate the creation of a just outcome, or at the very least to prevent or impede an unjust one from occurring.[51] Thus, should there be no real detrimental effects, a good indication is provided that any loss of legitimacy which the Amendment may suffer, especially as a result of Quebec not being a signatory thereto, is more apparent than real. That is, the force of the indictment regarding illegitimacy will lack true substance.

There are two main arguments supporting the charges made against the Charter, and these are consistent primarily with the second theme with respect to the preservation of language and the flourishing of Quebec society. The first argument is that the Charter weakens, to an unacceptable extent, Quebec's powers in this respect. The second argument is that the Charter holds dangerous assimilatory undercurrents running against the Québécois identity. Of course, in terms of visions of what the constitution should be reflecting, many see the Charter as too centralizing, especially by focusing on individual rights and not on the pursuit of collective Québécois goals, and many see multiculturalism as a rejection of biculturalism. The implications of the existence of these differing visions for the survival of the French language and the promotion of francophone society were discussed and will be discussed further. The theme of contrary visions will be more fully dealt with in Chapter 10 regarding the process of constitutional change in written constitutional text.

Language and society

The Quebec government possesses substantial powers to promote its francophone society and language, and the Constitution has not jeopardized this pursuit. The main provisions contained in the *Constitution Act, 1982* that are most relevant to the powers of the Quebec government directly affecting language are s. 23, minority education language rights, and, secondly, s. 2(b), freedom of expression. Although s. 23(1)(b) gives broader English language education protection than Bill 101 accorded, the predominance of French language education increased, while the level of English language education in Quebec decreased dramatically, particularly with respect to allophones. This situation is true despite the fact that s. 23(1)(b) cannot be overridden by the Quebec legislature.

Secondly, the freedom of expression provisions of the Charter, as with other fundamental rights and freedoms contained in sections 2 and 7 to 15, can be overridden by the s. 33 notwithstanding clause should the need arise; but, there is a high price for its invocation although less so in Quebec when the needs of the collectivity arise. Section 33 was invoked with respect to Bill 178, the language of outdoor advertising to maintain an *image linguistique*, but subsequently was not reinvoked. The Quebec Interministerial Committee on the Status of the French Language in Quebec concluded that one, even on Montreal Island, would see an *image linguistique* of a place occupied by a majority of francophones.

Third, and more importantly, the language of the workplace is, by and large, French and the French language predominates within the provincial government and in communications Quebecers have with the Quebec government. Bill 101, a kind of linguistic affirmative action legislation, played no small part in promoting the French language in the workplace of Quebec. Furthermore, the Charter is limited to "government action" and does not apply to the private sector, which may institute its own linguistic policy.

The economic union provisions of the Charter concern only the mobility of Canadians, and together with the economic union provisions of the 1867 *Constitution Act*, have minimal impacts on the Quebec government's ability to provide for the flourishing of francophone business. As demonstrated, Quebec's efforts are substantial in this respect, and such efforts may even give rise to interprovincial trade barriers, as we will see.

Finally, nothing in the Charter hinders Quebec's ability to facilitate the flourishing of Quebec culture and, indeed, the Charter can work to protect cultural expression.

Therefore, the empirical evidence demonstrates that any apparent limitations the Charter may place on the powers of the Quebec government in respect of language and society are more apparent than real, and the protection of the French language and the facilitation of the flourishing of francophone society in Quebec are not imperilled in the least.

Assimilatory effects of the Charter

It is maintained that the Charter holds dangerous assimilatory undercurrents for the Québécois as it models a new political culture structuring Canadians to think along pan-Canadian lines and to identify with Canada to the detriment of provincialist loyalties and identities.[52] It is argued that the Charter focuses on individual rights that are shared by all Canadians equally and without variation from coast to coast, as opposed to collective provincialist goals. It is said that the Charter, as a vehicle of national identity, is incompatible with Quebec's identity. Furthermore, it replaces a bicultural view of Canada with a multicultural one. Laforest argues that Quebec needs a greater integration:

> I do not believe that multiculturalism can be reconciled with the project of the promotion of a distinct society in Quebec.[53] (translation)

Finally, the Charter is ultimately enforced by a central institution, the Supreme Court of Canada, which hands down decisions binding on all of Canada.

Laforest argues that the Charter opposes the idea that the Québécois, given their situation in North America, should possess collective rights different from other Canadians.[54] Yet, even the argument that the consideration of rights cannot be modified by local considerations is not accurate. We already saw in the *Quebec Signs* case that the Supreme Court of Canada took into account provincial conditions in determining, under s. 1, whether the limits placed on the right amounted to such reasonable limits as can be demonstrably justified in a free and democratic society. The Court held that maintaining the "French Face" of outdoor advertising was a valid objective under the Charter as it addressed the vulnerable position of the French language in Quebec, Canada and North America. However, the problem was that the means used to pursue the objective was excessive since protecting the French language did not mean excluding all other languages from outdoor advertising. Furthermore, the Court in *Reference re Quebec Secession* explicitly recognized Quebec's distinctive qualities and acknowledged that the principle of federalism facilitates the pursuit of collective goals by territorially based cultural and linguistic groups. In addition to s. 1, there is also s. 33 of the Charter, which can be invoked if necessary to preserve the Quebec collectivity. Finally, and most importantly, the criticism neglects a more global perspective of the fundamental ways in which federalism acts to protect the French language in Quebec and to promote the flourishing of francophone society.

The assimilation argument applies to the ability of the provincial government or the Québécois to promote the French language in Quebec. The second aspect relates to the erosion of nationalistic bonds towards Quebec. It is clear from the empirical evidence that multiculturalism does not imperil whatsoever the integration of immigrants or ethnic minorities into the public and collective French speaking community and life of Quebec.

The second argument pushed to its extreme raises a concern that nationalism bonds are essentially psychological barriers, which have been diminishing as Quebec became less distinct from the other parts of Canada. Potentially, now, such bonds and barriers are being fatally assaulted by the Charter and by the lack of explicit distinct society recognition. At the very least, the Charter is seen as unacceptable by tending to consolidate the preponderance of the federal government to the detriment of Quebec. Yet, as we have observed in the Québécois case and as other Quebec francophone writers like Stéphan Dion argue, the more the people and their cultures resemble each other, the more they insist on stressing their difference. Indeed, Laforest, himself, admits this view.[55]

While many of the claims about the Charter may hold a good deal of truth for English Canada, which must by now surely regard it as a fundamental aspect of their society in a pan-Canadian context, the effects are not present to as great a degree in francophone Quebec. All of this is not to say that the Québécois do not support individual rights:

> However, on issues of the collectivity which have been explicitly linked to the survival of the collectivity there clearly is less deference to individual rights, the Charter, and the Supreme Court's leadership in interpreting the Charter. This essentially boils down to the question of language.[56]

We already discussed the tremendous grass roots movement opposing the Quebec signs decision under the banner *"ne touchez pas à la loi 101,"* in favour of invoking the s. 33 notwithstanding clause in support of Bill 178. Furthermore, Quebec governments demonstrate a strong commitment to preserve the French language and to provide for the flourishing of Quebec society. With respect to the perception of francophone Quebecers, the empirical evidence supports the conclusion that no evidence exists of the

Charter strengthening pan-Canadian sentiment or group solidarities *to the detriment of* territorially defined loyalties, or identification with Quebec's own institutions. Further examples include the vigilance with which every day Quebecers monitor outdoor signage compliance with the provisions of language legislation. Another interesting example involves the perceptions held by women's groups regarding the effect of a Quebec distinct society clause on the Charter's s. 28 guaranteeing gender equality. English Canadian women's groups saw it as a threat and mobilized against it; whereas, most womens' groups in Quebec saw no conflict.[57] The Quebec women's groups were prepared to look to the Quebec government and rely on Quebec's *Charte des droits et libertés de la personne.*

It is inconceivable that the Québécois, who have a vested interest in their own well-being and fulfilment by preserving their own language and promoting the flourishing of their francophone society, would allow themselves to be assimilated by the very existence of an entrenched bill of rights focusing on pan-Canadian rights, which does not, in any real or important way, interfere with the achievement of these goals. The fact that the Charter may elucidate values that Canadians value as a whole and which may increase their identification with Canada does not mean that the level of Québécois identification with the territory and government of Quebec is undermined, which clearly is not the case. Neither the cultural and societal convergence of Canadian francophones and anglophones, nor the Charter impede the desire or ability of francophone Quebecers to pursue and achieve their most fundamental goals. Indeed, federalism has acted to promote their achievement. The existence of multiple loyalties is not detrimental to the existence of Quebec's French speaking society, with respect to francophones, allophones or anglophone Quebecers. It is not surprising, however, that separatists or sovereignists are apprehensive at any strengthening of Québécois identification with Canada as such identification, far from undermining the French language or the flourishing of francophone Quebec society or identity, does adversely affect the separatist or sovereignist movement.

Chapter 8
The Constitutional Aspects of Federalism II:
The Route to Federalism

Significant and far reaching constitutional accommodation within Canada is possible, even if there are only modest changes in its written text. Since the beginnings of Confederation, Canadian federalism has been evolving and accommodating the needs and concerns of the participants and citizens in the federal system. Furthermore, it cannot be said that accommodations were not made pertaining to Quebec. Quite the opposite is true.

From Quasi to True Federalism

If the principle of federalism is that two levels of government are co-ordinate (or exercising divided jurisdiction) and independent from each other, then the *Constitution Act, 1867* set up a form of federalism that was quasi and not truly federal in nature.[1] A second aspect to the federal principle, which involves more process than form, is that the powers assigned to the two levels of government must be responsive to regional, as well as national interests. Again, on this point, there is a strong argument that on a plain reading of the *Constitution Act, 1867*, the provincial government did not have substantial powers, as compared with the federal government.

However, as a result of the political practices that developed and court decisions interpreting the federalism provisions of the Constitution, Canada progressed from being a quasi-federal, and potentially highly centralist country, to one which is truly federal in form and decentralized in nature. Indeed, one may legitimately argue that on the latter point, Canada became too decentralized.

In order that Canada be truly federal in form, it must meet the criteria of the two levels of government being co-ordinate and independent. What this means, in the Canadian context, is that both levels of government must possess an equality of status as true governments, and that the unitary features of the Confederation settlement had to somehow disappear.

Status of Provincial Legislatures

Although there may have been doubt at one time, the provincial legislature is a true government and possesses an equality of status with the federal government.

The nature of the *Constitution Act, 1867* is such that it is the British Crown which is the sovereign entity and the two orders of the Canadian government exercise jurisdiction within their respective spheres of power. This characterization is accurate as it is the British Crown, through its representative the Governor General or Lieutenant-governor, that formally makes the laws of Canada and of the provinces respectively. In practice, however, Canada functions as the sovereign entity, regardless of what the formal provisions of the Constitution might say.

The major section granting the federal government its legislative authority is s. 91 of the 1867 *Constitution Act*. Section 91 states that the Queen, on the advice and consent of the federal Parliament, possesses the legislative authority to make laws consistent with the parameters specified in that section. Whereas, s. 91 clearly states that the Crown is present in the federal Parliament, there is no such mention of the Crown being present in the provincial legislatures under s. 92 of the *Constitution Act, 1867*, which is the major section giving the provinces their power. The question then arose whether or not the provincial government in exercising its jurisdiction is equal, or somehow inferior to or dependant upon the federal government.

The question came to a head when the Receiver General of New Brunswick claimed the same status of creditor as held by the Receiver General of Canada, regarding the liquidation of the Maritime Bank.[2] Claiming the same status as creditor was based on the argument that the province enjoys the same status as the federal government. The highest appellate court, at that time, the British Judicial Committee of the Privy Council (the JCPC) held that: "the Lieutenant-Governor when appointed is as much the representative of Her Majesty for all purposes of provincial government as the Governor-General himself is for all purposes of Dominion government and consequently both are 'Parliament' and have the same status."[3] Therefore, when the provinces exercise their jurisdiction, the doctrine of Parliamentary Supremacy applies. Furthermore, the provincial executive possesses all the authority subsumed in Crown/royal prerogative. Thus, certain privileges attach to governments that possess the status of a true government or Parliament.

The doctrine of Parliamentary Supremacy provides that as long as the federal and provincial legislatures are acting within their assigned legislative spheres, their enactments cannot be rendered invalid by the Courts.[4] The doctrine is modified by the Charter. The second aspect is that no Parliament is bound by an act of its predecessors and can change or undo obligations established by preceding Parliaments. Neither can any Parliament be bound to do anything, for example, by the outcome of a referendum.[5] However, in addition to the Charter, Parliamentary Supremacy is mitigated by political, cultural, economic, psychological and other constraints.

Secondly, royal prerogative constitutes the residue of legal power passing through the Crown to Crown representatives, like the Governor General and the Lieutenant-governor. These offices are themselves created by royal prerogative. The powers associated with Crown prerogative are outlined in statues like the Letters Patent of 1947 and the *Constitution Act, 1867*. Such powers include the appointment of first ministers and their ministers, dissolving the elected chamber, and giving assent to laws passed by the elected assembly. The Governor General appoints ambassadors, signs treaties and declares war. With extremely rare historical exceptions, the Crown's representative acts on the advice of the first minister.

Use and Disuse of the Unitary Features

Although the provinces were equal in status, they were not coordinate in the sense of exercising their own jurisdiction without interference from the federal government.[6] Where the federal government could interfere with all or nearly all instances of the exercise of provincial jurisdiction, the Constitution would be in form more appropriately described as operating as if there were really only one true level of government and one ineffective or subordinate level of government, regardless of formal status. However, as a matter of political practice, the unitary features of the Confederation settlement have fallen to disuse. These events clearly demonstrate that constitutional change can, and does, occur without formal amendment. Instead, the change, in this respect, comes from constitutional convention.

The unitary features of the *Constitution Act, 1867* involve the reservation and disallowance power of the federal government, the reservation power of the Lieutenant-governor, the federal remedial power over education and the "declaratory" power. Each of these powers fell into disuse, with the partial exception of the federal declaratory power, as not being a part of Canadian political culture and in not being consistent with federalism.

The reservation power refers to the power to delay the coming into effect of legislation such that the legislation may be considered by that reserving body, or another body, as specified in the Constitution. Upon consideration of the legislation, the disallowance power allows the respective body to disallow that legislation such that it is without force or effect.

The British Crown possessed a reservation and disallowance power of its own over Canadian legislation in sections 55, 56 and 57 of the *Constitution Act, 1867*. As the Canadian colony progressed to a state of nationhood, this Imperial unitary measure was not acceptable from the point of view of political culture. Therefore, in 1878, Mackenzie and Blake secured from the Imperial Parliament letters of instruction to be sent to the Governor General to ignore those sections.

It would appear, therefore, that if the Imperial power did not apply in Canada, the federal reservation and disallowance was also undermined. However, these powers continued to be used by Prime Minister Macdonald. The centralist minded Macdonald was careful, however, to balance the unqualified legal power of disallowance with clear guidelines for and limitations upon its use, including the requirement of consulting with the province involved.[7] Essentially, through this policy of non-interference, the disallowance power would only be used in practice on jurisdictional grounds. Nevertheless, its use was a source of friction between the federal government and the provinces, particularly, Ontario.

This balance, however, regarding the use of the disallowance power was ignored with the *Rivers and Streams Act* of 1881. The legislation originated with a dispute between private parties. One of the parties attempted to prevent the other from floating their logs down a certain river, on the grounds that the former alone financed the dams and improvements making the river usable for driving logs. A court injunction was then secured to that effect. Ontario legislation entitled *An Act for Protecting the Public Interests in Rivers, Streams and Creeks* was enacted to allow the driving of logs in waterways upon payment of a fee to those responsible for its improvement. Macdonald nullified the Act without consulting the Ontario government on the grounds of private rights and natural justice.[8] Significantly, therefore, the Bill was disallowed on grounds that departed from the principle generally adhered to of limiting the use of that power to jurisdictional matters.

The then Premier of Ontario, Mowat, argued that disallowance violated the terms of the Confederation settlement in which the provinces were supposed to be supreme in their sphere of authority, and that such action destroyed the principle of constitutional responsibility to the people of the province. It was recognized that there was no rationale for exclusive jurisdiction if the boundaries of that jurisdiction could be impinged upon by the federal government under the pretext of "general interests of the Dominion". In total, the Ontario legislation was passed four times and disallowed three.

A second episode involving the disallowance power, as well as the remedial power over education was the *Manitoba School Act, 1890*, which purported to terminate public support for Roman Catholic Schools in favour of one public school system. The dilemma was that there was a demand from Roman Catholics, especially from Quebec, to disallow the Act; but, on the other hand, the Protestants supported the Act. Macdonald promised that while he would not disallow the legislation, if elected, he would use the remedial powers contained in s. 93(4) of the *Constitution Act, 1867*. Although re-elected, Macdonald died shortly thereafter before invoking the section. In a span of four years, there were four different Conservative leaders. Finally, Tupper lost the election to the Liberal Laurier. Laurier would not use the disallowance power. He would consistently argue that remedies for provincial legislation did not rest with disallowance, but, rather, with the people of the province.

Provincial autonomy was interpreted as independence from the federal level of government and fair sharing of powers with it. The corollary to the argument was that it was dangerous to allow one of the parties in jurisdictional disputes to be a judge in its own case.[9] Once disallowance could not be reconciled with the federal principle, there became too high a political price for its use; therefore, it was thought to be better to allow the Courts to decide the constitutionality of provincial statutes, rather, than to have the federal government criticized for the use or misuse of that power.[10]

Thus, the federal reservation and disallowance power has become unacceptable as a matter of constitutional convention. The precedents include the *Rivers and Streams Act* debates, the Manitoba school controversy, the fact that, especially during the 1930's, after a measure was disallowed it would be referred to the courts, and, finally, the use of disallowance was abandoned altogether as a power. The actors, in those precedents believed, in the beginning, that there must be, at least, some restraint on the use of that power and over the years ended with the belief that the reservation and disallowance power ought never to be used. The reason for the rule is grounded in the federal principle and the fact that it would be dangerous for the federal government to be both a party to a jurisdictional dispute and the judge. In fact, when it was offered by Prime Minister Trudeau to trade-off revoking the disallowance power in constitutional text in favour of a Charter of rights and freedoms, the proposal was laughed at because there was no real trade-off. Indeed, by the late 1980's, that power was never even considered to strike down Quebec's very controversial Bill 178, imposing unilingual French outdoor advertising and overriding the Charter in doing so.

A related aspect to the federal reservation and disallowance power is the Lieutenant-governor's reservation power under s. 90 of the *Constitution Act, 1867*. The Lieutenant-governor is a federal appointee through the Governor General. Once the legitimacy of the federal reservation and disallowance power was gone, so too was the Lieutenant-governor's reservation power. The reservation power of the Lieutenant-governor was not used after the early 1960's, when Bastedo's use of that power was repudiated by the federal government on the grounds of federalism.

The Manitoba School controversy simultaneously gave rise to another constitutional convention. Laurier did not use remedial legislation under s. 93 of the *Constitution Act, 1867* in favour of the principle of provincial autonomy. That section was never invoked in Canada.

The "declaratory power" enables the federal government to declare a local work to be "for the general advantage of Canada" and, thereby, to assume jurisdiction. Section 92(10)(c) of the *Constitution Act, 1867* states that provincial jurisdiction encompasses:

s. 92(10) Local Works and Undertakings other than such as are of the following Classes:-

> **(c)** Such Works as, although wholly situate within the Province, are before or after their Execution declared by the Parliament of Canada to be for the general Advantage of Canada or for the Advantage of Two or more of the Provinces.

The power was invoked over four hundred times, mostly involving local railways, but also with respect to tramways, canals, bridges, dams, tunnels, harbours, wharves, telegraphs, telephones, mines, mills, grain elevators, hotels, restaurants, theatres, oil refineries and factories of various kinds.[11] However, the power is used only sparingly in recent times due to its inconsistency with classical federal notions. The more recent declarations cited are the *Cape Breton Development Corporation Act* (1967–68) and *Teleglobe Canada*

Reorganization and Divestiture Act (1987).[12] Thus, it would appear that whereas this power has not fallen to complete disuse, as a matter of practice or constitutional convention, it is nevertheless used sparingly.

The Road to Decentralization: The Judiciary

The second aspect of the federal principle relates more to the processes underlying the Constitution and the country itself. This aspect of the principle is that the powers assigned to the two levels of government must be responsive to regional, as well as national interests. Responsiveness to regional or national interests involves adequate powers or jurisdiction, and adequate resources to exercise that jurisdiction.

The role of the judiciary will be examined in this section. The major components of the jurisprudence resulting in the decentralization of constitutional powers in Canada will be outlined, and the significance of these judicial decisions interpreting the Constitution will be given. In the end, many believe that, in fact, Canadian federalism became too decentralized.

The sections distributing jurisdiction between the federal and provincial levels of government under the Constitution are sections 91, 92, 92A, 93, 94A, 95, 101, 108, 109, 117 and 132 of the *Constitution Act, 1867*; the more significant of which are sections 91, 92 and 93. A plain reading of those sections would seem to indicate a centralized scheme in which the federal government would have greater powers. Section 91 states:

> **s. 91** It shall be lawful for the Queen, by and with the Advice and Consent of the Senate and House of Commons, to make Laws for the Peace, Order and good Government of Canada, in relation to all Matters not coming within the Classes of Subjects by this Act assigned exclusively to the Legislatures of the Provinces; and for greater Certainty, but not so as to restrict the Generality of the foregoing Terms of this Section, it is hereby declared that (notwithstanding anything in this Act) the exclusive Legislative Authority of the Parliament of Canada extends to all Matters coming within the Classes of Subjects next hereinafter enumerated; that is to say, -

The section originally listed twenty-seven matters falling under federal jurisdiction and now includes twenty-nine matters. The matters listed are significant, including Trade and Commerce, raising money by any mode of taxation, Defence, Currency, Banking, and Criminal law. That section goes on to say:

> **s. 91(29)** Such Classes of Subjects as are expressly excepted in the Enumeration of the Classes of Subjects by this Act assigned exclusively to the Legislatures of the Provinces.

And any Matter coming within any of the Classes of Subjects enumerated in this Section shall not be deemed to come within the Class of Matters of a local or private Nature comprised in the Enumeration of the Classes of Subjects by this Act assigned exclusively to the Legislatures of the Provinces.

Provincial powers, on the other hand, seem to be less significant and seem to be confined merely to local matters. Section 92 reads as follows:

s. 92 In each Province the Legislature may exclusively make Laws in relation to Matters coming within the Classes of Subject next hereinafter enumerated; that is to say, -

The section goes on to list sixteen matters, the most important of which being Direct taxation, Property and civil rights in the province, and Generally all matters of a merely local or private nature in the province. Section 93 gives the power over education to the provinces subject to the now unusable provisions concerning remedial legislation in education.

Other provisions that would indicate the centralizing nature of the document include, as we have seen, the unitary features of the Constitution and s. 94 allowing for the uniformity of all laws relative to property and civil rights and the procedure of the courts in Ontario, Nova Scotia and New Brunswick upon their consent.

Thus, it would seem that the provinces could only exercise jurisdiction on purely local matters, while the federal government could exercise jurisdiction on all other matters, including those enumerated in section 91. However, what began as a centralizing document became something quite different due to judicial decisions, particularly those of the JCPC.

The key to understanding this apparent shift lies in the fact that law, and particularly constitutional law, rarely dictates a clear answer, especially in harder cases. Mechanical and deductive reasoning cannot account for judicial decision-making, as general propositions cannot decide concrete cases. As one of the earlier jurists who recognized this relation stated: "decisions will depend on a judgement or intention more subtle than any articulate major premise."[13] Words are often ambiguous and create room in which several valid and logical interpretations can arise with respect to a given set of facts. Furthermore, we have already seen indications of how sections 91 and 92 overlap in their very wording. Accordingly, in the process of interpreting law, and especially constitutional law, judges play a legal function in interpreting the law and a political function in deciding which interpretation will be chosen. There is no clear law-policy dichotomy; however, that is not necessarily to say that law is arbitrary policy imposed by a judge.[14] Rather, it is based on reasoning and argumentation.

On a very general level one can say that certain trends in the jurisprudence can be detected during certain periods of time.[15] Generally, the JCPC acted as a constitutional counterbalance to the centralizing tendencies of the *Constitution Act, 1867*. The first period, spanning from 1880 to 1899 in which Lord Watson was the dominant figure, can be classified as "classical federalism". The JCPC aimed to prevent the powers of one level of government, primarily the province, from being absorbed by the powers of the other level. The decisions tended to uphold the validity of legislation. Thus, although sections 91 and 92 tend to speak in terms of exclusive authority, both levels of government were permitted similar laws in concurrent areas of jurisdiction.

The second period spanned 1911–1928, in which Viscount Haldane was the prominent figure and can be classified as "Provincialist". There was a tendency to find against the validity of legislation. Section 91 was restricted and narrowed. There is an argument to be made that these decisions were not simply provincialist, but, rather, were an attempt to restrict the scope of state action in the market in favour of competition and laissez-faire economics, as was being done in the United States.[16]

The final period of JCPC decisions (1929–1949), involved a period of conflicting jurisprudence. On the one hand, some of the Law Lords, like Sankey, approached the constitution as if it were a "living tree capable of growth and expansion within its natural limits."[17] Such an approach takes account of changing realities and does not rely on a narrow or legalistic approach, as was characteristically done in the past. This approach favoured the validity of laws, and would not allow sections 91 and 92 to be interpreted in a narrow fashion. On the other hand, during the mid-1930's, the JCPC was striking down national social welfare schemes such as unemployment insurance, and maximum hours and minimum wages. To do so, s. 91 was narrowly interpreted.

As a result of a growing sense of Canadian nationalism and independence, and the criticism that the JCPC impeded Canadian governments in dealing with economic problems, there was a movement to abolish appeals to that body. After 1949, the Supreme Court of Canada became the highest appellate Court of the land. The Supreme Court's approach can be characterized as playing a balancing role, or of countervailing power, in which the idea of absolute or unchecked authority was rejected. One good example, is the *Patriation Reference* decision in which the Court gave something to both sides. Although, the federal government could legally amend the Constitution unilaterally, there was a constitutional convention requiring a substantial degree of provincial consent. Again, in the *Quebec Veto Reference*, Quebec unsuccessfully asserted a veto by virtue of convention. Having a veto can be seen as a type of absolute authority over constitutional amendment.

Secondly, there was no great divergence from the jurisprudence of the past as the precedents of the JCPC were accepted. Between 1949–75, there was little constitutional litigation. Thus, from 1951 to 1975, it was not really significant that more provincial statutes or sections were found to be unconstitutional than federal ones. Furthermore, some commentators assess the overall impact of Supreme Court of Canada decisions on the evolution of federal government activity to be relatively insignificant.[18]

Some recent cases are beginning to recognize that perhaps the Constitution was interpreted in too formalistic and technical a manner, rather than being responsive to present conditions. Therefore, cases such as *Crown Zellerbach*[19] and *General Motors v. City National Leasing*[20] indicate a greater willingness to look at matters more functionally, and which may require some centralization on a principled and well defined basis in order to effectively deal with present day problems.

The question, then, is how did we start with an apparently centralized document and end up with a decentralized constitution. The major jurisprudential components of that transformation will be outlined through considering the two significant federal powers of peace, order and good government, and the trade and commerce power. The discussion on peace, order and good government traces its evolution in, first, being separated from the other powers in s. 91, and, secondly, in how that power was interpreted by the courts.

Section 91: Peace, Order and Good Government

In order to give full effect to the centralization apparently contemplated in the context of sections 91 and 92, one would have to see provincial jurisdiction encompassing only matters of local concern enumerated under s. 92, but, not including matters enumerated under s. 91, which is deemed to be federal jurisdiction. Federal jurisdiction would, then, include all other matters. The paramount enumerated heads under s. 91 are only examples of the federal residual power of peace, order and good government. Accordingly, the vast sphere of powers would be allocated to the federal government. This highly centralized view of the Constitution did not survive very long. Instead, the "three-compartment" view of the division of jurisdiction was established.

The *Local Prohibition* case of 1896 was a landmark decision concerning the federal residuary power.[21] The case established, in part due to its interpretation of an earlier case *Russell v. The Queen,*[22] the three compartment view of sections 91 and 92. Lord Watson divided the legislative authority of the federal Parliament into peace, order and good government and the enumerated powers in s. 91. A third compartment of the three compartment view would be provincial power in s. 92. The federal government's power would generally only be paramount, or supreme, over provincial power on matters strictly relating to an enumerated head in s. 91.

The second critical element for the three compartment view was Lord Watson's statement, in the *Local Prohibition* case, that s. 92(16) included all local and private matters in a province omitted from the sixteen heads of s. 92; whereas, peace, order and good government referred to all of the then twenty-seven heads of s. 91. The use of the peace, order and good government power had to be in relation to a matter going beyond local and private matters in a province.

The significance of the three compartment view was that, through grammatical construction and a judicial tendency to fit as many laws into enumerated heads, an expansive and exclusive sphere of provincial jurisdiction was established.[23] Indeed, the enumerated head of s. 92(13) of the *Constitution Act, 1867,* the provincial power over property and civil rights, as a result of the Judicial Committee became a kind of residual power of tremendous significance, and more important than the federal government's residual power over peace, order and good government. In distinguishing between civil rights, which included the area of private law and contracts, and the federal domain of public wrongs, a significant portion of jurisdiction was appropriated to the provincial government. Some further significant aspects of s. 91(13) will be outlined later regarding the treatment of the federal Trade and Commerce power.

At this juncture, one may summarize the effect of the three compartment view of sections 91 and 92 as creating a hierarchy of powers among the enumerated heads of s. 91, s. 92 and the peace, order and good government power. If the courts determined that the subject matter contained in the legislation properly (in "pith and substance") comes within the classes of subjects enumerated in s. 91, then the matter was one of federal jurisdiction, as those classes are deemed under the *Constitution Act, 1867* to be federal. If the matter did not fall under an enumerated head in s. 91, then the court would look to whether the matter properly falls within s. 92. If it falls within that section, then it was a matter of provincial jurisdiction, unless there was a national emergency justifying the use of the federal peace, order and good government power temporarily impinging on provincial jurisdiction. Finally, if it fell within neither of the enumerated heads in sections 91 or 92, one considered if it fell within the federal residuary power of peace, order and good government.

Theoretically, in an age of Parliamentary Supremacy before the Charter, the subject matter of the legislation must fall within one level of jurisdiction or both. On a practical level, however, it may be possible, in a given case, to structure legal doctrines in such a way that neither level of government possesses *effective* power to deal with a situation, which was precisely the suspicion raised regarding the JCPC's treatment of attempted government intervention during the Depression. In this way, the measures enacted by one level of government could be struck down knowing full well that the other level of government might not enact, or might not be capable of enacting similar legislation. If the enumerated heads of sections 91 and 92 were interpreted narrowly and the peace, order and good government power was confined to emergency legislation, there could be areas of jurisdiction practically inaccessible to either level of government. Presumably though, at least on a political level, with the exception of the Charter, no amount of judicial creativity could overcome a valid intergovernmental agreement in which both levels of government were pooling their power, so to speak, as the judiciary would be striking at the very heart of Parliamentary Supremacy.

As we observed in part and will continue to observe, primarily due to the theoretical overlap of federal and provincial powers, as expressed particularly in sections 91 and 92, the sections must be read together and not in isolation when applied to a certain matter. Furthermore, the various jurisprudential approaches reflect the decision-maker's views on Canadian federalism, be they "classical" or "provincialist" or whatever. Two other concepts are important to understand the relationship between federal and provincial powers. These are the Aspect and Ancillary doctrines.

Subject Matter and Aspect Doctrine

To complicate matters further, not only is it often unclear what level of government has jurisdiction, an issue may have both federal and provincial aspects and, consequently, both levels of government can legislate with respect to the same issue on the basis of their respective ground(s) of jurisdiction.[24] This situation is so because a particular problem may involve some aspects that are local in concern, and others that fall under the enumerated heads of s. 91, or are more national in nature. Again, the characterization of aspect is subject to interpretation by the courts.

To illustrate differing jurisdictions in subject matter and aspect, one may take the example of fighting inflation through wage and price controls. It quickly becomes clear that this issue involves an aggregation of subject matters regarding wage controls and price controls, with both federal and provincial components. Indeed, so much so that inflation fighting cannot, in jurisprudence, be properly characterized as a subject matter at all. Therefore, in such cases, the first step is to characterize what are the subject matters involved and who has jurisdiction in that respect.

Secondly, within those subject matters, various national and local (or provincial) aspects may arise. For example, over the subject matter of wage controls, the federal aspect includes the jurisdiction over wages and employment relations concerning federal civil servants. Provincial aspects of that area include wage and employment relations concerning provincial civil servants and, generally, with respect to the private sector within a province. The divisions of aspect may become far more complicated yet and the simple outline provided may be subject to modification. The point, however, is to demonstrate how federal and provincial aspects may arise regarding an issue and both levels of government may legislate on the same issue with respect to differing relevant subject matters or aspects, and, perhaps, in differing ways.

An abundance and variety of other examples relating to aspect exist. For example, there are similar provincial and federal offenses regarding the same offence, like driving without due care and attention, each resting on differing grounds and each consistent with the division of jurisdiction. In the area of securities, there is a federal and provincial overlap regarding the issuing of a false prospectus.

Ancillary or Necessarily Incidental

Legislation, then, exceeding its proper jurisdiction will be to that extent held invalid or *ultra vires*, unless the provision was so integral to the legislation that the whole of the legislation must be struck down. However, action taken by one level of government properly within its jurisdiction may impinge upon the jurisdiction of the other level of government, so long as such impingement is ancillary or necessarily incidental to otherwise valid action.[25] Therefore, aside from concurrency explicitly stipulated in the *Constitution Act, 1867*, in practice, a substantial area of concurrency arises providing for a broadened area in which federal and provincial governments may operate.

The doctrine of paramountcy exists to reconcile the conflicts between inconsistent laws of the two levels of government. Where there are inconsistent or conflicting federal and provincial laws and both are valid, the federal law prevails. As such, the way the courts interpret the applicability of this doctrine can either broaden the scope for provincial power, or narrow it.

The doctrine is interpreted in such a way that the provinces retain their broad area of jurisdiction. Usually, the doctrine is confined to situations of impossibility of dual compliance; that is, the compliance with one law involves breach of the other. Where there is a conflict in the operation of federal and provincial laws, and both laws can be complied with by following the stricter rule, the doctrine of paramountcy will not come into play. One case even suggested that for the provincial law to be invalid in this respect, it is not sufficient that it effects the exercise of federal jurisdiction, it must "sterilize it in all its functions and activities."[26]

Thus, on a theoretical level, repugnancy can only come into play regarding legislation that is regulatory in nature. It would not apply to any other sort of legislation, for example, in setting fiscal or social policy. The area within which such legislation may operate outside of the potential scope of the doctrine is vast.

On the other hand, there is some authority to suggest that if the federal government occupies a field of federal jurisdiction, and by express words, or through the operation of a complete treatment of the federal subject matter intends to exclude provincial jurisdiction, then it may do so. However, only the most explicit wording or a very complete scheme is required in this respect. Such a situation is very rare indeed. In *Irwin Toy Ltd. v. Quebec (Attorney-General)*,[27] the Court suggested that if the federal government made its lower standards the sole governing standard relating to the standards of television broadcasting, there may have been occasion to invoke the doctrine of paramountcy. The Supreme Court of Canada, by a majority of five to four, in *Workers' Compensation Board v. Huskey Oil Operations Ltd*,[28] held that the provinces cannot create priorities between creditors, or change the scheme of distribution in a bankruptcy situation. This case involved matters of deemed exclusive federal jurisdiction under s. 91(21) of the *Constitution Act, 1867*. Such provincial legislation was held to be in operational conflict with the federal legislation. The court will scrutinize the substance and form of the legislation, as well as the effect of the legislation, and not just the intent of the provincial legislature. The minority of the Court would impose a stricter test of operational conflict, whereby, only provincial laws that directly improve the priority of a claim upon the actual property of the bankrupt over that accorded by the *Bankruptcy Act* would be inoperative under the doctrine of paramountcy.

One may make two observations regarding these cases. First, *Irwin Toy* was a regulation case, and *Huskey Oil* is also a kind of regulation case in terms of regulating the process of bankruptcy. Secondly, and, most importantly, these cases deal with policy areas of exclusive federal jurisdiction, like broadcasting and bankruptcy. They do not constitute authority to allow federal legislation to be made in areas of provincial jurisdiction. Furthermore, few policy areas of significance, in a contemporary setting, are ones that involve exclusivity of jurisdiction, but, rather, involve an overlapping of federal and provincial jurisdictions, and more often involve an aggregation of subject matters. These cases are not persuasive authority to extend the doctrine's application to exclude the exercise of provincial powers in broad policy areas of mixed jurisdiction, such as fiscal or social policy, especially by simply occupying the policy field through the use of federal legislation.

Even when the doctrine of paramountcy applies, a provincial law is rendered inapplicable or inoperative, as the case may be, only to the extent of the inconsistency, unless that part is inseparably linked to the other constituent parts in which case all of the provincial law is inoperative. Once the federal law is repealed, the provincial law is automatically revived.[29]

Peace, Order and Good Government: The Power

The extent of the narrower role assigned to the peace, order and good government power itself was a matter of dispute in jurisprudence. At first, it might appear that if one were to accept the three compartment view, because of s. 92(16), private or local concern applies to all provincial powers, then the peace, order and good government power must embrace all other matters that go beyond a merely private or local concern. Even, this view was not necessarily accepted, as the history of the national concern and national emergency interpretations of the peace, order and good government power indicate.

The significant beginning of the national concern doctrine originated in the *Canada Temperance Federation* case in which it was asserted that if the subject matter is such that:

> ... it goes beyond local or provincial concern or interest and must from its inherent nature be the concern of the Dominion as a whole, then it will fall within the competence of Parliament as a matter affecting the peace order and good government of Canada though it may in another aspect touch on matters specially reserved to the provincial government.[30]

Otherwise, impinging on provincial jurisdiction was not permitted, or, it was thought that provincial autonomy would be destroyed.

However, the "Provincialist" era of jurisprudence was emerging and an even more restrictive interpretation of the peace, order and good government power was given. With Viscount Haldane, beginning with *In re Board of Commerce Act and Combines and Fair Prices Act*,[31] then in *Fort Francis Pulp and Power Co. v. Manitoba Free Press*[32] and culminating in *Toronto Electric Commissioners v. Snider*,[33] the emergency doctrine was established. That is, the peace, order and good government power could only be invoked in times of national emergency involving a "sudden danger to social order," and the legislation was necessary for the preservation of national life.[34] Such legislation could only be of temporary duration and once one could show that the emergency did not exist, the power could no longer be used.[35]

At varying times, the national concern or the national emergency view of the peace, order and good government power prevailed. In 1976, the matter was confronted directly by the Supreme Court of Canada in the *Anti-Inflation Act Reference* dealing with a comprehensive federal program of wage and price controls in key areas of the private sector, the federal public sector, and government employees of the provinces that opted into the scheme.[36] A majority of the court agreed with Mister Justice Beetz that the national concern and the national emergency doctrines are different, and both exist under the peace, order and good government power to support federal legislation. Should there be a national emergency, the federal government may temporarily legislate on provincial matters. The national concern doctrine operates as if certain heads were added to the subject matters enumerated in s. 91. Three criteria were required to be satisfied in order to invoke the national concern branch of peace, order and good government:

1. There is a gap in federal-provincial powers;

2. The subject matter of the legislation is characterized by a singleness, distinctiveness and indivisibility distinguishing it from a provincial concern; and

3. The subject matter is new.

It was more recently held that the test will be more functional, and less legalistic and abstract, to effectively deal with present day problems. In *Labatt Breweries*, the national concern branch was held to include a subject matter that "goes beyond local or provincial concern or interest and must from its inherent nature, be a concern of the Dominion as a whole."[37] The subject matter did not necessarily have to be "new" in the sense of not existing at the time of Confederation.

The *Crown Zellerbach* case involved a corporation's challenge to a charge laid under federal statute of dumping woodwaste wholly within provincial waters. The decision was significant due to its treatment of the criteria 'singleness, distinctiveness and indivisibility' of the subject matter distinguishing it from provincial concern. In this context, the court will consider the effect on "extra-provincial" interests of a provincial failure to deal effectively with the control or regulation of the intra-provincial aspects of the matter.[38]

In other words, the peace, order and good government power may be used to fill in the gap relating to that provincial inability to deal with a problem. Therefore, the "gap" test, as stated in the *Anti-Inflation Act Reference*, was no longer necessary to be satisfied. Thus, the two important aspects of the "singleness, distinctiveness and indivisibility" test are that the matter must be distinguished from matters of provincial concern, and, secondly, the degree of impact on provincial jurisdiction must be reconcilable with the fundamental distribution of legislative powers under the Constitution.

The Court in *Crown Zellerbach* held that marine pollution was a "single, indivisible matter" distinct from the control of pollution by dumping in other provincial waters. It was "indivisible" because, from a functional perspective, the difficulty in ascertaining federal and provincial waters created an unacceptable degree of uncertainty for the application of regulatory and penal provisions. Finally, the distinction of fresh and salt water dumping was seen to have ascertainable and reasonable limits, with respect to provincial jurisdiction.

Trade and Commerce

A second example of how an apparently broad federal power was limited to give greater scope for provincial power, particularly s. 92(13) property and civil rights, is the federal Trade and Commerce power. In *Citizens Insurance Co. v. Parsons*, the JCPC held that s. 91(2), the federal Trade and Commerce power, was not intended the full scope of its literal meaning because the mention of other classes of subjects like Banking would not be necessary.[39] Incidentally, the same linguistic principles were invoked to justify the separation within s. 91 of the residual power of peace order and good government from the enumerated heads. When there was a conflict of jurisdiction, the terms of sections 91 and 92 were interpreted to give practical effect to both sections, and to prevent the powers of one level of government from being absorbed by the other. Accordingly, the Trade and Commerce power was limited to international or interprovincial trade, or, the general regulation of trade affecting the whole of the Dominion. It did not include the power to regulate a particular business or trade.

Later, in the *Board of Commerce* case of 1922, Viscount Haldane further limited the Trade and Commerce power in stating that it could only be invoked in furtherance of a general power which Parliament possessed independently of it. Therefore, this power was virtually nullified and the provinces, thereby, enjoyed greater power. It appeared that the most the central government could do was to permit the incorporation of federal companies.[40]

Clearly, the *Board of Commerce* case was unacceptable in the Canadian context in which the federal government, also, represents Canadian citizens and must possess some general powers over trade and commerce. In 1931, the JCPC reversed its earlier holding and rejected that narrow idea of s. 91(2).[41] Nevertheless, the federal government was not permitted to acquire jurisdiction by creating sweeping legislation under s. 91(2) either.[42] In fact, until recently, other than regarding interprovincial and international trade, the federal government's power respecting the general regulation of trade affecting the whole Dominion was practically non-existent.

Even though the federal government possesses jurisdiction over interprovincial and international trade, the provinces exercise their jurisdiction to affect such trade. A brief discussion on interprovincial trade illustrates the point.

Interprovincial Trade

In terms of interprovincial trade, a province may regulate a transaction of sale and purchase within its boarders even between a resident and a person outside of the province.[43] The reason is that the regulation is in respect of contracts and not trade as trade.

Provincial regulation may, in fact, affect interprovincial trade and is not necessarily outside its jurisdiction unless the regulation was made "in relation to the regulation of extraprovincial trade and commerce."[44] The impact of the regulation is one factor in determining the purpose of the legislation. Therefore, provincial marketing schemes that include persons or corporations who bring their products inside the province, may very well constitute a valid exercise of provincial power.[45] Furthermore, incidental effects on interprovincial trade are not necessarily invalid. However, a regulation controlling the free flow of trade into the province, or, obtaining the most advantageous marketing for that province's producers will not be acceptable.[46]

In this way, a large spectrum of valid provincial measures affect and distort the interprovincial free flow of goods and services, despite the fact that interprovincial trade is a federal power. One might ask how this state of affairs can exist in the face of s. 121 of the *Constitution Act, 1867*, which states:

> **s. 121** All Articles of Growth, Produce or Manufacture of any one of the Provinces shall from and after the Union, be admitted free into each of the other Provinces.

This provision was read narrowly, being largely confined to custom duties, excise duties and the like, but, does not comprehend non-fiscal impediments, as the case of *Atlantic Smoke Shops* v. *Conlon* demonstrates.[47] Mr. Justice Rand, in *Murphy* v. *C.P.R.,* had this to say about s. 121:

> I take s. 121, apart from customs duties, to be aimed against trade regulation which is designed to place fetters upon or raise impediments to or otherwise restrict or limit the free flow of Commerce across the Dominion as if provincial boundaries did not exist. That it does not create a level of trade activity divested of all regulation I have no doubt; what is preserved is a free flow of trade regulated in subsidiary features which are or have come to be looked upon as incidents of trade. What is forbidden is trade regulation that in essence and purpose is related to a provincial boundary.[48]

As a result, provinces are permitted to impede interprovincial trade in important respects through trade regulated in "subsidiary features," or non-tariff barriers to interprovincial trade. Such provincial non-tariff barriers to trade, also, effect international trade.

To be fair, federal government policies, also, distort interprovincial trade, although, one might see such policies as properly falling under the Trade and Commerce power. Furthermore, the Ancillary doctrine cuts both ways and valid federal measures may be used to impinge on provincial jurisdiction. For example, in *Caloil v. Attorney-General of Canada*,[49] the Court considered the National Energy Policy (NEP), which provided regulation to control the importation of oil to foster development of Canadian oil resources by restricting oil importation to defined areas. The Court concluded the regulation was of the character of an extraprovincial marketing scheme, and the impingement on provincial jurisdiction was necessarily incidental.

General Regulation of Trade

In terms of the Second Branch of the Trade of Commerce power enunciated in the *Parsons* case, that is, the general regulation of trade affecting the whole dominion, it was practically non-existent until some signs of life began to emerge in 1977. It was not until 1989 that real meaning was given to it, while, at the same time, strict limits and criteria were imposed to prevent wholesale encroachment on provincial powers. The previously cited case of *General Motors v. City National Leasing* recognized the proper and constitutionally valid role of the federal government in the workings of the national economy of Canada, and not just regarding international and interprovincial trade.

The *City National* case involved an allegation of price discrimination and the constitutionality of the *Combines and Investigations Act* under which the allegations were raised. The Act's provisions provided for a private civil right of action against certain anti-competitive practices.

The court considers the constitutional validity of the federal government acting under the Second Branch of the Trade and Commerce power by employing a three step approach. First, the court will determine to what extent does the relevant provision impinge on the provincial power. For example, creating a civil right of action is *prima facie* intrusive. The extent of impingement is determined by assessing whether the provision is remedial or substantive in nature.[50] Remedial provisions are thought to be less intrusive. Secondly, the court determines whether the intrusion is limited or general in nature.

Once the extent of the impingement is determined, if any, the court will then examine the whole legislative scheme, which involves the consideration of certain factors. First, there must be the presence of a regulatory scheme. The three components of a regulatory scheme involve: the defining of offensive conduct, the establishment of an investigating mechanism, and the existence of criminal/administrative redress. Secondly, one looks at the validity of the regulatory scheme by considering the following non-exhaustive list of factors, of whether:

a) the scheme operates under the oversight of an agency;

b) the legislation is national in scope, i.e. it is a regulation of trade in general and not of a particular industry;

c) the deleterious effects of the problem (like anti-competitive practice) transcend provincial boundaries and are a national concern; and

d) there is a need for national regulation and the scheme would be ineffective if the legislation was confined to intraprovincial trade. Thus, the court will consider a provincial inability test to deal with the situation.

Finally, one considers the extent of the intrusion and the "fit" of the intrusive provision in the scheme of the legislation. A sliding scale is employed. If there is great intrusion, then a strict test is required such as the intrusive provision must be "truly necessary" or "integral".[51] The less intrusive the provision, the less vigorous is the test, such as a necessarily incidental standard and moving towards the less strict "functionally related" test.[52]

Therefore, from a seemingly centralized Constitution in which it appeared that the federal government controlled all the important powers, as a result of constitutional convention and judicial interpretation, the provinces exercise a tremendous amount of jurisdiction. In fact, at certain times, judicial opinions were so extreme that important federal powers were not given much recognition or efficacy. However, exercising control over expansive jurisdiction may not, in the end, be of great significance if the relevant level of government does not possess the resources to adequately exercise that jurisdiction.

Adequate Resources

The second aspect of a federal system, in addition to an appropriate distribution of powers, is that of adequate resources to exercise jurisdiction. This aspect of the equation deals with the revenue raising powers of the respective level of government, as contained in the Constitution.

Essentially, the key provisions dealing with taxation are sections 91(3) and 92(2) of the *Constitution Act, 1867*. The federal power extends to the raising of money by any mode or system of taxation, while the provincial power is limited to direct taxation within the province in order to raise revenue for provincial purposes and regarding licensing fees.

The seemingly limitless federal power over taxation was given limits by the judiciary. One leading study by G.V. La Forest on the taxing power under the

Constitution is particularly insightful regarding the limits on federal taxation and many of the comments and observations contained therein are reflected in this section.[53] First, although it may seem obvious, the federal taxation power is limited to raising money by taxation. As such, the courts are required to characterize the substance of the provision to determine whether it properly falls within the taxation power. A levy designed to regulate intra-provincial marketing, rather than raising money, was held not to be a tax.[54] However, the raising of revenue need not be the sole purpose of federal legislation as s. 91(3) may be combined with other federal powers such as peace, order and good government, or other federal enumerated powers, like those relating to the monetary system.

The second limitation to which the federal taxation power is subject is the so called direct/indirect doctrine. Where one level of government cannot constitutionally directly use its jurisdiction or powers to legislate in a given area, it will not be permitted to do so indirectly, for example, by using is taxation power to regulate that area.

Essentially, if the legislation in the form of tax is found in aspects and for the purposes exclusively within the provincial sphere, it will be held to be invalid.[55] In essence, the limitation is thought to be inherent in the federal system itself. As was stated by Duff C.J. in *Attorney-General of Ontario v. Reciprocal Insurers*,[56] which was adopted with respect to taxation by Viscount Dunedin in *In re Insurance Act of Canada*:

> ... the Parliament of Canada cannot by purporting to exercise taxation powers under s. 91, head 3, appropriate to itself exclusively a field of jurisdiction in which, apart from such a procedure, it could exert no legal authority, and that if, when examined as a whole, legislation in form taxing is found, in aspects and for purposes exclusively within the Provincial sphere to deal with matters committed to the Provinces, it cannot be upheld as valid.[57]

Furthermore, if federal taxation legislation is linked with such an illegal object as described, it too will be declared unconstitutional.[58] In the *Insurance Act of Canada* case, the Privy Council struck down federal legislation requiring foreign insurers doing business in Canada to obtain a federal licence, and struck down a provision imposing a 5 percent tax on premiums paid to insurers who did not possess a federal licence. The latter provision was struck down as being linked with the illegal object of the former provision.

In another example, a federal law prohibiting the operation of a fish cannery without a licence was held to be *ultra vires*. In the *Fish Cannaries* case,[59] the federal government admitted that the statute could not be justified under the taxation power, but, tried unsuccessfully to support that legislation on its power over Sea coast and inland fisheries. Also, in the *Reference re Employment and Social Insurance Act,*[60] it was doubted that compulsory employee and employer contributions to an Unemployment Insurance fund was a tax as it was seen as a special fund for a particular purpose and had special levies. In essence, the scheme was seen as a premium for compulsory insurance, being, at that time, a matter of provincial jurisdiction.

Provincial taxation, is limited by four criteria contained in s. 92(2) of the *Constitution Act, 1867.* The taxation must be direct. Its incidence must be within the province. It must be exercised in order to raise revenue and the revenue must be for provincial purposes. In 1867, the direct taxation power was not seen by some to be significant. Indeed, it is estimated that nearly four-fifths of the former provincial revenues were given to the new Dominion Government under the 1867 *Constitution Act.*[61] Despite its humble beginnings, the provincial taxation power grew to be highly significant.

In *Bank of Toronto v. Lambe,*[62] the JCPC held that a tax on a corporation was a direct tax, even though it is a commercial fact of life that a corporation can essentially shift the tax to the consumer through higher prices. This shifting of the tax burden was still held to be direct, in this case, because the tax was demanded from the very persons from whom it was intended should pay. Therefore, this case opened up the area of business taxation to the province. Furthermore, in *Atlantic Smoke Shops v. Conlon,*[63] the JCPC held that a tax on retail sales such as tobacco was direct because the province framed its legislation in such a way that it was aimed directly at the consumer. Every retailer was deemed to be an agent of the province to collect this tax at the point of sale.

A significant case emerged in 1978 regarding the ability of provinces to levy royalties with respect to natural resources. The Supreme Court of Canada held, in *Canadian Industrial Gas and Oil Ltd v. The Government of Saskatchewan,*[64] that the royalty surcharge on the production of natural resources on Crown owned lands did not fall under provincial jurisdiction in s. 109 of the *Constitution Act, 1867,* which deals with property in lands, mines, minerals and royalties belonging to the province at the time of Union. Rather, it was a tax, and an indirect one at that, because oil producers passed it on in the form of higher prices. In essence, it was an export tax as 98 per cent of Saskatchewan's oil was exported to other provinces and the United States.

This case was reversed in 1982, through the constitutional amendment s. 92A. Essentially, s. 92A gives to the provinces authority regarding the exportation for non-renewable natural resources in the province, as well as the development, conservation and management of non-renewable natural resources, forestry resources and electrical energy. The Amendment gives further powers over exportation relating to such resources, but, prohibits one province from discriminating in prices, or in supplies exported to another part of Canada. Finally, the province may employ any mode of taxation, direct or indirect, with respect to non-renewable natural resources and forestry resources in the province, including the primary production therefrom, and regarding sites and facilities in the province for the generation of electrical energy, including the production therefrom, whether or not such production is exported. Schedule Six of the *Constitution Act, 1867* deems non-renewable natural resources and forestry reuses to be "primary production" if:

s.1(a)(i) it is in the form in which it exists upon its recovery or severance from its natural state; or

(ii) it is a product resulting from processing or refining the resource, and is not a manufactured product or a product resulting from refining crude oil, refining upgraded heavy crude oil, refining gases or liquids derived from coal or refining a synthetic equivalent or crude oil.

Production from a forestry resource is "primary production" if it consists of sawlogs, poles, lumber, wood chips, sawdust or any other primary wood product or wood pulp, and is not a product manufactured from wood.

Thus, the provinces wield an enormous amount of taxation power, including personal and corporate income taxes, sales taxes, property taxes, licensing fees, and so on. It is, therefore, impossible to maintain that they do not possess adequate powers over taxation, as contained in constitutional text.

Chapter 9
The Continuing Legacy of Accommodation:
The Successes of Fiscal Federalism and other
Constitutional/non-Constitutional Change

Up to this point, much was made of the fact that Canada progressed from being a quasi-federal country to one that is truly federal in character, featuring two levels of government co-ordinate and independent, sharing a fair distribution of jurisdiction and resources to match. Some emphasis was placed on the importance of the role of the judiciary in interpreting the Constitution allowing for this decentralization to take place. However, that role should be put into the broader perspective of Canadian federalism and the changes occurring within the workings of the constitution.

Chapter 1 discussed the basic elements of Canadian federalism, including the role of the judiciary. It was stated that the legal results of judicial decisions may not even be the most important element influencing Canadian federalism. This is so because the way the constitution actually operates likely has more to do with the actions of federal and provincial governments, and the relations between them, including through intergovernmental agreements, than the constitutional decisions of the judiciary, although the latter are important. It is, particularly, due to the increased role of government in society; the fact that many problems involve an overlap or uncertainties associated with federal and provincial jurisdiction; and that one level of government may not be able to act alone, for example due to inadequate resources, that both levels of government must to work together to manage these interdependencies.

As with other areas related to Canadian federalism that were discussed, the relations between the two levels of government from a fiscal perspective are also characterizable by decentralization in significant aspects. There was, as well, centralization in certain respects. Through the use of the federal spending power, some, like Guay and Rocher, go so far as to charge that the federal government has been using its spending power to destroy the division of jurisdiction recognized in 1867 of exclusive areas of provincial jurisdiction and its use radically changed fiscal relations.[1] Consistent with battles over citizen conceptions and loyalties, some Quebecers condemn federal intervention regarding the welfare state, especially because it focuses on the individual and not the regions.[2]

However, the area of fiscal federalism demonstrates clearly that Canadian federalism, in significant ways, and with respect to important matters, has successfully evolved to meet the needs and interests of both levels of governments and to better provide for the needs and interests of the citizens to whom such expenditures are directed. It is, perhaps, this area of fiscal federalism that is one of the most important aspects of Canadian federalism.

Fiscal federalism refers to the relations and understandings between both orders of government, as it relates to public revenues and expenditures. As such, its essential features are government taxation and expenditures. The more important agreements that such intergovernmental relations deal with include the sharing and division of taxation, and expenditures related to shared cost programs and income security.

The spending responsibilities of one level of government can be higher at certain times, or in certain circumstances, than that of the other level. Therefore, adjustment may be necessary with respect to government revenue. For example, Baby Boomers created the need for increased education, and an aging population gives rise to escalating health care costs, both of which are primarily responsibilities of the province. The possibilities for revenue adjustment involve the ways in which each level of government raises revenue and controls expenditures and/or involves reallocating revenue sources either by grants or transfers from one level to another, or by one level of government obtaining more tax room.

All major federations recognize a spending power even in areas not strictly within a particular government's legislative jurisdiction. The spending power is not formally set out in the Constitutions of some federations, particularly the older ones, while it tends to be formally set out in more recent ones. In any event, such a power is recognized as constitutionally legitimate. The legal basis for federal grants or transfers with respect to matters falling under provincial jurisdiction originated in the *Employment and Social Insurance Reference* case, which struck down the special unemployment insurance fund set up under Bennett's New Deal legislation to deal with the Depression. The JCPC went on to say that as long as the federal government was spending money from the Consolidated Revenue Fund, which is a general account in which federal taxes are paid, it may dispose of its public property on any matter it chooses, including with respect to matters within provincial jurisdiction. The reason it could do so was a combination of the 1867 *Constitution Act's* ss. 91(1A) Public Debt and Property, like the Consolidated Revenue Fund, and 91(3) the federal taxation power. Furthermore, the federal government may transfer that money with conditions and the recipient may decline or accept such monies. The use of the spending power was again sanctioned by the courts, most recently in 1989, 1991 and 1997 so long as its use does not constitute in substance legislation on a provincial matter.[3]

Several important themes are identified with respect to Canadian fiscal federalism.[4] One theme is that of federal autonomy versus provincial autonomy. Each method by which revenue adjustment can be structured involves varying considerations with respect to the theme of autonomy. Generally speaking, reallocating tax room provides for the greatest amount of autonomy for both levels of government in the sense that neither level of government may be required to do anything more. A grant, on the other hand, may require the person or body receiving it to do something, and the person or body giving the grant to continue funding; therefore, there may be a loss of autonomy for both levels of government. Of course, the type of agreement giving rise to revenue adjustment may modify the considerations outlined with respect to autonomy, or indeed, reverse them. For example, a grant may be structured in such a way that it provides for complete autonomy, whereas, reallocating tax room may involve numerous constraints and conditions.

One final consideration with respect to reallocating revenue and autonomy, is that of political responsibility. Were the federal government to simply transfer some of its revenue to the provinces, it would be taking political responsibility for such grants. On the other hand, reallocating tax room to the provinces means that the province takes on its own political responsibility for the use of those funds. In Canada, both tax room and grants were, and are, being used.

A second, and related theme, is that of intergovernmental entanglements and disentanglements. This theme relates to the extent to which federal government involvement is determined by decisions actually made by the provinces, and provincial decisions being determined by federal funding. This loss of federal autonomy in controlling its expenditures has been a major issue for the federal government.

Third, is the theme of interprovincial diversity versus interprovincial disparity. In a federal system of government, national and provincial governments reflect their own diversities. Interprovincial diversities yield interprovincial disparities. Equalization, a principle now entrenched in the Canadian Constitution, was established to address the issue of interprovincial disparities between "have" and "have not" provinces so that each province can provide a diverse range of public goods and services to the people within that province.

The fourth theme relates to symmetry and asymmetry. This theme relates to the extent to which intergovernmental relations are essentially symmetrical, or asymmetrical (i.e. different) featuring compartmentalized relations between the federal government and a province. It is important to note that under this theme, Quebec has been the subject of numerous distinct or asymmetrical relations pertaining to taxation and transfers. A second aspect is the extent to which policy outcomes themselves are essentially symmetrical/asymmetrical notwithstanding whether or not intergovernmental relations are symmetrical or asymmetrical in a given circumstance.

Finally, federal reallocations of revenue, and the agreements underlying such reallocations, demonstrate the federal government's preoccupation with important programs that Canadians value.

Fiscal Federalism

Taxation

As eluded to previously, the federal and provincial governments share concurrency over direct taxation. The primary problem relating to this area of taxation is not to determine the respective limits of federal and provincial power, but, rather, to restrict and co-ordinate its use, and to prevent its abuse. As a result, these substantial issues of Canadian federalism are resolved through intergovernmental agreements, and such agreements allow for the balancing of the essential features of Canadian federalism.

The most significant issue that federal-provincial taxation agreements deal with relate to income taxation, both personal and corporate. As the years have gone by, more and more personal income tax (PIT) room, as a percentage of basic federal tax, has been allocated to the provinces, whereas, corporate income tax (CIT) was raised by one percentage point in favour of the provinces. The reason for this significant shift in taxation is that provincial spending responsibilities increased dramatically.

A related aspect to tax room is that the allocated tax room does not necessarily limit a government's ability to tax in excess. During the early 1960's, all provinces levied PIT according to their then allotted tax room of

16 points of basic federal tax, except for Manitoba and Saskatchewan who taxed more. It has long since been the case that each province taxes beyond their PIT tax room of 44 points.

During the Second World War, the provinces agreed to temporarily vacate the PIT and CIT fields in return for compensation based on a province's choice of one of two formulae, whichever would serve it best. The province could claim compensation either on the basis of the amount collected from those sources during the year ending nearest December 31, 1940; or, the cost of servicing the net debt paid by the province during the financial year (exclusive of payments to the sinking fund), less the revenues derived from succession duties during that period.[5] Later, the federal government entered into further agreements with all provinces except Ontario and Quebec. Subsequently, the agreement of Ontario was secured.

New agreements were negotiated for the period 1957 to 1961. Eight provinces agreed to permit the federal government to collect its taxes with standard rates of abatement constituting the provincial share. The standard rates included 10 percent of federal PIT (increased to 13 percent in 1955) and 50 percent of the federal tax on estates.[6] Ontario rented its PIT and received compensation; however, its CIT was at a rate 2 percent higher than the federal abatement and Ontario imposed its own succession duties. Quebec imposed its own PIT and CIT at rates higher than the federal abatement.

Provincial responsibilities increased dramatically beginning in the 1960's, leading to demands for a greater share of available taxation revenues. Under the Federal-Provincial Fiscal Arrangements Act of 1962, the tax rental arrangement was replaced by a tax collection agreement whereby the federal government collected without charge the PIT and CIT levied by the provinces. The federal government withdrew from PIT by 16 percent in favour of the provinces and continued to withdraw at a specified rate.[7] It, also, withdrew from CIT by 9 percent.[8] Again, Ontario collected its own CIT, while Quebec collected its own PIT and CIT.

Under the 1967 Federal-Provincial Fiscal Arrangements Act, the federal government withdrew from PIT a further four percentage points from the 1966 level, now totalling 28 percent.[9] It, also, vacated a further point in CIT, totalling 10 percent.[10] Relevant to this period is the cost sharing of post-secondary education (PSE) undertaken by the federal government to the amount of 50 percent of the cost. This cost sharing was effected through further tax room as specified (4 PIT points and 1 CIT point), supplemented by cash transfers sufficient to raise the yield of that tax room to half the amount of PSE.

In 1972, the standard PIT abatement was raised to 30.5 percent of basic federal tax.[11] Due to new rules regarding tax calculation, the provincial tax base became smaller. With the smaller tax base, 30.5 PIT points equalled what 28 PIT points would have before the change.

In 1977, the 30.5 PIT abatement rose to 44 percent, representing an increase of 13.5 points. This increase represented the replacement of shared cost programs pertaining to hospital insurance and medicare with Established Programs Finance (EPF). Since that time, changes contemplated in tax room have not been dramatic until perhaps with the Canada Health and Social Transfer, 1995, which may entail further tax abatements.

The evolution of shared cost programs resulted in tax changes, and affected the way in which such programs are funded. Recalling the themes of autonomy and disentanglement of the two levels of government, the trend is towards a more decentralized federation. Accordingly, an outline will be provided in order to put the overall fiscal relations into perspective, and to provide background for the next section dealing with the special arrangements between Quebec and the federal government.

Shared Cost Programs

The first shared cost programs emerged in the 1920's and were in the form of categorical conditional grants. These grants were very specific federal grants for very specific program purposes based on federal cost-matching of provincial spending. By the early 1960's, many specific categorical grants were in place relating to such matters as pensions for the blind and disabled, and with respect to health care. Vocational education related to agriculture and apprenticeship. The federal and provincial governments were becoming aware of the problems surrounding such grants. In particular, categorical conditional grants tended to produce too much with respect to a particular program, and too little regarding programs without conditional grants. Although specific purpose cash transfers still exist, for example, with respect to bilingual education and services for young offenders, by and large, they declined.

The next stage in the evolution of shared cost programs was the development of broad percentage cost sharing. Pursuant to this arrangement, the federal government payed 50 percent of the cost of all provincial social welfare expenditure. The Canada Assistance Plan (CAP) was initiated in the mid-1960's. Health Insurance and Medicare represented another huge area of shared costs. Post-Secondary Education (PSE) was timed to accommodate

Baby Boomers who were reaching college and university age. Given these broad areas, policy distortions were avoided in that there would be no favouring of one program aspect over another. Provincial autonomy was, therefore, enhanced. The federal government was becoming worried about its own autonomy with the high increase of spending, and the fact that provincial decisions were driving up federal spending. As costs were ascending dramatically, the federal government put a 15 percent cap on PSE.[12]

The third phase of fiscal relations arose with Established Program Finance (EPF). This funding is characterized as block funding, involving federal transfers and tax room. By the late 1980's, in order to fight burgeoning deficits, federal increases in EPF funding was at a rate under the percentage growth of Gross National Product. In the 1986 year, the federal government limited the growth in EPF transfers by reducing the GNP escalator by 2 percent.[13] There were special per capita adjustment payments to ensure that growth in EPF kept pace with inflation. For the 1990–91 year, the federal government reduced the growth in EPF to the growth in GNP minus 3 percent, but still guaranteed that the rate of growth would not fall below the rate of inflation. EPF per capita entitlements were then frozen to the end of 1994–1995.

Essentially, the provinces determined CAP spending. In February of 1990, the federal government placed a ceiling of 5 percent on increases in spending for provinces not in receipt of Equalization; that is, Ontario, Alberta and British Columbia, at that time. British Columbia challenged the federal government's unilateral change in the joint agreement and succeeded at the Court of Appeal level. The Supreme Court of Canada upheld the federal government's appeal in August 1991, when it ruled that the nature of the agreement and federal responsibility over national policy justified such unilateral measures.[14] The limit was extended to the end of 1994–95 by the 1991 federal budget. The only conditions that needed to be met for federal participation were that a needs test had to be satisfied, an appeals mechanism was required to be set up by the province, and, generally, no residency tests were permitted.

In the 1995 federal Budget, a major change was announced for the 1996–97 year and thereafter. Transfers for social assistance were combined with those for health and post-secondary education, and the overall amount of federal contribution declined. The new block transfer is called the Canada Health and Social Transfer (CHST), and is allocated in the same proportion that the provinces received under the previous system.[15] Conditions under the *Canada*

Health Act still apply, as well as the prohibition of minimum residency requirements with respect to social assistance.[16] Where conditions are not met, the federal government may withhold some, or even all, of its transfers. Notice and consultation mechanisms are envisaged in the case of such breach.

An Agreement on Health by First Ministers on February 4, 1999 was constituted by an exchange of letters the previous month. The Premiers committed themselves to the five principles of medicare, that increases in federal transfers are to be used for health care services and programs, to making health care as effective as possible, to making information about the health care system available to Canadians, and to working in partnership with the federal government to help achieve these objectives. Related to the commitments are two further documents, the Record of Decision from the Federal, Provincial, Territorial meeting of Health Ministers (September 1998) and the Future Directions and Priorities, and the accountability section of the Social Union Framework Agreement, which will be later described. The 1999 federal budget provided an additional $11.5 billion over five years specifically for health care. Of that amount, $8 billion is provided through future year increases in CHST and $3.5 billion as an immediate one time supplement, thereby, establishing a predictable and stable funding arrangement. The 1999 budget also announced significant increases in Equalization (especially due to the economic growth in Ontario), projected as an additional $5 billion over the previous five years or $50 billion in total. As Equalization is non-conditional, the provinces are free to determine such spending, including for CHST items.

Thus, block funding is essentially unconditional funding with the exception of what may be termed "circumscribed unconditionality"[17] contained in the *Canada Health Act*, committed to by the Provinces and Territories in the Agreement on Health, as well as the prohibition of residency requirements for social assistance, all of which have strengthened and clarified federal conditions for financing.

With respect to health care, under the regulations, the provinces must clearly recognize in its public documents, advertising or promotions the federal financing role. There is also an obligation for the provinces to provide certain information to the federal government as prescribed. The public administration of health care must meet certain criteria, such as being conducted on a non-profit basis and that the body administering the program must be responsible to government. The program must be comprehensive by covering all insured health services. It must be universal, in the sense of being available to all insured persons on uniform terms and conditions. No minimum residency requirements are permitted greater than three months and one is covered if one moves to another participating province, or is temporarily absent from one's province. There must be reasonable access to health service for all insured persons, and health care providers are to receive reasonable compensation. Finally, extrabilling by physicians is prohibited. Aside from these general exceptions, block funding is essentially a cash transfer to the province, which further enhances provincial autonomy.

Opting Out

Although the history of standard abatements shows that Canadian federalism has been sensitive to provincial needs and interests, other special accommodations and distinctive agreements were made with respect to Quebec. Of particular note in this respect is the acceptance of the "opting out" principle in 1964. This principle allows a province to contract out of certain programs in return for tax room to recognize money that would otherwise be spent in that province by the federal government. Only Quebec avails itself to such arrangements.

The university episode occurred in 1953 when the federal government, on recommendation of the Massey Commission, attempted to give direct grants to universities. The then Quebec Premier, Duplessis, interposed the state, in the form of the premier (i.e. himself), between institutions of provincial jurisdiction and the acceptance of federal money. The university was obliged to decline this money, or Duplessis would cut back provincial money. This episode gave rise to the first instance of contracting out and Quebec received one point of CIT.

Duplessis treated federal shared cost programs as a shopping list, choosing some like social assistance and rejecting others, especially, health and technical training. Refusals were based on classical federalism notions. The Quebec government, at that time, was generally laissez-faire, therefore, little provincial money was spent in these areas.

The Quebec Liberals under Lesage accepted all programs to gain federal spending activity, but, contracted out of those programs for tax room. The amount could be calculated on the basis of forgone grants. The PIT abatements were used by Quebec in such a way as to produce a tax yield that grew faster than the percentage growth of national income. Quebec contracted out of hospital insurance, technical training and social welfare.

The 1967 fiscal arrangements resulted in the federal government transferring

4 PIT points and 1 CIT point. As the cash PSE and university grants were terminated under these arrangements, the 1 CIT point for Quebec was no longer necessary and was terminated. At this time, the provincial standard abatement was 28 PIT and 10 CIT points.

When hospital and health insurance was transferred to EPF, the scope for contracting out was further reduced. In terms of EPF, Quebec contracted out for 8.5 PIT points.[18] Furthermore, Quebec receives 5 PIT points after social welfare was transferred to CAP.[19] The federal government treats these two items as money withheld that Quebec would otherwise receive. Pursuant to this arrangement, Quebec must submit to Ottawa a statement of what it spent pertaining to CAP and EPF.

In addition to these two matters in which Quebec contracts out, there is a third related to Youth Allowance. Ottawa paid Family Allowances for each child from birth to fifteen years of age. In 1961, the Lesage Liberals extended Youth Allowances to sixteen and seventeen year olds. The federal government later did the same. With the 1974 overhaul of Family Allowance policy, provinces could "configure" the amount of federal family allowance to age and rank in the family, which was exactly what Quebec did. As a result, the Youth Allowance episode was over and the opting-out provision no longer applicable. The three points of additional tax room is bought directly from Ottawa by Quebec for cash. For example, in 1996, Quebec paid $438.5 million for that additional tax room.[20]

Therefore, in total, Quebec contracts out or purchases 16.5 PIT points,[21] which remains true under the Canada Health and Social Transfer. Of that amount, the 8.5 PIT points for EPF and 5 PIT points for CAP essentially represent reduced cash payments from the federal government to Quebec. Secondly, Quebec buys 3 PIT points directly from Ottawa. However, the CHST may entail further decentralization of tax room, which would likely make the position of the other provinces more similar to that of Quebec in terms of health care, post-secondary education and social assistance funding.

What is, the significance of these 16.5 tax points? Quebec's personal income tax is distinctive, as it involves a 16.5% subtraction or abatement from basic federal tax. One may inquire, then, as to the significance of this distinctive personal income tax arrangement.

Tax Collection Agreements

Nine provinces, not including Quebec, have personal income tax collection agreements with the federal government to promote simplicity for the taxpayer, and uniformity of the tax structure relating to exemptions, credits and rates. In return, the provinces receive the service of tax collection free of charge. The provincial rate is expressed as a percentage of the Basic Federal Tax (BFT). The system is unravelling in the sense that the BFT is becoming less significant to provincial taxation, or to the uniformity of the tax structure as expressed in the tax collection agreements.

One particularly significant event, explaining the unravelling of the system, is the 1987 Tax Reforms, which reflected a worldwide trend away from income distribution. The reforms affected the BFT and provincial revenues. The federal government was not able, as in the past, to ease the transition through income tax abatements. However, even by the early 1970's, the unravelling was occurring. During that time period, the then Liberal Finance Minister, John Turner, indexed the tax structure to inflation, measured by the Consumer Price Index, resulting in less favourable yields of tax revenue, and exacerbating the problem of deficits as government spending has been sensitive to inflation. Provinces began levying taxes in excess of their 44 point allotment since the tax base was not raising fast enough.

Independent of the BFT, there are surtaxes imposed and reductions for low income groups. Provincial taxation began to differ province by province, and even the federal government levies its own surtaxes. The existence of collection agreements do not preclude provincial autonomy in creating such differences. Canada is a long way away from tax structure uniformity making the distinctive position of Quebec less distinctive.

Quebec's personal income taxation was never part of the tax collection agreements. Quebec did not levy a PIT until 1954 when it began to spend more. Quebec created its own tax structure and tax forms due to Premier Duplessis' view that the power to tax was the power to govern. That taxation structure did not really differ all that much from those outside the province. However, one important difference arose in 1974, when the Liberal Premier Bourassa did not index PIT to inflation as Turner did. The result was a more favourable yield of income tax. Because Quebec's revenue was more 'elastic', it could forgo some of that revenue for tax breaks. One such tax break was the creation of the Quebec Stock Savings Plan by the Quebec Finance Minister, Jacques Parizeau.

The 1988 reforms of the Quebec tax structure resulted in its tax structure being along the same lines as that of Ottawa. For example, Ottawa reduced the number of progressive rate brackets, so did Quebec. One difference that remained was Quebec's Dependent Children's Credit, which was in addition to the federal credit and reflected a demographic policy.

A number of other provinces wanted to have a Stock Savings Plan, as instituted by Quebec. Four provinces including Newfoundland, Nova Scotia, New Brunswick and Alberta built stock savings plans into their provincial income tax. Ontario is a rich province and does not need a stock savings plan, but, does worry about home ownership. Ontario set up the Home Ownership Savings Plan.

The tax collection agreements feature less simplicity and less overall uniformity. The taxation structure is more like that of Quebec, which never entered into any such agreement, and the differences are diminishing. In 1997, the Federal Minister of Finance, Paul Martin, made an announcement supporting enhanced flexibility for the provinces in the design of their income tax systems within the context of federal-provincial tax collection agreements. For example, instead of imposing income tax as a percent of BFT, the provinces may be able to impose such tax directly and use federal collection.[22]

Observations

Several important features emerge from the discussion on fiscal federalism. In considering these observations, one must bear in mind the importance of intergovernmental agreements regarding fiscal federalism as a tool for making constitutional adjustments. Although such agreements are not "legal" *per se*, in the sense of a private law agreement binding either level of government as the *Ref re Canada Assistance Plan* case demonstrates, they are nonetheless important political agreements that can and do affect the workings of federalism to a greater extent than do purely constitutional provisions.

Due to the nature of intergovernmental fiscal agreements and the nature of fiscal issues themselves, fiscal federalism evolved to meet the needs and interests of the respective governments involved, and to provide more effective programs for the Canadian citizen. Thus, although numerous constitutional modifications did not occur in written text, understandings of a political nature modified constitutional relations between the two orders of government in concrete ways. These arrangements provide predictability with respect to how those governments will act given the particular matter concerned. Accordingly, modifications of intergovernmental relations occurred resulting in constitutional adjustments and modifications on a *de facto* level.

Quebec has always been a party to distinctive agreements within the context of fiscal federalism, particularly with respect to opting out of federal shared cost programs for extra tax room, and by having its own PIT forms and tax structures allowing for innovative incentives. In this way, Quebec's distinctiveness is accommodated and the constitution has provided for flexibility in order to allow adjustments and accommodations to be made. Clearly, a large impetus for the profound decentralization that Canada experienced came from the province of Quebec and as a result of the activism of Quebec governments.

As we observed, Quebec was not the only party to those agreements whose needs and interests were accommodated. Overall decentralization accommodated the interests of provincial autonomy. As such, in view of the overall decentralization, the distinctive nature of the agreements Quebec entered into are being matched by the activism of the other provinces with respect to program funding and taxation issues. For example, the differences between block funding and contracting out are not all that significant from the perspective of autonomy. Essentially, all the provinces possess a substantial amount of autonomy regarding those shared cost programs.

Given this context, it is difficult to appreciate the criticism made by some Quebecers regarding federal spending in areas of exclusive provincial jurisdiction and the charge that the use of that power undermined the Confederation agreement of 1867. Notions of "watertight compartments" of clearly delineated federal and provincial powers or issues are no longer conceptually or practically possible if ever they where. All major federations provide for a "spending power" in areas that do not strictly fall within legislative jurisdiction. Additionally and significantly, in Canada, it has been used less often and with fewer conditions then in virtually any other federation. As Stephan Dion notes, federal initiatives considered perfectly normal in other federations, like the federal post-secondary student scholarship program, are criticised in Canada as a violation of the Constitution and spirit of the federation.[23]

That notwithstanding, the federal spending power was further limited voluntarily as announced in its 1996 Throne Speech, and also through the collaborative approach established in the Social Union Framework Agreement, which was agreed to on February 4, 1999 by the federal government and all the provinces and territories, except Quebec. With respect to any new Canada wide initiatives funded through intergovernmental transfers for health care, post-secondary education and social welfare, the federal government and a majority of the provinces must agree on priorities and objectives. The actual design of the programs/policies consistent with the priorities and objectives will be left to the province or territory to tailor to its needs. Finally, agreement is to be achieved on an appropriate accountability framework. Where a province or territory already provides a similar program, it can reinvest dedicated federal monies in the same or related area. In cases where the federal government makes direct transfers to individuals or organizations with respect to Canada wide objectives in health care, post-secondary education and social welfare, it will prior to implementation give at least three months notice and offer to consult. Governments participating in the consultations will be accorded the opportunity to identify potential duplication and to propose alternative approaches to achieve flexibility and effective implementation. Such provisions are truly without parallel in other federations.

Particularly with respect to the issue of autonomy, Quebec contracts out of the largest and most significant of those programs and receives extra tax room, therefore, autonomy is not an issue with respect to the tax abatement, tending to comprise approximately one-quarter of the cost of health care, social assistance and post-secondary education. The other three-quarters financing is received in the form of block federal cash transfer, with the rather minimal conditions attached, to which the other provinces are subject.

Also, given that the major building blocks of the social welfare state and regional economic development programs are in place, the existence of a significant federal debt, the increased support for separatism in Quebec, and demands from the West for more decentralization, it does not appear likely that the federal government could realistically substantially increase the number of shared cost programs although new ones will likely be created as needed (and agreed to). Furthermore, the lessons derived from the very history of shared cost programs, including the university episode, suggest that any future shared cost program, even without the Social Union Framework Agreement, will balance the various concerns involved such as those of autonomy and disentanglement of spending, as well as addressing the overlap problem. Finally, in some areas relating to industry or the economic fields, there are trends favouring and/or reflecting a declining government involvement and, perhaps, a growing private sector involvement.

If recent events provide any indication at all, for example federal-provincial occupational training and infrastructure agreements, these clearly demonstrate that shared cost programs are more decentralized than ever. The decentralization in these areas is characterized by the federal government abandoning the program design and delivery role, which ensures greater provincial control at that level, while the conditions attached tend to be minimal or easily satisfied, particularly with respect to infrastructure works, being essentially governed by performance criteria. Neither of these cases are characterizable as being exclusively provincial jurisdiction since each area contains significant federal aspects, for example, occupational training and infrastructure relating to telecommunications. Therefore, such devolution appears to reflect a disentanglement of overlap/duplication philosophy, as well as a policy effectiveness goal, and perhaps even political pressures for decentralization. Ironically, the provinces, including Quebec, are not objecting to federal spending in these areas, which are often asserted to be exclusively provincial jurisdiction, especially related to infrastructure.

What is left, therefore, by way of criticism, appears substantially to be symbolic in nature; that is, objecting to the fact that the federal government is even spending money in areas of provincial jurisdiction and in support of national programs Canadians desire. On the other hand, these arrangements balance the needs and concerns of governments and provide for more effective treatment of a policy area.

The federal government's national interests are accommodated by ensuring the existence of nation wide programs relating to social welfare, health care, hospital insurance and post-secondary education, as well as, more recently, by having its participation in these programs acknowledged to a greater extent. Furthermore, the federal government is finding ways to disentangle itself from its spending being dictated exclusively by provincial decisions.

From the perspective of effective programs, provincial autonomy will prevent the problems of imbalance created by the categorical shared cost programs, while increased autonomy means greater scope for provincial experimentation, and federal-provincial duplication is reduced. On the other hand, the pan-Canadian dimensions contributed to higher levels of equity and efficiency in the design of the welfare state than a more decentralized approach would likely have produced, and minimized distortions in the mobility of capital and labour.[24]

Finally, and perhaps the greatest impact and significance for the workings of the Canadian federal system has been the substantial decentralization of taxation and revenues. As a result, effective power shifted from the federal to the provincial level of government. The extent of that shift may be illustrated by considering the following figures:

... In 1946, the federal government accounted for 71.8% of total governmental expenditures (including intergovernmental transfers), the provinces and the municipalities together accounting for 28.2% (15.5% and 12.7% respectively). In 1956, comparable figures were 56.1% federal and 43.9% provincial and municipal (23.3% and 20.6% respectively). In 1975, the figures were 43.7% federal, 56.2% provincial and municipal (38.5% and 17.7% respectively). In those 30 years, the percentage gap between federal and provincial proportions of expenditures narrowed from over 59% to almost 5%, and the provincial and municipal governments accounted for well over half the total government expenditures in Canada.[25]

This shift in spending pattern continued. Often times, little or no public attention is drawn to the extent to which Canada became decentralized, and, often times, such decentralization occurred at the behest of Quebec.

Other Constitutional Change: Constitutional Amendment

Some other examples of constitutional change in the workings of the federal system are found in the area of Income Security. In 1940, in response to the JCPC decision of the *Employment and Social Insurance Reference*, the constitutional amendment s. 91(2)(A) was passed transferring unemployment insurance to the federal government.

In 1951 and 1964, s. 94(A) of the *Constitution Act* came into being. Old age pensions and supplementary benefits, including survivor and disability pensions, are now concurrently under federal and provincial jurisdiction with paramountcy belonging to the provinces. This arrangement gave rise to further distinctiveness with respect to Quebec. The Canada Pension Plan applies to nine provinces while Quebec created its own. The Caisse de dépôt is the body that administers the Quebec Pension Plan. It became instrumental in the formulation and consolidation of the "new business class" in Quebec, and relieved that provincial government of some of the province's dependence on English-Canadian and American capital markets. The Caisse, employing pensions and benefits, is distinctive from the Canadian Pension Plan, which invests in safer instruments such as bonds. The Caisse's investments include holding common shares as an instrument of economic policy. Although the Alberta Heritage Savings Trust Fund shares some similarities with the Caisse, the Caisse controls significantly greater funds.

Continuing 'Constitutional' Change

It is clear then that substantial and far reaching changes have occurred to the Canadian constitution and federalism despite the fact that only modest changes were made to its written constitutional text. Moreover, Canadian federalism adapted and evolved to meet the concerns of the participants in the federal system, including Quebec. Therefore, to say that Quebec's concerns have not been recognized in the context of the constitution and that Quebecers and other Canadians have interests that cannot be reconciled is to ignore the realities and history concerning Canadian federalism.

The 1990's bears witness to a continuation of the evolution of federalism by non-constitutional means. Harvey Lazar argues that the failure of the Charlottetown Accord and the election of the federal Liberals in 1993 marked a turning point in intergovernmental relations in Canada by reinventing the federation through non-constitutional means.[26] What is different is not so much the process of constitutional change on a *de facto* level, which always occurs, rather, the strong and determined focus of the federal Liberals to avoid constitutional talks in favour of an overt approach of renewing the federation through non-constitutional means, thereby, conclusively demonstrating that such an approach exists and is effective. Such 'Constitutional' and quasi-Constitutional reform on a *de facto* level is characterized by higher levels of intergovernmental collaboration, cooperation, a clarification of roles and responsibilities, and decentralization. The instances of non-Constitutional renewal in the 1990's is quite vast and cannot be dealt with comprehensively in this book. Rather, a few examples will be provided for the purposes of illustration.

'Constitutional' Reform

In terms of direct 'Constitutional' change without Constitutional amendment, several initiatives figured prominently in the federal approach. In the final days leading up to the 1995 Sovereignty Referendum in Quebec, the federal government gave its undertaking that it would, within the bounds of its constitutional authority, recognize Quebec's distinctiveness and assure Quebec a *de facto* veto power over future amendments. Pursuant to this promise, in December of 1995, the House of Commons and Senate tabled and adopted a resolution recognizing Quebec as a distinct society within Canada that includes a French-speaking majority, a unique culture and a civil law tradition. The Premiers, in the context of the Calgary Declaration, themselves recognized that all provinces are equal, but Quebec is 'unique'. The second federal initiative occurred in February of 1996 when Ottawa passed a Bill guaranteeing that Canada would not make any constitutional changes affecting Quebec or any other of the major regions of the country without their consent. There was an explicit and voluntary limitation of federal power. In its 1996 Throne Speech, the federal government promised not to use its spending power to create new shared-cost programs in areas of exclusive provincial jurisdiction unless the consent of a majority of the provinces was obtained, accompanied by a right to opt out with compensation if equivalent or comparable initiatives are undertaken. The substance of these initiatives are, of course, familiar and reflect some of the major provisions contained in the Meech Lake Accord. It is interesting to note that any of a number of these initiatives may furthermore attain a status of constitutional convention. Fourth, with respect to Quebec, but also offered to the other provinces, the federal government initiated a process leading to constitutional amendment enabling the Government of Quebec to modernize its educational system and establish linguistic school boards, which was an issue in Quebec for thirty years. Under the *Constitution Act, 1982*, this Amendment only required bilateral agreement.

As discussed, the Social Union Framework Agreement, which limits the use of the federal spending power, was signed by the federal government and all provinces and territories, except Quebec. The Agreement creates a more collaborative model for intergovernmental relations. It sets out various Canadian principles and fundamental values, such as equality, respect for diversity, fairness, individual dignity, mutual aid and our responsibilities for one another. It addresses topics such as mobility within Canada, public accountability and transparency, working in partnership for Canadians, limitation on the federal spending power, dispute avoidance and resolution, and a commitment to review the Social Union Framework Agreement on or within three years and to make appropriate adjustments. Although Quebec did not sign the Agreement, the federal government made the commitment to see Quebecers benefit from it as much as possible.

Quasi-Constitutional Reform

It is argued that reform on the 'quasi-Constitutional' level involves an attempt to clarify roles and responsibilities of the two levels of government by finding new models of federal-provincial co-operation, to bring services and decision-making closer to citizens, and to make federalism more efficient and better reflect the specific needs of different regions.[27] The emphasis is on good government, job creation, the fiscal situation, and away from transferring authority to produce formal asymmetry.

Perhaps, the most important initiative in this respect is in relation to the social union and most notably the CHST replacing EPF. Fewer conditions were accompanied by an initial reduction in transfers, until the February 1999 budget which provided an additional $11.5 billion investment in health care.

The *Canada Health Act* enjoys widespread support among Canadians, therefore, the provinces endorsed its five principles. However, the provinces wanted to develop a new consensus with respect to the evolving health system and to clarify roles and responsibilities. In September of 1997 a press release was made in which the federal and provincial Health Ministers agreed to consider and develop a protocol for governments to discuss a joint process of interpretation regarding the *Canada Health Act*, reflecting a co-determination model. Otherwise, under the CHST, the federal government alone possesses the legal authority to interpret the five principles of the CHA.[28] In February of 1999, the Agreement on Health was established by the federal government and all provinces and territories, including Quebec.

In terms of labour markets, the new *Employment Insurance Act* involves a major restructuring, including matters of entitlement, active labour market programs to help the unemployed reintegrate, and even the possibility of delegating programs to the provinces. Bilateral labour market agreements signed between the federal government and eight provinces assure greater provincial responsibility for the design and delivery of programs under the *Employment Insurance Act*, together with a transfer of resources. The agreements involving Alberta, Manitoba, New Brunswick and Quebec provide agreement in principle to devolve that authority from the federal government; whereas, those involving British Columbia, Newfoundland, Nova Scotia and Prince Edward Island are characterized by co-management, with continued federal delivery.[29] Under the devolution model, the federal government bound itself to transfer a certain sum annually for at least three years, and also delegated authority to deliver some services of the National Employment Service, like the local aspects of employment counselling. The goal is to eventually provide a single window delivery for federal and provincial programs. Minimum residency periods are prohibited, the federal role must be given recognition, and there is a federal-provincial agreement on criteria to evaluate results. Since program performance is defined by criteria without reference to the provincial labour market, but in terms of re-employment generally, it is argued that there is a provincial incentive to train even if the trainee moves out of the province, which would not otherwise be the case.[30] The federal government has responsibility over a national system of labour market information and exchange.

The child benefit system is the best example of the collaborative approach to social union. This area is traditionally characterized by ineffective and inefficient overlap and weak coordination. One particular problem was that the federal government typically exerted political pressure on the province to raise the welfare rate for families with children whenever the federal government raised tax benefits for children. The result was an improvement in the income of welfare families, but no improvement in the incentives to work and the provinces did not like such pressures anyway.[31]

The response to this situation was the National Child Benefit System. The federal government's Canada Child Tax Benefit enlarged and simplified the child tax benefit to strengthen the national foundation of income support to all low-income families with children. The 1997 Federal Budget increased federal spending to $1.7 billion in total funding by the year 2000. The provinces are free to reduce their social assistance payment on behalf of children by the amount of federal increase and to reinvest it in complementary programs targeted at improving work incentives, benefits, and services to low income families with children. Additionally, Quebec receives a $150 million margin of flexibility inviting it to reinvest in programs for low-income families and/or children. Several Ministers' meetings were held and work is proceeding on how to reinvest those funds, including on the development of a national reinvestment framework to "flexibly guide" reinvestment. All of which brings welcome prospects of significantly improved policy outcomes. In this circumstance, intergovernmental collaboration holds promise to be more successful than unilaterally acting federal and provincial governments.

The challenge with respect to the service for the disabled is to integrate programs. In August of 1996, the Provincial premiers recognized as a priority to overcome the lack of coherence in this area, and work is being undertaken by federal and provincial Ministers of Social Services. The aim includes income support, and services to the disabled to enable them to participate more fully in labour markets. However, the two major federal and provincial programs, the CPP and workers compensation, are financed by contributions and for different purposes, posing problems for integration. Therefore, the approach will likely focus on certain problem areas.

The federal government mounted significant moral pressure on the provinces to better secure the economic union in Canada. In 1980, the federal government proposed an amendment to strengthen s. 121 of the *Constitution Act, 1867*. The idea was rejected by the provinces, being concerned over its affect on their own authority. Other initiatives included the Macdonald Commission, the Charlottetown Accord, and various other federal-provincial committees and conferences. In March of 1992, the First Ministers agreed to accelerate the process to reduce internal trade barriers, to strengthen domestic linkages and to minimize competition for investment. When Constitutional reform failed in December 1992, a re-invigorated non-constitutional process emerged, with the federal government starting the process. The Agreement on Internal Trade was in effect by July of 1995. Although the agreement is criticized and with good reason, it does provide at the very least a general normative framework to which the federal and provincial governments agreed and it serves to structure their interaction. Furthermore, there are some successes in this area, for example, in the area of government procurement and further sub-agreements were or are in the process of being made. But, significantly, the agreement accomplished what could not be done by other means, including through constitutional reform. The federal government pledged to work with the provinces and private sector to achieve a more open agreement, and both levels of government met to expand the scope of the Agreement, especially regarding the public sector. The Framework on Social Union itself contains a section devoted to mobility within Canada.

The Canada Food Inspection Agency is an attempt to deal with an area that executive federalism is yet to be successful in generating effective, co-operative action. The federal government reorganized and refocused its own involvement through the direct federal role in a new agency, while at the same time undertaking a variety of federal-provincial initiatives, in close consultation with industry and consumer groups.[32] One of its successes is the National Dairy Code.

Any of a number of a multitude of other initiatives may be cited reflecting a clarification of roles and responsibilities, efficiency goals and/or devolution of powers. For example, federal-provincial agreements were reached transferring social housing to the provinces, clarifications of responsibility were made regarding the environment, and a number deal with greater responsibilities over natural resource management being devolved to the provinces, as with respect to freshwater fisheries, mining and forest development. The federal government also took steps to withdraw from the areas of recreation and tourism.

Separatists and sovereignists downplay this vast and extensive history of Canadian federalism. Bald statements are made such as agreeing that Canada is one of the most decentralized federations in the world, but, because of Quebec's unique place in Canada, this fact is not significant and Quebec should be independent, or, at least, sovereign. On the surface and ignoring the realities of Canadian federalism, such statements may, to some, appear to be sensible. However, given the history and evolution of Canadian federalism, and the accommodations that have been made with respect to Quebec and the other provinces, which addressed the concerns of those within the Canadian federalist system including its citizens, such statements are exposed for the illusions that they truly bear.

Chapter 10
The Process of Constitutional
Change in Written Text

Quebec governments contributed significantly to the creation and proliferation of a process that resulted in the inability of or extreme difficulty in attaining constitutional change in written text. Symbolic demands made by Quebec governments for special status and massive decentralization were not met, resulting in those governments withholding their consent for Constitutional amendment, as was seen in Chapter 4, particularly from the Victoria Charter to the *Constitution Act, 1982*. The decentralization demanded in the Meech Lake Accord was mostly fairly moderate, while special status was still sought. It is incorrect or somewhat self-serving for separatists and sovereignists to attack federalism on the grounds that Constitutional change in written text cannot occur, or, more importantly, that the lack of such explicit change in constitutional text imperils the survival of the French language or hinders the flourishing of Quebec francophone society.

To fully understand the process which developed, some background will be provided. Constitutions have been adeptly defined in the following terms:

A constitution is a set of fundamental laws, customs and conventions which provide a framework within which government is exercised in a state. A constitution contains essentially (1) the basic principles, objectives and rules which command the political life of a society; (2) the definition of the principal organs of government in all four branches - the legislature, the executive, the judicial and the administrative—their composition, functions, powers and limitations; (3) the distribution and co-ordination of powers between the two orders of government ...; (4) the definition of relationships between the governors and the governed, particularly the rights of the latter.[1]

To this definition one may add the requirement that a constitution must provide a framework allowing succeeding generations to adapt the role of government in light of contemporary circumstances. By these measures,

Canadian federalism has worked very well in meeting the needs and concerns of the participants in the system, and of its citizens.

However, the purpose of constitutions and constitutionalism in Canada became something quite different. Instead of focusing on how well, in reality, the constitution is serving the needs of its participants and citizens, constitutions are seen as a battleground for political actors and social groups searching for special status, which results in status anxieties for other actors or groups. In essence, much of its perceived value is derived from its symbolism, and not necessarily its operation. These groups view the Constitution as more than a legal text, but, a combination of symbols, values and emotions that "make" a country, leading some Quebecers to feel that: "[i]n Canada, it does not seem that the Quebec society is part of that combination."[2] It must be recognized that conceptions of a country such as pan-Canadian nationalism, provincialism, Quebec nationalism and those held by groups and individuals are on the surface incompatible, therefore, giving rise to battles to explicitly entrench one government's or group's position.

The origins of constitutional status seeking can largely be traced to the late 1960's with Premier Daniel Johnson's status claim *Égalité ou Indépendence* asserting the urgency of early and radical constitutional reform regarding Quebec. That status claim, as well as other status seeking constitutional demands by successive Quebec governments, in turn, created status anxieties for the federal government relating to the loss of nationhood bonds, and led to the agony of Constitutional reform. Constitutional politics that relates to a polity's most fundamental or essential level is an infinitely different game than the other aspects of constitutional politics relating to the consideration of the merits of specific constitutional proposals to address concrete and discrete issues. Rather, it involves a battle over the very nature of the political community on which the constitution is based:

> [m]ega constitutional politics, whether directed towards comprehensive constitutional change or not is concerned with reaching agreement on the identity and fundamental principle of the body politic.[3]

The *Constitution Act, 1982*, itself, conferred status and created status anxieties. A non-exhaustive list of examples follows. With the Charter, social groups became new actors in the constitutional process. Their desires and values were factored into the Charter and these groups continue to be vocal in the Constitutional arena. Included, within those groups of social pluralists are rights activists, multicultural groups, aboriginals, and gender equality groups. Furthermore, the Charter was also seen by the federal government as a nation building instrument to bind Canadians together through the sharing of common values.

The province's status seeking mission was answered through an amending formula that required provincial legislation, rather than a national referendum. Section 33 of the Charter was in the provincial interest, including that of Quebec. Finally, s. 40 is provincialist and 'Quebec centred' given that if an amendment is made under the general amending formula in s. 38(1) transferring provincial legislative powers relating to education or culture from provincial legislatures to Parliament, Canada must provide reasonable compensation to any province that opts out of the amendment. At the same time, status anxieties arose in Quebec, particularly due to the fact that it did not give its legislative consent to the *Constitution Act, 1982*.

Constitution-making now involves competitions to restructure the relationships between governments, between government and the individual, and to transform citizens' identities and conceptions of community. Because of its fundamental nature and its connection with a citizen's sense of identity, constitutionalism in Canada has become exceptionally emotionally charged and intense. Constitutions are political resources to be used as symbolic weapons in political battles. They are also instructions to judges in legal battles. As a result, vague status phrases like "distinct society" hold tremendous potential for usage, especially in the political arena.[4]

Because the four elements of Canadian federalism, namely Canadian nationhood, provincialism, Quebec distinctiveness and social pluralism, are to some extent incompatible as ideal types, there must be balance in which all of these legitimate visions can thrive. To constitutionalize one vision is to symbolically reject other visions, whether or not such visions nevertheless exist and are protected in reality. If one actor's or group's vision is not mirrored in constitutional text, in part due to the symbolism constitutions can provide and in part due to the relative permanence of such documents, that group will see itself as being on the outside of the constitution and will reject that text.

The Meech Lake Accord is highly instructive about the degeneration of constitutionalism into a process of status seeking and the resulting and combatting of status anxieties, which, in the end, was both its impetus and its death knell. Meech began as an attempt to bring Quebec back into the constitutional fold, which, itself, was status based. The topics of Senate reform and annual First Ministers Conferences were added to obtain provincial compliance.

Provincialism was a victor in the process, as reflected in the text of the Accord. The provinces received status from the ability to compile lists of Senators and Supreme Court judges, from which the federal government would make appointments. Provinces would be able to opt out of federal spending programs in areas of exclusive provincial jurisdiction and receive compensation if the provinces instituted similar programs consistent with national objectives, as opposed to the higher threshold of national standards that nationhood advocates preferred. Section 40 of the *Constitution Act* was expanded to include compensation in all areas of constitutional amendment derogating from provincial jurisdiction.

Nationhood advocates could still maintain that no province possessed any special veto powers, but gained little more.

'Quebec distinctiveness' was another winner as Quebec would be labelled a distinct society. The linguistic duality provisions reflected a definite segmentalist tilt, arising from the differing roles of the federal and Quebec governments. The role of Parliament was to "preserve" the fundamental characteristics of Canada referred to in s. 2(1)(a) of the Accord:

> **s. 2(1)(a)** the recognition that the existence of French-speaking Canadians, centred in Quebec but also present elsewhere in Canada, and English-speaking Canadians, concentrated outside Quebec but also present in Quebec, constitutes a fundamental characteristic of Canada.

The role of the Quebec government is to "preserve and promote" the distinct identity of Quebec referred to in s. 2(1)(b) of the Accord:

> **s. 2(1)(b)** the recognition that Quebec constitutes within Canada a distinct society.

Questions arises regarding the meaning of "distinct society" and whether it is different from the linguistic fundamental characteristic of Canada outlined in s. 2(1)(a) with particular respect to Quebec. If they are the same, then the Quebec government's role with respect to the French language is to "preserve and promote"; whereas, the federal role is to "preserve". If they are different, what is the effect of "distinct society" recognition?

Section 2(4) of the Accord states that nothing in the section derogates from the rights of legislatures and governments. The second part of that subsection states: "including any powers, rights or privileges relating to language." As s. 2 is an interpretation section rather than one conferring power, the language rights contained in s. 133 of the *Constitution Act, 1867*, and ss. 23 and 16–20 of the *Constitution Act, 1982*, would not be overtaken as these matters are outside of the division of jurisdiction. Still, there is much uncertainty regarding the effect of "distinct society".

Quebec received explicit asymmetry in the "distinct society" clause, the "preserve and promote" clause of the linguistic duality provisions, and subsections 101(B),(C) in which three judges of the Supreme Court must be from Quebec and be nominated by the government of Quebec. There was potential for asymmetry for Quebec and the other provinces in ss. 95, 106 and 40 of the Accord. Section 95 would constitutionalize bilateral agreements between the federal and provincial governments with respect to immigration, or, regarding the temporary admission of aliens. Section 106 would allow any province to opt out of new shared cost programs in areas of exclusive provincial jurisdiction with compensation if the province carries out its own program that is compatible with national objectives. Finally, s. 40 would provide reasonable compensation to any province opting out of a constitutional amendment transferring legislative powers from the province to Parliament.

Not surprisingly, given the degeneration of constitutionalism in Canada into a process of symbolism, status seeking and the combatting of status anxieties, the Accord was criticized in all its provisions and from all perpectives. "Distinct Society" is political currency for Quebec and status anxiety elsewhere. It runs counter to the nationhood view of Canada. It worries some provinces about implications of first and second class provinces and Canadians. It worries social pluralists regarding its effect on the Charter.

In terms of the Accord, generally, social pluralists disagree with the approach of the Accord that territorial peculiarisms are the definitive cleavages in Canadian society. The Charter created new cleavages and there was concern regarding the Accord's effects on Charter rights and freedoms.

Aboriginal groups were anxious as their claims were not yet settled. Multicultural groups did not like the focus of the Meech Lake Accord only on English and French speaking Canadians.

Separatist and Sovereignist minded Quebecers were status anxious due to the fact that the Accord legitimized Quebec in the federal structure. Section 106 of the Accord would recognize federal spending in areas of provincial jurisdiction and that gave rise to status anxieties within those who disagreed with any such spending, and who would advocate further massive decentralization of taxation, leaving the federal government with little in that respect. Finally, Quebec would still not have supremacy over language legislation as a result of the Charter.

Nationhood advocates argued that "distinct society" runs counter to a single bilingual and multicultural Canada. "Preserving and promoting" linguistic rights deals with government roles and not language rights *per se*. Federal spending will be weakened and national standards will not be protected. Opting out of federal spending programs would be encouraged. The provisions taken together would set the foundations for the balkanization of Canada. A provincially appointed Senate could hamper federal government functioning. There was no deadlock breaking mechanism in the Accord in the event that the federal government did not chose to appoint a Supreme Court judge nominated by the provinces.

The shopping list of criticisms can go on and on. It is not surprising that the Accord, the federal Senate's Resolutions, and the Charlottetown Accord all failed in this process of symbolism, status seeking, status anxieties, and the fatigue generated by constitutional reform talks. The very approach to constitutions and constitutionalism that Quebec politicians began and encouraged eventually killed the Meech Lake Accord, which they themselves wanted. Still, in the context of symbolism and status seeking, if demands made were agreed to, the Quebec government would win in tremendously augmenting its power. If such demands failed, as they almost certainly had to, at least in terms of demanding massive decentralization, the Quebec government would still win in the sense that it could state to Quebecers that Quebec is being rejected, whether or not that was, in fact, true.

If one paid attention only to this constitutional wrangling, it would seem abundantly clear, albeit illusory, that the Canadian constitution is not working. Yet, the reality shows quite the opposite. Canadian federalism has, as we have seen over and over again, evolved and adapted to meet the needs of the participants in the federal system, including Quebec. All of this change and evolution occurred despite the fact that changes and balancing *prima facie* incompatible conceptions and ideals in constitutional text are not likely, or perhaps even possible, in a context where constitution makers and players seek to confer status and combat status anxieties. Whereas conceptions such as pan-Canadian nationalism, provincialism, Quebec nationalism and views held by groups and individuals are on the surface irreconcilable, needs and interests can be accommodated and compromises can occur to achieve those accommodations, as fiscal federalism demonstrates. Provisions conferring status are not so amenable. If one vision is entrenched, then others are rejected. Constitutionalism in Canada has become a game of "ins" and "outs".[5]

The test of a valid and useful constitution is not whether one's vision is explicitly embodied in Constitutional text, but, rather, whether the Constitution functions effectively to allow for the fundamental values of its society to exist, and to allow for the adaptation of the role of government in light of contemporary circumstances. From Quebec's perspective, Canadian federalism is functioning and evolving successfully to meet the needs and concerns of its society, and of its successive governments.

Chapter 11
Federalism as Competition

This part of the study once again becomes broader in perspective in order to provide an overview of the Canadian federalism landscape, as well as to better explain the changes in its workings that were discussed earlier, especially the decentralizing ones. Again, we return to several familiar themes. The overall theme is that competition is a dynamic inherent in the Canadian federal system.

In the first part, an abstract overview is provided of Canadian federalism. Secondly, provincial assertiveness, including the forces that gave rise to it and its implication of intergovernmental competition, will be discussed. Contemporary factors, such as the increased role of government in society, aggravated that federal-provincial competition and conflict by exacerbating the jurisdictional overlap and interdependency problem. Two other implications of overlap and interdependence relate to the financial cost associated with government duplication and the federalism impact on policy, including disharmonized policies. Yet, none of the outlined grounds serve as a justification for massive decentralization in the Canadian context, let alone separatism or sovereignty. Rather, the issues require a willingness on the part of both levels of government to find solutions, which may mean giving up as well as acquiring powers. It is not just the form and processes of federalism that give rise to competitions, there exist underlying regional or provincial differences that are articulated and which governments may represent. The organizational aspects of government contributing to federal-provincial competition will be discussed. Then mixed into the federalism cauldron will be the variable of government leaders and party politics in Quebec, which contributed to an overemphasis publically and in federal-provincial relations on seeking explicit change to the Constitution. Finally, the balance of the Chapter will show that federal-provincial competitions are not just battles over jurisdiction, they involve an even more profound process of competition over citizen loyalty.

Overview of Federalism

Federalism is a form of government that allows symbiotic national and territorial communities to define and even redefine their identities, and provides for the defining and redefining of the relations with one another. Although federalism does not necessarily protect all values, it does give particular salience to territorially based ones, and it is through federalism that the diversity of territorial and national concerns are respected.

Federalism is as much about governments as the communities they represent. Institutionally created governments, as in Canada, have a fair amount of autonomy of action from those communities and, as such, take on a life of their own. Government, then, as an institution, is a variable in the federalist system contributing to a dynamic of competition among federal and provincial governments in order to expand jurisdiction and to avoid blame.

As outlined in Chapter 1, the dynamic for competition is enhanced by the territorial division of power ordained by the *Constitution Act, 1867*; the theoretical and practical overlap of those powers giving rise to an interdependence between the two orders of government, particularly in a context where the increased level of state activity in Canada involves matters not exclusively assigned under the Constitution; the Cabinet-Parliamentary system of government, which tends to require federal-provincial adjustment to be made through interstate federalism; the political economy of Canada; and, the existence of compartmentalized dual citizenship giving rise to the ability of each level of government to draw upon the same citizen support for different purposes. Canadian federalism features a symbiotic relationship characterized by the relations between the two orders of government resulting in policy adjustment reflecting both national and territorial concerns and, also, features a competition over citizen loyalties and conceptions of community.

The Rise of Provincial Assertiveness

These same forces just discussed generated the rise of provincial assertiveness and its long term implication was competition between the two orders of government for jurisdiction, the avoidance of blame, and over citizen loyalties and conceptions of community. Quebec was not even the first province to begin such competition. As Armstrong writes, "Ontario premiers from Mowat onward, attempted to extend the sway of 'Empire Ontario' and in doing so would increase their own power and authority."[1] All governments compete for more power. In this respect, Quebec is no exception to the rule, and is quite similar to other governments.

In broad terms, the sources of this competition can be largely traced to the constitution, as well as the underlying territorial societal interests and the political economy of Canada. The former was important to influence the norms of constitutionalism to ensure Canada would operate as a truly federal country, which, in turn, provided the provinces with the status and the ability to effectively engage in province-building. The latter factors are also significant in explaining the decentralization of Canada as a result of the process of contending forces identifying their interests with different levels of government.[2] The political economy of Canada was, and continues to be, a primary determinant in this respect, with perhaps the exception of Quebec, whose main focus is its underlying societal composition. Three sectors began to emerge as highly important to the Canadian economy, each with divergent interests and concentrated in different provinces and regions. The patterns of economic development in these sectors of secondary manufacturing, export oriented agriculture and the export oriented resource industries resulted in a predominate reliance on the provincial, as opposed to the federal, level of government in representing their interests and to assist in economic activity. Secondary manufacturing is heavily concentrated in Ontario. Because of Ontario's wealth and prosperity, it possessed the financial means to pursue economic policies that contributed to further economic development. Industrialists looked to the Ontario government to pursue their interests. Furthermore, with greater American control, the industrialists became indifferent to the federal tariff. Export oriented agriculture is predominate in the West and its interests were traditionally in opposition to the manufacturing sector, therefore, this business conflict took on regional dimensions in which Saskatchewan and Albertan governments represented those regional interests, which, furthermore, became federal-provincial conflicts. Export-oriented resources was the area of greatest expansion after World War II and it was this sector that was most intimately associated with provincial jurisdiction.

Thus, the political economy of Canada provided the major impetus for provincial involvement, while geographic location of industry, ownership patterns and the division of jurisdiction provided for the relevancy of such involvement. In the end, province-building as well as nation-building are extremely important in Canada.

In terms of constitutionalism in Canada, by 1890, the provinces became strong enough to influence its norms. The principle of provincial autonomy became a fundamental constitutional principle in Canada. Sources of this provincialist doctrine were found in the *Constitution Act, 1867*, itself, especially the division of jurisdiction. Language contained in constitutional text can have political uses more powerful than legal ones and jurisdictional disputes entail visions of sovereignty and status.

As Robert Vipond argues, during the first thirty years after Confederation, the 'provincial rights' movement developed a distinctive approach to the Constitution which rested on two principle claims.[3] First, there was an expansive understanding of provincial autonomy. Second, the Constitution was conceived as a set of formal rules and principles superior to and, indeed, largely independent of broader considerations of policy. The result was to transform questions of federalism into questions of constitutional principle. Provinces could argue that in defending provincial power or opposing the extravagant use of federal vetos, their object was to purify the Constitution, not to undermine it.[4] However, once the founding myth about provincial autonomy was established, it became almost impossible to contain.[5]

One significant impact of the provincial rights movement was, as we observed, Canada's progression from a quasi-federalist state containing unitary provisions to a truly federal state involving a sharing of jurisdiction that was more appropriate in representing territorially based communities. Secondly, the Compact Theory of Confederation was used as a tool to demand that no change could be made to the *Constitution Act* without the consent of the provinces. The degree of provincial consent was one of the major obstacles to patriating the Constitution since 1927. The Compact Theory was even used by Quebec to justify its concluding international arrangements with other countries on matters respecting provincial jurisdiction. Provincial sovereignty and province-building remain central concepts to Canadian politics and discourse even today, unlike the situation in the United States with respect to the relationship between the federal and state governments.[6]

The 'financial compact' and the fight to control resources were critical to both the provincial movement to influence constitutionalism and the ability of provinces to build their own economies and societies. Financial resources, especially derived from taxation, which, in turn, is a function of the strength of the provincial economy, provide the provinces with financial means and facilitate the development of the institutional capacity to exercise its jurisdiction effectively and to compete with the federal government. Provinces emphasized the close relation between financial resources and provincial autonomy.

During the years after Confederation, Ontario competed frequently with the federal government over resource development. Ontario premiers resisted demands for disallowance and insisted on the right of the province to manage the development of hydroelectricity. Because of its size and wealth, successive Ontario governments were able to compete vigorously with the federal government. While Ontario may have been at the forefront of the provincial rights movement, other provinces were playing a role and regional interests were being asserted. One example is the broad based Maritime Rights movement of the 1920's, protesting various sources of political discontent like the regional effects of national transportation policy, which forced freight rate concessions from Prime Minister Mackenzie King. The Western protests in the 1930's against tariff and exchange rate policy was another example.

With the crisis of the great depression in the 1930's, the provinces began to argue that their revenue sources should be appropriate to their responsibility. In the years following the Second World War, provincial expenditures increased dramatically and fiscal autonomy was demanded and obtained by the provinces through a reallocation of tax room and not merely higher grants or subsidies.

Provinces began to assert themselves and became far more active in society and the economy than previously, as the federal government was already doing. Federal-provincial competitions increased substantially. During the 1960's, Quebec's Lesage government took the lead in battles over taxation, shared cost programs and federal incursions into provincial jurisdiction; but, all provinces were increasingly competitive in this respect. All provinces were undertaking initiatives to develop their respective provincial societies. With the discovery of oil and natural gas in the West, resistance to central policy proliferated, especially from Alberta over energy policy and development.

Provincial assertiveness and the development of provincial societies are perhaps best illuminated by the explosion of provincial government activity. Combined provincial and municipal expenditures rose dramatically from $5.397 billion in 1960 to $23.404 billion in 1970, to $89.987 billion in 1980.[7] Federal expenditures were in excess of the provincial and municipal one, but that would no longer to be the case. In 1960, federal expenditures totalled $6.584 billion, rising to $15.728 billion in 1970, and $67.880 billion in 1980.[8]

Provincial expansionism in the economy and society is further reflected by the virtual explosion of provincial regulatory agencies and crown corporations. The question must surely have arisen whether the movement for provincial autonomy was unstoppable. The provinces armed with the federal principle, were not required to explain or justify why provincial autonomy should prevail, but only that it was threatened. [9] As such, the provinces were often successful in competing with the federal government for more power and the players seemed to acquiesce, until Prime Minister Trudeau, who challenged that game. The result of the process, as Vipond argues, was a deficiency of debate in terms of political philosophy by artificially separating the constitutional from the political, rather than discussing the two together.[10] As such, issues would be discussed in terms of constitution and autonomy, to the detriment of the functional considerations of what policy is most appropriate in the circumstances.

In response to the decentralizing, centrifugal forces threatening to tear Canada apart, Prime Minister Trudeau attempted to create or bring to the forefront values and a national identity that bind Canadians together as a people. Those principles for him were the principles of freedom and equality of opportunity.[11] These principles informed the national government's attempts to maintain national standards in important policy areas such as social welfare, post-secondary education, health care and hospital insurance. The national government sought to avoid the balkanization of those programs, as well as the taxation system, particularly in not allowing one province to wield special powers that the others did not enjoy. For example, the Quebec government's opting out of various shared cost programs, although asymmetrical and meeting concerns emanating from that province, was not really all that distinctive since the other provinces receive block funding.

It was primarily the provisions contained in the Charter that were aimed at making explicit those unifying nationhood ideas and to establish the primacy of the Canadian individual over the state. First, the Charter outlines rights and freedoms enjoyed by all Canadians equally. Bilingualism and multiculturalism were elucidated as fundamental characteristics of Canada through explicit entrenchment in the Constitution. Second, the Charter provides for equality of opportunity through government equalization payments; linguistic rights; rights of multicultural, aboriginal and gender based groups; and, through mobility and equality rights. There is a general statement of commitment in s. 36(1) on the part of the federal and provincial governments to promote equal opportunities regarding the well being of Canadians, regional economic development, and to provide a basic level of essential public services to all Canadians. There was some minimal attempt to combat the "balkanization" of the economy through mobility rights, which allows every Canadian to take up residence and to pursue the gaining of a livelihood in any province.[12] The Canadian personality is, thus, expressed in terms of diversity based on shared values and solidified by equality of opportunity.

Contemporary Aggravating Factors: Increased Government in Society

A factor aggravating federal-provincial conflict was the explosion of government involvement in Canadian society after the Second World War. The result is a proliferation of issues overlapping federal and provincial jurisdictions due to the increase in the number of fields of state activity that fall outside the categories contained in the formal Constitution, or that cut across jurisdictional lines. This overlap, combined with the increased involvement of both levels of government in the majority of new fields, and in the more traditional ones as well, means that most fields of jurisdiction are now shared and very few are exclusive to a single level of government.[13]

It is simply incorrect to say that it is only the federal government that may act in areas of exclusive provincial jurisdiction through its spending power. The Aspect Doctrine is proof enough of that statement. The provincial governments involved themselves in many areas of federal jurisdiction, be it through unilateral action or by agreement. Some examples include provincial involvement in international trade and commerce, Newfoundland being active in federal jurisdiction over the fisheries, several provinces having civil aviation officials, and Alberta operating savings banks under the guise of "Treasury Branches".[14] State, society and the economy are now so interwoven that the "local/national" distinction underlying the division of jurisdiction is not really all that helpful since policy fields contain both aspects.[15] As such, the Constitution provides broad boundaries to the abilities of each level of government to act in unrestrained ways.

Another example reflecting a growing area of government attention is the environment. One study examined the overlapping jurisdictions regarding the subject area of the environment.[16] The following summarizes that overlap demonstrating that each level of government possesses ample powers to involve itself in important policy fields. Furthermore, it illustrates the extent to which policy fields may overlap jurisdiction.

In terms of federal power, the emergency branch of the peace, order and good government power could be invoked to deal with massive spills and issues that could pose an immediate and serious safety or health risk, such as a Mississauga train derailment type of situation. The national concern branch could be used to regulate pollution of interprovincial waters,[17] or to prevent dumping of substances in marine waters.[18] The power over public debt and property could be used in support of measures dealing with Canadian waters outside provincial boundaries, and in respect of federal lands. The federal taxation power may provide for incentives and disincentives. Other powers may include the criminal law power, native lands, fisheries, navigation and shipping, aviation, interprovincial transportation, and jurisdiction over nuclear power.

Provincial power extends over property and civil rights, which encompasses most aspects of business regulation and environmental standards, including emissions. The jurisdiction over municipal institutions involves water treatment, land use and waste management. Direct taxation may provide for incentives and disincentives. Other powers include jurisdiction over local works and provincial lands.

Therefore, there are ample powers possessed by the federal and provincial governments to involve themselves in this policy area. Furthermore, the degree of overlap demonstrates the substantial degree of interdependence of the two levels of government.

In terms of the likely areas in which competition will likely manifest itself, economic squeezes on government revenues tend to curtail expansion in the social policy field. Some commentators note that the shift from fiscal relations and shared cost programs to regulatory matters resulted in an increased level of intergovernmental conflict for revenue and short term economic benefits.[19] This competition makes agreement on longer term strategies difficult.

Two other implications of overlap are the financial costs associated with duplication and the way in which policy is impacted by federalism, including the issue of disharmonized policies. The later implication relates to the efficiency of policy formation, the effectiveness of policy, and the intergovernmental competitions that may arise.

Certainly, one of the criticisms made by separatists and sovereignists about Canadian federalism is that Canadian federalism does not work because there is too much overlap in the functions of the two orders of government and, as a result, there should be massive decentralization, or Quebec should be sovereign. This criticism is really a ruse for a 'sovereignty' power grab, most perniciously as an attempt to exclude any federal involvement in many important areas, and constitutes a self-serving comment that does not make any real sense.

Since, as we have seen over and over again, federalism has worked well to protect the interests of Quebecers, the overlap issue does not apply to the question of whether Quebec's interests are protected within the federation. Quebecers already hold sufficient powers within the Canadian federation to protect their society's needs and interests, and Canada is already a highly decentralized federation. What is even more ironic is the fact that such overlap significantly contributed to or was the outcome of the decentralization of Canada. Today, Canadian federalism is characterized by a high degree of functional concurrency. Both levels of government possess sufficient authority to intervene in virtually any significant policy area of the 1990's.[20] Thus, proposals like the Allaire report calling for massive decentralization do not, to any great extent, increase provincial jurisdiction as the provinces are already active in most of these areas.

Accordingly, a cleaver but false dilemma is created in that Canada must be criticized for the overlap, but, on the other hand, Canada must be criticized if there were no overlap because it would be too centralized. In short, Canada must be criticized because it is Canada. Underlying that criticism is really a 'sovereignty' power grab primarily by attempting to completely exclude any federal involvement in certain policy areas, and it distorts the realities of how Canadian federalism works or how it may be improved. If the criticism then is a simple economic or efficiency based one, as it must be, then the conclusion of the need for massive decentralization is not supported in the Canadian context.

The Costs of Duplication

Overlap, and the duplication of efforts that it spawns, may become a serious problem in terms of the financial health of a country, or, can result in overregulation. The actual costs of duplication result ultimately in higher deficits and higher taxes. The financial costs relate to such matters as salaries and expenses of administrators performing parallel tasks, and for the upkeep of buildings. Governments incur costs in monitoring each other. Therefore, it is likely that the efficacy of the public sector deteriorated somewhat.[21]

On the other hand, some overlap and duplication is inevitable and, indeed, desirable in a federal country. Transferring exclusive jurisdiction to one level of government would entail either massive centralization or decentralization, neither of which is consistent with federalism principles in that either the provincial or national values will no longer retain their salience. Both sets of values are seen as important in Canada. Also, massive transference of jurisdiction will not cut out all of the costs associated with the other level of government. For example, the level of government with the newly acquired jurisdiction must hire more people to deal with the total policy area delegated to it, whereas, before, only parts of that area may have been focused upon. Therefore, one cannot say that all the costs associated with running the relevant bodies of the other level of government will be saved with only one level of government exercising exclusive jurisdiction. The question is an empirical one to be determined in each circumstance. On the other hand, separatism would likely cause substantial job losses to Quebec federal bureaucrats (among other types of workers), especially those concentrated in certain areas, like l'Outaouais, which could not be absorbed.

Secondly, tremendous waste through overspending or bloated bureaucracies often comes from within a level of government itself, and has little or nothing to do with federalism or federal-provincial interactions. To so blame federalism in such circumstances would be to misdirect blame. Furthermore, and to demonstrate how much a ruse the overlap criticism is, there is overlap and competition within the departments and agencies of either of the two levels of government. One does not see separatists or sovereignists calling for the abolition of government in Quebec as a solution.

Finally, and significantly, in terms of its structure regarding the overall size of government, number of employees and fiscal commitments to the welfare state, Canada differs little and ranks near the middle in comparison with other advanced industrial countries.[22] Clients of services do not seem to complain about this state of affairs. Indeed, some, like Jean Mercier, argue that the Japanese experience demonstrates that efficiency gains may be realized by deliberately creating a certain level of duplication or overlap;[23] a point I will briefly return to later.

Although duplication may result in wasted expenditures, it is simply impossible to blame government deficits and debt on federalism. The previously highly underestimated phenomena of inflation and economic stagnation are of tremendously greater significance to deficits and debt then the structures of or relations arising within the context of federalism ever were. Furthermore, the federal government and some provinces are achieving successes in balancing their books by eliminating deficits and, indeed, realizing surpluses.

The Federalism Impact on Policy

A second, and, perhaps, more important problem arising from overlapping jurisdiction and interdependence is the threat of disharmonized policies. Governments may act competitively and at crosspurposes, which may in turn frustrate each other's policies, or prevent effective policy development and co-ordination. The result of federal-provincial, provincial-provincial competitiveness, and the assertion of regional identities give rise to trade distortions within Canada. Additionally, on the whole, with the exception of bidding up subsidies, tax breaks and other assistance to industry, some commentators argue that it is not possible to demonstrate substantial negative effects arising from such competition.[24] Nevertheless, competitiveness and overlapping jurisdiction provide ample room for federal-provincial acrimony and "competing unilateralisms."

Secondly, state autonomy is exercised in the role of actor and umpire in society. Political and bureaucratic elites have their own goals for society, their own interests to protect, and massive resources and power to support the pursuit of such goals and interests. Government, be it at the provincial or federal level, is a continuing organization in which all past actions continue unless they are changed. Government actors have neither the time nor the knowledge to overhaul more than a small fraction of policies, which are embedded in bureaucracies and linked in a symbiotic relationship with clientele groups.[25] Many government actors such as crown corporations and regulatory agencies enjoy autonomy from government control to varying extents. Therefore, change to policy generally occurs at the margin. While, such a process occurs within each level of government, it, also, affects relations between levels of government.

These processes hold implications for the way government actors act and respond. As Cairns points out, given these "circumstances of built-in rigidities and vetos, it is scarcely surprising that federal and provincial political élites increasingly resort to a unilateralism of 'act first and pick up the pieces afterwards.'"[26] Some examples of federal government unilateralisms are Ottawa's extensive program of wage and price controls introduced as a Bill in 1976 to combat inflation, the unilateral change in fiscal arrangements regarding physician extra-billing, and Trudeau's threat to unilaterally patriate the Constitution if agreement was not forthcoming.

Provincial governments unilaterally become involved in many areas of federal jurisdiction. Some provinces, like Quebec and Alberta, assert a right to deal directly with foreign governments on a variety of issues and involve themselves in international trade and commerce.[27] The West and Quebec intruded on federal jurisdiction over "Indians, and Lands reserved for Indians" which was, at times, viewed disfavourably by the Natives.[28] Alberta operates savings banks under the guise of "Treasury Branches". In the long run, competing unilateralisms can destroy civility, undermine the spirit of the constitution and encourage further competing unilateralisms.[29]

Aside from competitive unilateralisms, the rigidities in the system may create a pattern of delay in policy formation, or, the existence of overlap may result in areas of uncoordinated action. Policies in one province may affect other provinces, for example, in competing for new businesses. One may consider the effect of a lack of a sales tax within a certain province. Generally, leading commentators conclude, though, that the policy impact of federalism is largely indirect:

> Federalism has influenced the terms and character of political debate; it has influenced the timing and pace of innovation and has significantly influenced the kinds of policy instruments that governments have brought to bear ... Yet the overall pattern of policy in Canada has developed in ways remarkably similar to those of other advanced countries, both those that are more centralized federal states and those that are unitary states.[30]

Federalism may contribute to a pattern of delay, it certainly does not result in paralysis:

> Failure to achieve concerted government action on the pressing economic problems of the 80's probably relates more to the intractability of these problems (which were difficulties faced by other countries) then to the federal system.[31]

One need only look to the controversy over the National Energy Policy to demonstrate how divergent regional economic interests can make consensus on national policies difficult to achieve. Other factors might include a mistrust of shared jurisdiction and competition among the political actors.

On the other hand, some suggest that efficiency gains may be realized from competitive or unilaterally acting governments. Albert Breton, for example, argues that competition between centres of power (like federal and provincial governments and bureaucracies) can forge a strong behavioural connection between the quantity/quality of goods/services supplied and the tax prices for which citizens must pay, which in turn minimizes utility losses.[32] Of course, the nature of the competition itself must be stable to prevent self-destructive behaviour. This point is highly important since competition is not necessarily, or even mostly, associated with negative implications.

If there is an overlap problem in Canada leading to disharmonized policies, imagine the disharmonization that would occur if Quebec were to be sovereign or independent. There would be two independent sources of sovereign exercises of power. One would be Quebec, supported by its bureaucracies, and the other being Canada, which, in turn, would include the federal and/or provincial level(s) of government(s) and their respective bureaucracies, as the case may be, and there would be less incentive and no institutional structures to provide for the harmonization of policy between the two sovereign entities. This is so because the stated goal of sovereignty is Quebec's exclusive control of politics within its boarders and only trade association with Canada. Furthermore, there will be a fundamental backlash in Canada in the event of independence or sovereignty to allow any Quebec voice on political matters within Canada or in any other way, including with respect to economic or trade agreements that are not to the decided benefit of the rest of Canada.

Thus, this matter of political and economic separation is far more complicated than portrayed, particularly, by the separatists and sovereignists. Economic agreements will necessarily place constraints on the political powers of government, which may, in fact, be very substantial. Secondly, disharmonized political and social policies may result in substantial effects on the functioning of a contemplated economic union. The European Community experience demonstrates these conclusions very well. It is clear, though, that the separatist or sovereignist option with its stated goal of achieving an exclusive say over political matters within its borders would be far more detrimental to policy harmonization than the situation that exists today in Canada. In the alternative, Quebec governments will likely be required to give up significant control over their political destiny in order to achieve true economic union; ironically, a situation in response to which separatists and sovereignists cite as a need for Quebec sovereignty!

Harmful federal-provincial competition and uncoordinated action is not a necessary and always occurring outcome of the federalist system, nor is competition necessarily bad. Indeed, governments tend to collaborate more than they fight. Furthermore, there are techniques to facilitate co-operative solutions. An overview on the workability of Canadian federalism yields several observations. Executive federalism works very well when relations can be characterized as "functional" in which intergovernmental officials of the same training and backgrounds focus on discrete technical issues and deal with agreements that are subject to further modification where ongoing relations create "trust" ties in those officials.[33] The commitment of federal monies is, of course, conducive to achieving intergovernmental agreement. It is far more difficult to obtain agreement on global issues where there are numerous governmental departments of both orders of government and central agencies involved.

These observations and conclusions should not be taken to mean that Canadians should not strive to further improve the workings of Canadian government, be it federal, provincial, or, the relations between the two. However, the underlying issues just do not support separatism or sovereignty.

The Real Issue

If the real issue is managing the overlap of jurisdiction and the interdependencies that give rise to wasted expenditures and disharmonized policies that are inefficient or in some way unbeneficial, which is what should be done especially in certain policy areas, then that is what should be focused on. It may very well be that joint decision-making and action by the two levels of government may be required in certain circumstances, while in others competing or unilaterally acting governments provide the best option. The overlap/interdependence issue should not and logically cannot be used to support separatism or sovereignty. Federalism successfully allows for the two orders of government to function well together, particularly with respect to major areas of policy, as fiscal federalism demonstrates. Furthermore, those expenditures require massive outlays of money irrespective of overlap. What must be done then is to identify important areas in which federalism or intergovernmental relations are not working well to solve problems facing the country, and to devise solutions to improve those structures and relations.

What the solutions are or should be in those particular areas requiring greater rationalization were never really the focus of enough governmental attention and action. This lack of attention arises, in part, due to the focus on symbolism, particularly in the arena of the written constitutional text giving rise to status seeking/status anxieties inherent in that game. Thereby, important attention has been deflected, although not exclusively by Quebec governments, away from improving the federation. What really is required is that both levels of governments be willing to compromise to better manage the interdependencies and overlap, which, in turn, may mean both giving up and acquiring power. Symbolic demands only get in the way of achieving solutions to already difficult problems such as developing an effective and coherent industrial policy (or policies) for Canada. Other provinces do not always appear to be altogether too enthusiastic about finding solutions and to give up or forego some of their jurisdiction, if need be, as well as acquiring other powers to achieve solutions. It is only relatively recently that some real steps were taken as an attempt to improve interprovincial trade within Canada. However, even that attempt is far from a full and complete solution to the issue.

Conclusions: Overlap and Interdependencies

The conclusions that one may draw from the history of Canadian federalism is that it has worked well, in reality, to provide for the major programs and expenditures that Canadians want. Overlapping jurisdictions have not caused deficits; inflation and economic stagnation are the major culprits, and government policies and spending contributed significantly to the problem, while overlap certainly aggravated that problem. Overlapping jurisdiction provides greater freedom of action for both levels of government to act and provided for a great amount of decentralization. Massive decentralization only really results in, intended or otherwise, excluding any federal involvement in important policy areas. It is self-serving for separatists and sovereignists to claim that there are problems associated with overlap as an argument for separatism or sovereignty when governments of Quebec themselves diverted important attention away from finding solutions by choosing to pursue the process of symbolism and status seeking, especially in the constitutional arena. Finally, it is not clear that disharmonized policies and competitive policies of the federal and provincial governments are necessarily bad. Each circumstance must be assessed on its own merits.

If more attention were focused on addressing problems arising out of overlap and inderdependencies, the tool of constitutional wrangling could not be used by separatists or sovereignists to promote the dismembering of Canada. Indeed, such participation would be a symbolic defeat for separatists and sovereignists, as it would be appearing to legitimize Quebec's role in Confederation. Furthermore, real successes might be achieved resulting in further improvement to Canadian federalism, while Canadians and Quebecers alike would more often be exposed to the reality that Canadian federalism is working well. In the end, the argument of overlapping jurisdiction used by separatists or sovereignists is little more than a ruse.

Clearly, not all areas of overlap should be managed. Areas that are seen as nationally important, such as creating effective industrial policy for Canada (or effective policies given the multitude of aspects comprising industrial policy), or managing areas that create substantial waste of expenditures, where the benefits of such co-ordinated action outweigh truly competitive or unilaterally acting governments, would be suitable candidates for such co-ordinated action. Overlap, is otherwise healthy in a federation as it allows for regional diversity and autonomy for the two orders of government, especially for the territorial level, as well as potentially promoting efficiency of program creation and delivery.

Executive Federalism and the Institutionalized Cabinet

Another aspect contributing to the competition between the two orders of government is not a federalism issue *per se*, but, relates to the organizational aspects of government. The way decision-making within Cabinet is structured can effect significantly the nature of relations between the two orders of government be they competitive or co-operative, and for the relations within a single level of government. The two characteristic modes of cabinet operation existing in Canada after the First World War were the Departmentalized Cabinet and the Institutionalized or Collegial Cabinet.

Executive federalism refers to the relations between elected and appointed officials of the federal and provincial governments, which can be bilateral or multilateral. The relations can either be at the summit level involving first ministers, and usually their Finance and/or Justice Ministers, or they can be "functional", being articulated by the Minister whose portfolio is affected.

Therefore, in addition to the mode of cabinet operation, the other variable that contributes to competitive or cooperative relations intergovernmentally or intragovernmentally relates to the types of officials dealing with an issue, which, in turn, is, in large part, determined by the nature of the issue itself.

Functional relations are ones most likely to bring about co-operative federal-provincial relations and to transcend federal-provincial differences. Summit federalism can produce relations that are "functional", like relations between Ministers whose portfolios are affected. The story of fiscal federalism bears out this latter proposition with, perhaps, the exception of the *Canada Health Act*, which deviated from the functional model with respect to extra-billing.[34] Institutional Cabinets tend to be less facilitative of functional relations than do the Departmentalized Cabinets, but certainly do not prevent them, nor do they prevent successful relations or workable outcomes.

Departmentalized Cabinet

Indeed, the period between 1940 and 1960 was an era often described as cooperative federalism, and one characterized by a Departmental model of Cabinet operation, together with a functional model of federal-provincial relations. Under the Departmentalized model, ministerial decision-making concerned a Minister's area of responsibilities, and there was a trust that colleagues in other areas were performing satisfactorily. Ministerial decision-making was therefore not collective. Individual departments were expert in their areas and their opinions went unchallenged.[35]

Federal-provincial relations, whether they be multilateral or bilateral, were functional in nature. Intergovernmental relations were conducted at the level of federal and provincial program officials, who shared a commonality based on common values and a technical vocabulary from common training. These commonalities percolated upwards to the Deputy Minister and Ministers and portfolio loyalties meant that Ministers would articulate these commonalities.[36] Structures were formed, and with those commonalities, further "trust" networks were developed helping to transcend federal-provincial differences.[37] These relations were further facilitated when there was money, particularly federal money, forthcoming in order to administer the program.

As time went on, problems were perceived with respect to the Departmentalized system. There was too little shared knowledge among Ministers and too much ministerial dependence on the civil service. The system reflected very little overall planning, and government was reacting on a fire fighting basis. Finally, there was seen to be too much special interest influence on government.

Institutionalized Cabinet

With the growth of government intervention in society and the fact that issues overlap the jurisdiction of various departments, a new type of cabinet decision-making was required, the Institutional or Collegial Cabinet. The Institutional Cabinet features collective responsibility for decision-making. Cabinet is structured into committees with overlapping responsibilities. The committees formed are the principle institution of collegial decision-making. Institutionalized decision-making then represents combinations of formal committee structures and established central agencies, with budget and management techniques infused into collegial decision-making, within the framework of government wide priorities and objectives to manage decision-making.

The committee scrutinizes ministerial proposals, therefore, the individual Minister becomes less of a decision-maker and more of a decision proponent supported by expert officials. Decision-making became more adversarial and competitive pitting experts from one department against experts of another. Officials and agencies concerned with particular programs came increasingly to lose autonomy in interacting with their professional counterparts in the other level of government.[38] Due to greater scrutiny and expertise of the committee, there was more scrutiny of specialized interests. Finally, and perhaps most importantly, the emphasis is now on government wide objectives, as opposed to discreet functional ones.

Therefore, the expanded areas of government intervention, resulting in substantial areas of overlap and interdependence of the two levels of government, and the expertise and more global perspectives of the Collegial Cabinet, gave the two orders of government greater incentives and the institutional capability to compete with each other.

The development of the Institutional Cabinet does not mean that the functional relations model characterizing intergovernmental relations is eliminated or that the participation of central agencies prevents such relations; far from it. For example, among the most significant programs in Canada are the social shared cost programs, which are characterized by functional relations in the summit context. A special kind of functional relations model developed in the mid-50's relating to meetings of Finance Ministers, together with an expert infrastructure of officials. The two bodies that emerged were the Continuing Committee on Fiscal and Economic Matters and the Tax Structure Committee. Another example of functional relations is the Canadian Council of Ministers of the Environment (formerly the Canadian Council of Resource and Environment Ministers), an established body of federal and provincial Ministers functioning to provide a forum for intergovernmental consultation and contact since the early 1970's. Of course, well structured functional collaborative relations do not always necessarily result in optimal policy outcomes or agreements, as in the environmental field.

Federalism and Bureaucracy

Thus, variables inherent in the Canadian federal system, such as two constitutionally ordained levels of government sharing divided, and practically and theoretically overlapping jurisdictions, set up a dynamic of competition. Added to those federalism variables are the organizational aspects of government, which can enhance competition or cooperation. The Institutional

Cabinet tends to increase competition both within a government and between the two orders of government, as politicized central agents display a greater tendency to involve themselves in the symbolic jurisdictional and electoral aspects of issues.[39] However, this situation does not prevent relations or structures that facilitate co-operation.

Furthermore, executive federalism tends to work better in some contexts than in others. The more issues depart from being discreet and isolated, begin to involve more than one type of official not sharing the same "commonality", and where structures of interaction giving rise to "trust ties" are not established, the more difficult it will be to obtain agreement and the more the interactions will be characterized by competition or acrimony. Of course, the commitment of federal funds is also helpful in achieving co-operative action. It is furthermore argued that:

> Collaboration can be managed well or badly and not all forms of collaboration are equal. Collaboration that requires the agreement of both orders of government on a regular basis or that requires the agreement of all provincial governments, as well as Ottawa, risks inaction.[40]

Although there is much dynamism for competition inherent in the Canadian federal system, it is wrong to say that intergovernmental relations are always, or even mostly, characterized by competition, or that competition is necessarily bad. It is highly important to note that federal and provincial governments tend to collaborate far more than they fight. A continuous process of federal-provincial consultation and negotiation is at the heart of the Canadian federal system and further allows for policy adjustment to take into account regional interests.

Therefore, phrases such as 'Quebec and Canada do not see eye to eye', or 'Quebec keeps Canada back and Canada keeps Quebec back', due to these federal-provincial competitions are banal and ultimately do not make sense given the nature, processes and history underlying Canadian federalism. Quebec is not a special case by competing with the federal government for more power. All provinces compete for more power. Competition and change are by-products of the federalist system in Canada. Although Quebec governments are often more vocal and at the forefront of decentralizing changes in Canada, it is not really all that different from the other provinces in terms of its willingness to compete for more power or advantage. Instead, those features that make Quebec distinct are fully protected and respected within the federalist system and, as such, in important ways, Canada and the provinces, including Quebec, *do* see "eye to eye" on the most fundamental and crucial matters.

Indeed, it is interesting to note that separatism did not even originate in Quebec, nor is separatism exclusively a Quebec phenomenon in Canada. Nova Scotians were the original separatists, consistently opposing Confederation at the outset. They were brought into Confederation by the Conservative Premier Tupper, who would not submit the question to a vote in the Legislature.[41] The sentiments of Nova Scotians were made clear in the federal and provincial elections of 1867. Eighteen of nineteen seats in the federal Parliament went to separatists and, provincially, Tupper's Conservative party was almost eliminated.[42] There were even calls, based on business and economic rationales, in support of joining the United States, as an alternative to Confederation. The secessionist movement would thereafter wane in the face of British opposition and increasing economic prosperity.

Western alienation in Canadian federalism represents a longstanding and widespread disaffection with the national government, due to the perception of the federal government favouring "central" Canada. As a result, the West is much less likely to be supportive of Quebec's demands for special status and greater powers. Studies conducted regarding the 1979–85 period indicate that approximately one in twenty Western Canadians advocated separation or union with the United States. [43] Clearly, however, the greatest threat of separation in contemporary Canada comes from Quebec.

The real problem that must be faced within the federal system in Canada is not in essence competition at all. Rather, as indicated earlier, the main issue is managing the overlap and interdependencies of the two orders of government in selected areas.

The Variable of Government Leaders and Party Politics in Quebec

Another variable, in addition to the ones outlined relating to the systemic dynamics inherent in the Canadian federal system, and those related to the organizational aspects of governments and the structure of their interaction, is that of the leaders and party politics in the Canadian federalist system. Although competition is a dynamic inherent in the Canadian federal system, the exact nature and focus that those competitions will take are not necessarily determined by the federal system.

It is quite clear that federal-provincial competitions occur over a broad range of areas, and at various levels. At the formal constitutional level, it was certain that this area of federal-provincial interaction would play a very large role because, especially after 1927, it was necessary for Canada as a fully independent country to acquire all the trappings of an independent state, including possessing its own constitutional amending procedure. If the dynamic of competition is inherent in Canadian federalism, there could be no better forum in which to play out that competition than the constitutional arena. Any government with a desire to forward an agenda could withhold its consent to an amending formula until its demands were satisfied. An amendment without the consent of all the parties concerned would result in negative implications for relations and give rise to ill feelings within the federal system, especially with respect to the dissenting province(s). These negative relations would likely arise despite the fact that the amendment may constitute good law, binding on all within the state and was otherwise legitimate.

However, what the variable of party politics in Quebec and the variable of individual leaders added to the federal system is an overemphasis on changing the written constitution, which overshadowed in perceived importance, the other, and more important aspects of the workings of Canadian federalism. As a result, important attention was diverted from the successes of Canadian federalism, as well as away from creating new processes to deal with problem areas for which chosen processes, like executive federalism, were not able to produce optimal solutions. This focus on constitutional text is accompanied by successive Quebec government leaders searching for some form of symbolism or special status, which, in turn, led to the degeneration of constitutional reform in written constitutional text into a process of status seeking and addressing status anxieties. Furthermore, some government leaders have been more successful than others in the pursuit of separatism.

The Embedded Game

The overarching goal of governments from Quebec, be it with respect to constitutional text or otherwise, has been to maximize that province's cultural, fiscal and political autonomy, particularly by expanding the scope of provincial powers and to seek special status. The second important aspect, then, regarding government leaders in Quebec, is that due to the past conduct of successive government leaders, the competition for more power in Quebec became an embedded game in Quebec politics, including electoral politics. As Daniel Latouche argues, although in the early 1960's Quebecers were scarcely aware of the existence of constitutional debates, it was becoming increasingly apparent to Quebec political parties that there were immense electoral advantages to be derived from nationalist rhetoric.[44] Therefore, as Latouche goes on to say, Quebec was hardly in a hurry to bring the constitutional game to an end by formulating concrete constitutional proposals to sustain a constitutional reform it claimed to want, and there was not even consensus on any given question.[45] A brief history of government politics in Quebec illustrates this process that emerged.

The Liberal government headed by Lesage can be characterized as searching for non-isolationist autonomy and proactive nationalism, including cooperative federalism in intergovernmental relations.[46] Previously, Duplessis' position was that Québécois culture could best survive in isolation from the rest of Canada. Lesage, on the other hand, took an active involvement in intergovernmental relations in an effort to recoup lost political power, prestige and fiscal resources needed for the development of Quebec state and society.

On the written constitutional front, the Fulton-Favreau amending formula of 1965 was rejected on the basis that it did not guarantee Quebec the power to participate in the development of national policies, the development of the French Canadian language and culture, and, ultimately, the means to maximize Quebec governmental authority.[47] Furthermore, Lesage objected to federal refusal to delimit its then existing power to amend parts of the Constitution concerning exclusive federal jurisdiction. Also, the unanimity principle, which would give Quebec a veto, was strongly opposed by Lesage because further constitutional reform would be made more difficult to achieve.

Lesage asserted that Quebec would not agree to any Constitutional amendment until issues such as Quebec's powers and role in Confederation, as well as safeguards for francophone minority rights were settled to the satisfaction of Quebec.[48] This assertion, also, became the position of subsequent Quebec governments.

Having rejected the Fulton-Favreau formula and faced with losing votes to Daniel Johnson in the 1966 election, the Lesage government became more nationalist and provincialist by shifting its position from equality to special status for Quebec. Pension negotiations resulting in the creation of the Quebec Pension Plan was a case in point.

The Liberal government sought a greater role in interprovincial and foreign relations. Indeed, in 1960, Quebec convened a Premiers Conference, which was to become an annual event. Quebec attended the international Francophonie conference and concluded several agreements in relation to cultural and economic matters with the French government. At times, Quebec forays into the international scene gave rise to tension with the federal government, but on many occasions such participation occurred with federal government approval.

There was an effort to maximize provincial programs and fiscal authority by opting out of shared cost programs, demanding tax room, and by establishing provincial welfare and development programs independently of the federal government.

The Union National, between 1966 and 1970 under the Johnson and Bertrand, demonstrated a continuity in demands for constitutional and fiscal reform, and for greater powers and status in domestic and international relations. However, there was a change in tone and perspective. The importance of the process of status seeking and the combatting of status anxieties in constitutional text originated with Johnson's campaign slogan *Égalité ou Independence*. Now, the threat of separatism was lurking in the background of the constitutional reform process regarding its written form, as a final option where all else failed. Bertrand stressed special status and collective rights including the right of national self-determination.[49]

For Johnson and Bertrand, "equality" meant equality between the representatives of the two founding linguistic groups; whereas, for Lesage it essentially meant equality among the provinces.[50] Johnson and Bertrand furthermore demanded that the federal government get out of certain areas like pensions, manpower training, family allowances, and health and welfare.

With the Liberals back in power, between 1970 and 1976, under Premier Bourassa, decentralization was sought along with profitable federalism and cultural autonomy for Quebec. On the issue of reform of the written constitution, Bourassa's goal was to give Quebec special powers and resources thought necessary to promote the binational character of the federation and to assure Quebec's cultural sovereignty; not the "dual alliance" of the two founding linguistic groups approach of Johnson and Bertrand. In seeking its mandate, Bourassa made reform of the *Constitution Act* one of the major components of his platform. Support for patriation was dependent on the new constitution including Quebec's "traditional demands", such as a Quebec constitutional veto, the right to opt out of federal spending programs with compensation and so on.

Still, this dual objective of cultural autonomy and profitable federalism was not enough for electoral victory over the Parti Québécois in 1976, who would remain in power until 1985. Initially, the Parti Québécois refused to seriously consider the renewal of Confederation, as its stated objective was sovereignty-association, which involved political sovereignty and economic association.[51]

In 1985, in the aftermath of a lost referendum and the patriation of the Constitution, the Parti Québécois presented the Mulroney government with its *beau risque*, "Draft Agreement on the Constitution" containing twenty-two conditions for signing a constitutional accord, including a Quebec veto, more provincial power in communications, immigration, international relations, limitations on Charter application in Quebec, and distinct society recognition. Thus, that Party temporarily settled for special status, when, only six years earlier, it criticized special status as a dangerous illusion for Quebec and the rest of Canada.[52] Again, under Pierre Marc Johnson, sovereignty-association was said not to be abandoned, but, the immediate goal was to gain concessions from Ottawa that maximized Quebec's status and autonomy.

The election of the Liberals under Bourassa in 1985 meant a return to cultural autonomy and profitable federalism. The Bourassa government's initiatives for reforming the text of the Constitution centred on five points, which made up the core of the Meech Lake Accord, and the follow up constitutional conference, the Langevin Block. Again, such demands included "distinct society" recognition, a Quebec veto regarding Constitutional amendment, and limiting federal spending in areas of provincial jurisdiction.

Again, the post-1995 referendum phase of Quebec politics features a debate on how much decentralization is to be demanded. The Liberal opposition, under Daniel Johnson, stated its intention to wait for Ottawa to make proposals to Quebec in respect of granting special status to Quebec and decentralization in written constitutional text. On the other hand, the former Bloc M.P., Bouchard, now leader of the Parti Québécois, stated unequivocally his intention to hold another referendum on sovereignty after the next election, and presumably a multitude of other times after that until Quebecers finally vote in the way he wants them to. In the meanwhile, Bouchard stated that he too was waiting for offers from Ottawa, but, in the end, admitted that he was a committed sovereignist, thereby, implying that offers from Ottawa are not really desired in and of themselves as a solution. Jean Charest, formerly leader of the federal Progressive Conservatives, replaced Daniel Johnson as leader of the Quebec Liberal Party. His stated priority is the Quebec economy and not the Constitution.

Individual Leaders

Some Quebec government leaders may be regarded as more influential in their attempts to bring about separation. The two leaders that stand out in stature are René Lévesque and Lucien Bouchard. Lévesque was a kind of folk hero, passionate in the cause, characterized by his excessive cigarette smoking and ability, at times, to speak without the aid of notes in what seemed an impromptu performance. Bouchard, on the other hand, is the charismatic public speaker. Many Quebecers see him as possessing good leadership qualities. Indeed, in the case of the latter, the campaign for the second referendum in Quebec did not make any real progress until Bouchard took the helm. In this way, the personality of Parizeau, being more reserved and aloof, did not appeal to Quebecers, who did not necessarily see him as capable of leading an independent Quebec.

Thus, some leaders, appear to be trusted and respected to a greater extent than other leaders, and give greater credibility or momentum to the separatist campaign. What is curious though is that during the second referendum campaign, for example, the issues were still the same before and after Bouchard took the helm. Furthermore, separatist and sovereignist supporters seemed to disregard what appeared to be the Parti Québécois putting off the second referendum until more favourable polling results were obtained; or, that the referendum question was not released until the last minute, not least because it gave an opportunity for the P.Q. to have various questions market tested. Finally, as many referendums are promised by Bouchard until the sovereignists win the referendum. These actions can be seen as attempts by the P.Q. to manipulate the public and to disregard the intentions of Quebecers as expressed through their votes in previous referendums. The second referendum question itself was not seen as honest by many Quebecers, and it was since reported that Jacques Parizeau may not have had any intention of even honouring the terms of that question, but would have moved for Quebec to secede the day following a Yes vote.

The danger, as in any case, of placing too much confidence in a government leader is that not everything that the leader says might be thoroughly evaluated by the citizen. Although there was extensive discussion concerning the sovereignist agenda, the claim that separatism or sovereignty is necessary for Quebec was never really discussed critically by examining the actual workings of federalism in relation to the preservation and promotion of the most basic interests of Quebec francophones, that is, the French language and the flourishing of francophone Quebec society. Secondly, the assertion that after separation relations between Canada and Quebec will not change except insofar as Quebec would be politically independent was never really challenged in the campaign. Or, claiming that there will be a "transition period" after sovereignty is likewise not a forthright response. Tremendously difficult issues will likely arise for Quebecers and Canadians, not the least of which involve Quebec's share of the national debt, the protection of minorities within Quebec, the broader question of borders, and the fact that Canada will treat Quebec as an independent state and make trade or other arrangements only in Canada's best interests. Any of a number of these issues hold the potential to create great acrimony and should have been more fully discussed. Finally, the secessionists made bold statements that an independent Quebec will automatically become part of NAFTA and so its economic future will be secure. However, the Americans themselves indicated that this would not be the case and that Quebec would be required to negotiate separately. Not only would the U.S. likely take Ottawa's lead as a courtesy, it would likely seek major concessions such as ending Quebec's 'dairy subsidies'. Quebec's future will then be far worse off.

Of course, complete blame for the lack of this type of discussion cannot be placed on the confidence some Quebecers maintain in certain leaders. The federalist forces were not fully discussing the issues either at that time, and they were the advocates of the "No" position.

Overview

Regardless of whether or not Quebec may possess adequate powers regarding the needs and concerns arising out of that province, Quebec governments are expected to compete for more power and to seek special status. No party in Quebec with any reasonable aspirations of becoming the governing party can be successful without participating in this embedded game and in pursuing its objectives. The objectives may entail demanding the ability to opt out of shared cost programs, or may involve more extreme proposals such as massive decentralization or sovereignty, or may involve distinct society recognition in written constitutional text. Successive Quebec Parties and governments are constantly defining and redefining the objectives of the embedded game. The general trend reflects a move beyond the recognition of Quebec specificity as confined to the survival of language, religion and the Civil Code, to encompass almost all aspects of civil society such as health, education, the economy, and the workplace. The game itself, however, is accepted without question and partially reflects the desire of citizens as provincial voters to elect a provincial government they perceive will best and most vigorously forward their interests. Party politics and electoral competition are presented to the voter in terms of the embedded game and the only debate is what objectives are to be pursued in the context of the game.

The point of examining the history and processes of Canadian federalism is to challenge the underpinnings of the embedded game since Quebec and Quebecers possess adequate powers and the ability to protect their needs and concerns, and that intergovernmental relations and the resulting agreements and understandings they produced are sensitive to Quebec's position in Canada. Of course, Quebec governments are not the only ones to engage in the game for greater status and decentralization. However, the game is an embedded one in the party and electoral politics of Quebec, and the extremes to which it is taken is what distinguishes Quebec from the other provinces. Provincial competition was necessary to bring about the decentralization of Canada, which, in turn, better reflected the processes underlying Canadian federalism; however, once that state of affairs was accomplished, the justifications for further demands for decentralization, in and of itself, cease to exist. Like a runaway train, the decentralization mentality and embedded game blaze on ahead without a track and with little or no end in sight. These games took on a life of their own despite their principled justifications ceasing to exist.

Indeed, so entrenched is this game that it is feared, Quebec and other provincial governments accustomed to playing the decentralization game, will be loath to enter into agreements that might limit their power, even if accompanied by a limitation on other governments, in order to deal with important issues. Such issues might include improving trade within Canada, or attempting to harmonize policy in important areas like industrial policy to deal with the problems facing Canada in a globalized setting. Such agreements would be beneficial to all citizens. What appears to be needed is a change of attitude, and the creation of structures to allow for effective discussion and resolution of problems in certain important areas that traditional forms of executive federalism were not able to deal with adequately, and to determine what areas are better dealt with co-operatively rather than competitively, or vise versa. Co-operation, in turn, requires that governments of both levels be willing to compromise and exercise power on a principled basis to create greater efficiency in Canadian federalism. Perhaps, it is a telling reminder that the pro-separatist government of Quebec has not to date entered into the Social Union Framework Agreement.

Competition for Citizen Loyalty

Much is made of federal-provincial competition being a dynamic inherent in the Canadian federal system. To be sure, federal-provincial competition in the Canadian context is not just about battles over jurisdiction, it includes an even more profound process of competition over citizen loyalty by activist national and provincial governments. These battles are most evident at the level of refashioning symbolism in the Constitution, but, are certainly not limited to the same. Secondly and relatedly, in recent decades, there is a tighter fusion of state and society due to the virtual explosion of government involvement in society and the economy. This process simultaneously fragments the state as the two orders of government pulled, and continue to pull, society and the economy into a framework of Canadian-wide or provincially centred concerns.[53] This situation arises as a result of the policy significance of a citizens' simultaneous membership in national and provincial communities. The process is, thereby, institutionally structured by the form of federalism.

Since the 1960's, the concept of national community is being threatened by the growing activism of provincial governments, and the increasing competitions with the federal government undermined some citizen attachment to the national community and to the national level of government. Accordingly, the status anxious federal government attempted to shape conceptions of the national community, particularly in the context of constitutional struggles and especially through the Charter, as we have seen. The federal government also attempted to see certain concerns of the national community addressed in provincial policy areas that were highly significant to the country as a whole, for example, through social shared cost programs. Furthermore, the federal government rejected attempts at the balkanization of the economic union, tax system, and fundamental rights and freedoms.

Varying definitions of community result in differential consequences for a government's effective authority, including in the context of intergovernmental relations. This process is reflected in the competition between Quebec and the federal government for citizen allegiance. Such competition modifies the self-conceptions of citizens and the significance of provincial and national communities to which the Canadian citizen relates.

The rise of sovereignist sentiment in Quebec speaks volumes about the national government's relative ability to compete with successive Quebec governments to affect citizen conceptions and loyalties in Quebec. A remarkable aspect of the lessening or lack of national affinities in separatists or sovereignists towards the nation is that Canadian federalism is working well in reality and its successes are traceable, to a significant extent, to the constitution, and, secondly, to the federal government and its interactions with the provinces, including Quebec. Of course, this is not to say that most Quebecers do not value both provincial and national communities and levels of governments. Generally, Quebecers rightly see no need to choose between the two and such a choice is neither necessary nor desirable. This position is not in the least bit contradictory, as was continually observed. Multiple loyalties, be they to province, country, family or whatever, are not necessarily incompatible or antagonistic.[54]

It is not surprising that Quebecers, and particularly francophone Quebecers, display a strong affinity towards the provincial level of government. Indeed, the rationale for federalism is that territorial governments possess adequate powers to preserve territorial interests. Accordingly, the province of Quebec is looked to by francophone Quebecers to protect language and to promote the flourishing of its society. This goal is in large measure accomplished through francophone control of territorial government, and the Quebec economy and business world. All of these powers are ones that the provincial government and Quebecers possess in constitutional text, through intergovernmental relations or agreements, and through the actions or initiatives of Quebecers themselves.

What is surprising is that among a significant proportion of Quebecers who are separatists and sovereignists, there is not a simultaneously strong natural affinity towards Canada. Such a view of community is surprising because Canadian federalism is working well to provide for the flourishing of francophone Quebec society and its French language.

To a significant extent, the reason for the rise of sovereignist sentiment and the corresponding decline of national affinity relates to the visibility to Quebecers of the success stories of Canadian federalism, and the visibility of the importance of the national community and federal government in contributing to the well being of Canadians and Quebecers alike. In this respect, the federal government is being outcompeted by Quebec governments. There are several possible reasons for this state of affairs. The powers possessed by the Quebec government are highly relevant to Quebecers, and Quebecers must look to a significant extent to the provincial government to pursue their goals and to provide for the flourishing of their society. Secondly, the history of Canada, up to the end of World War II, also helps to explain Quebecers' affinity towards Quebec. Quebecers historically looked to the Quebec government to represent or satisfy their interests. Many can remember a time when Quebec's business world was not dominated by francophones and, which, gave rise to some feelings of resentment. Finally, the media and education in Quebec also played an important role contributing to this state of affairs. These factors taken together instill a confidence in Quebecers for the province and their provincial level of government, which they may see as most necessary or relevant to many issues perceived to be of important to them. Finally, the successes of Canadian federalism are in a sense shielded from Quebecers by Quebec governments, even if indirectly or unintentionally, especially, due to their unquestioning participation in the "embedded" game of demanding special powers and further decentralization, and by the attention of Quebecers being focussed on wranglings associated with written constitutional text. The result of this fractional attention is that far from exposing the successes and benefits of membership in the Canadian community, and with respect to the federal government, they are incorrectly portrayed as being unwilling or unable to recognize the needs and concerns of Quebecers. An 'ideology' is even created for some that the only true Quebecer is one who stands for an independent Quebec.

One example of the embedded game relates to "opting" out. Demands for the opting out of shared cost programs are symbolic in the sense that block funding available to other provinces is essentially unconditional and, therefore, autonomy is not an issue. However, there is a deeper effect on citizen loyalties because the federal government's role in Quebec life appears to be less significant. In other words, its role lacks visibility and Quebecers may only largely see the provincial government as being relevant to them. Indeed, there are great incentives for Quebec governments to resist federal spending or other programs, which, thereby, inject national concerns and national conceptions of community within Quebec. Furthermore, Quebecers would gain a greater sense of the relevance and beneficial role of the national community and federal government, as well as the successes of Canadian federalism.

By far, the Quebec government is the actor most visible to Quebecers. Quebec has its own personal and corporate income tax forms, it controls and uses powers integral to francophone Quebec society, the provincial government controls education, and francophone Quebecers possess the effective ability to promote their views in cultural mediums, like broadcasting and the print media of Quebec.

On the other hand, the federal government has not been nearly as visible to Quebecers. Equalization payments by the federal government reflect a national revenue average in which payments are made to provinces who fall short of that average. Quebec, for instance, in the 1989–90 fiscal year, enjoyed an Equalization entitlement of $3.354 billion and an actual payment of $3.7075 billion, taking into account payments and recoveries for previous years, which constituted a significant proportion of that province's revenues.[55] Indeed, in the 1989–90 year, Quebec received $552 per inhabitant.[56] Quebec receives approximately one-half of all Equalization.[57] The amount of Equalization since rose for Quebec. By 1994–95, that entitlement amounted to $3.9655 billion and a cash payment of $3.5427 billion, including payments and recoveries for previous years.[58] Such transfers combat interprovincial disparities and reflect national concerns to maintain a reasonable national standard of public goods and services within a province. However, as these amounts are given to provincial governments, they are not visible to ordinary citizens.

One of the few areas in which the federal government is visible is old age security and unemployment insurance payments. Every person who qualifies receives a cheque each month and, therefore, recognizes a federal presence in their lives. However, greater attempts at gaining more federal recognition are being made in recent times, as with the Canada Health and Social Transfer.

The Charter is a significant area whereby national conceptions of community are established in constitutional text by focusing on rights and freedoms and equality of opportunity shared by Canadians.

Finally, given the trust and confidence Quebecers demonstrate in favour of their provincial level of government, that government's advice to Quebec citizens regarding the need for more power and status may go unquestioned to any serious extent. Secondly, there is an informational gap, on the part of individual citizens that creates difficulties in assessing the merits of government proposals or action.[59] As a result of these factors of the strength of the natural affinities towards Quebec, trust, informational gap, and lack of federal government visibility, the game of seeking more power and status, particularly in the constitutional forum, has been established and followed by successive Quebec governments such that it became and continues to be an embedded game in that province. Furthermore, the game must be followed if there is to be any chance of success in becoming the governing party; therefore, the embedded game cannot presently be challenged by any political party in Quebec seeking to govern.

In this context, further decentralization will always be required absent some dramatic change in outlook regarding the appropriate role of party and electoral politics in Quebec, which, at present, seems unlikely. Secondly, given the focus on constitutional reform in its written text and the inherent difficulties in gaining agreement in that area, Quebec governments focussed attention away from the successes of Canadian federalism and the appearance of an unworkable federation arose. It might be noted that there is no real down side to Quebec governments pursuing symbolic goals in the arena of written constitutional text because if the effort fails, that Quebec government still wins citizen loyalty in Quebec since it can be said that the rest of Canada rejected Quebec, whether or not that is in fact true.

Thus, the extent to which separatism or sovereignty grew in significance can, to a significant degree, be seen in terms of the national community's representative, the federal government, being at a competitive disadvantage in bringing to light the advantages and successes of the nation, and in competing with Quebec governments and sovereignists regarding the conceptions of community held by Quebecers. In essence, the separatist or sovereignist sees the provincial level of government as the natural one and the national level as an artificial construct valued only for its convenience (if at all). A major element explaining why the federal government has been outcompeted by Quebec governments centres on visibility. In this respect, the Quebec government has been highly visible, and seen as highly relevant and essential to Quebecers. However, except for certain matters, such as old age security and unemployment insurance, the federal government is not as visible to Quebecers and, hence, its relevance to Quebecers may be less well known. Furthermore, the benefits of federalism are not always immediately perceivable or tangible and yet they always exist in the background.

Indeed, visibility is precisely the reason why relief aid and money in the millions sent from the rest of Canada to those struck by the 1996 flood in the Saguenay region of Quebec or for the ice storm victims of 1998 may very well do more to combat separatism in those areas than all the success stories of Canadian federalism put together. The reason is that these residents can see first hand that Canadians outside Quebec are concerned about all Canadians, including Quebecers, in ways that really matter. Yet, in terms of dollar amounts, this relief money pales in comparison to all the benefits and rewards Quebecers experience within Canada.

What is, furthermore, surprising is that proponents of the national community, particularly the federal government, are not more energetically bringing to light to Quebecers and Canadians alike the successes and realities of Canadian federalism. In this respect, the national community is not being adequately represented. Perhaps, one explanation lies in the concern that due to the fact that Quebec governments and sovereignists have outcompeted the federal government, the federal government is hesitant to take more active steps to outline the successes of Canadian federalism, which may result in the further alienation of Quebecers.

Yet, despite the competitive advantages possessed by Quebec governments in competing for citizen loyalties, it is clear that a majority of Quebecers demonstrate a significant degree of attachment to the national Canadian community and the national government, to which the results of two referendums on sovereignty bear witness. Separatism or sovereignty would deny to Quebecers the deeply rooted Canadian part of their identities.[60] Despite lower visibility levels of the national government and community, Quebecers do experience and generally do recognize the benefits of membership in the Canadian community. The benefits are abundant including economic prosperity, a good standard of living, and the belonging to a society that values tolerance and respect for individuals, cultures, and groups, such as francophone Quebecers. There is enough community in Quebec and Canada to go around for everybody, particularly with respect to the national and territorial levels of community and government.

Conclusion

And so our journey through the landscape of Canadian federalism, both past and present, has taken us far and wide yielding in depth observations about Canadian federalism and about the province and society of Quebec.

The question that must ultimately be answered, particularly by Quebecers who are being constantly asked through successive referendums for their support for separatism or sovereignty, is whether or not there exist substantial and reasonable grounds to justify secession. When separatist or sovereignist governments make such solicitations of the people, which might drastically alter the lives of the citizens within that territory and within the nation as a whole, the imperative must be on those separatist or sovereignist governments or supporters to justify their ends. Being witnesses on our journey through Canadian federalism taught us that far from there existing substantial and reasonable grounds for separatism and sovereignty in Quebec, the conclusion is quite the opposite and that substantial and reasonable grounds support Quebec remaining in Confederation.

Indeed, as with any examination of all the layers of a matter until true understanding is reached, the nature of Canadian federalism, as well as its elements, form, purpose, processes and history were analysed in order to determine its nature, essence, workings and the successes or lack thereof, especially with respect to Quebec. What we found, after extensive inquiry, is that Canadian federalism has been working well to provide for the flourishing of Quebec society, its needs, concerns and the preservation of its French language. Even francophone Quebecers who are critical of Canadian federalism and who advocate separatism must admit that: "[i]t is honest to start by saying that the Canadian experience has been globally positive for most of us on a personal level."[1]

However, by focusing only on limited aspect of that complex of relations, processes and history, the appearances of powerful justifications for separatism or sovereignty may appear to emerge. These justifications relate to the themes of differing visions of the country held by Québécois and other Canadians, assimilation of the French language and the inability to secure the flourishing of Quebec francophone society, as well as calling into question the very legitimacy of Canada itself. Other arguments point to the increased support for secession, or characterize federalism as being too inefficient or competitive. Focusing on selective facts and periods of time also results in obstructing from view the realities of Canadian federalism, thereby, giving rise to the possible appearance of reasonable and substantial grounds for separatism and sovereignty.

These highly detailed and complex realities of Canadian federalism, once known and understood by Canadians, will provide the basis supporting critical assessment by Canadians and Quebecers alike for their choices regarding the future of Canada. Furthermore, citizens will be better able to monitor and assess government action and policies with respect to separatism and sovereignty or intergovernmental relations, and make demands upon their governments to act more on a basis that will allow for the improvement of federalism.

First and foremost, Canadian federalism is made up of various elements that are constantly being balanced. Federalism as a form of state organization is one that seeks to reflect the natural affinities and interests of citizens simultaneously through national and territorial governments. Although federalism does not protect all cleavages existing within a society, it gives salience to cleavages that are territorially based, as defined in the Constitution. This state of affairs helps to explain why francophone minorities outside Quebec face a much more difficult time in preserving their language and culture, and why the francophone majority within Quebec is able to preserve their language and to provide for the flourishing of their society, even though it exists within a country that is otherwise predominately English speaking. Federalism provides for territorially based groups to promote the flourishing of their differences, primarily through the jurisdiction exercised by that territorial level of government, regardless of the views held elsewhere either in support or to the contrary. Federalism, therefore, successfully allows differing and, indeed, 'contradictory' conceptions of community to exist simultaneously within its boarders.

Federalism as a form of government reflects the natural affinity of citizens towards both the national and territorial levels. For federalism to ultimately survive, it must maintain those dual affinities. In Canada, in more recent years, the affinities towards the national level have been weakening, especially in Quebec.

It must always be remembered that the overriding concern of francophone Quebec society is to preserve its French language and promote the flourishing of its francophone society. Francophones constitute a majority in Quebec, but, a minority in the context of Canada and North America. Contemporary forces resulted in francophone Quebec society being far less distinct than in the 1950's. Federalism's purpose is to give salience to territorially based cleavages. For Quebec, that means the protection of the language and society of francophones within its borders. It is, perhaps, this factor that to the greatest extent galvanizes Quebecers and as well it should. The problem that may occur is that the natural affinities of Quebecers towards Canada may be undervalued even when federalism works well to create a framework within which the French language and francophone society may flourish and in fact does flourish.

What is lamentable about this state of affairs is that the perception of federalism not working well to allow for the beneficial co-existence of francophones and anglophones is based on a certain focus. This focus relates to certain time frames or events in terms of political, economic and especially constitutional histories, without taking account of the entire workings and history of Canadian federalism.

There was significant conflict at the political-historical level. The Conquest still today somehow serves as a reminder that the French and their descendants are a conquered people. The survival of *Conquétisme* is surprising, not least because the Conquest was little about the defeat of New France, who although heavily outnumbered were for many years surprisingly successful against the British. Indeed, the Conquest was much more about France abandoning her colony in North America in favour of more lucrative ones elsewhere.

Secondly, and perhaps more importantly, for there to exist a legitimate concern over *Conquétisme*, with its danger that Quebecers are second class citizens within Canadian federalism, there must exist some continuing reminder to Quebecers of that inferior status. Yet, there is none. There were no serious or realistic attempts to assimilate the French Canadians, at least after the Royal Proclamation of 1763. Confederation, itself, represented the coming together of leaders from four areas in order to arrive at agreement in creating a country. The leaders, and the areas they represented, were viewed as equals and the ultimate agreement had to be acceptable to all parties.

Federalism, then, was a compromise, including with respect to Quebec. This situation, notwithstanding, Canadian federalism still proved to be too centralized and further adaptations were made, often at the behest of Quebec. If Quebecers were second class citizens, they often received more rights and accommodations, and often possessed more bargaining clout than first class citizens, who were, presumably, the other provinces.

It is true that prior to the end of the Second World War, English and French Canadians came into conflict with each other on issues of language, religion, and matters relating to Britain. The view of the majority anglophones usually triumphed on issues attaining a national focus and taking place outside of Quebec; whereas, within Quebec, consistent with federalism which protects the interests of territorial groups, the majority francophones were victorious regardless of how vociferous Canadian anglophones might be. It is, furthermore, understandable that there might be resentment by Quebecers of the fact that anglophones within Quebec were thriving, whereas, francophones outside of Quebec were losing their rights and privileges, and even their language. As such, Quebecers began to look more and more to the Quebec government to represent and satisfy their needs and aspirations, and devoted less energy to linguistic, religious and other cultural matters occurring outside of Quebec.

The arduous process characterizing the attempts at patriating and reforming the Constitution is a main source of grievance for many Quebecers. Successive Quebec governments focused much effort on the process of Constitutional reform to pursue their objectives. As a result of the wrangling, the Constitution was not patriated until 1982 when the matter reached a critical point and patriation would occur with or without substantial provincial consent. At that time, Patriation did occur with the consent of the federal government and all the provinces except Quebec. It is maintained by some that Quebec was left out of the deal and betrayed. However, the facts do not support such a conclusion. Rather, the facts point to a complex and intense negotiation period during a last ditch effort to arrive at agreement, not a grand Machiavellian trap for Quebec. Indeed, Quebec contributed to its own isolation by breaking ranks with the "Gang of Eight". While one may not necessarily conclude that it was Quebec's fault that it was not a signatory to the 1982 Amendment, the language of betrayal is simply not accurate. Nonetheless, the fact of not being a signatory to the 1982 *Constitution Act* remains in the consciousness of many Quebecers.

Furthermore, there is no dispute that the Amendment procedure observed was consistent with democracy and the prevailing constitutional values or principles of the time. On a democratic level, the manner and content of Patriation were driven, to a large and significant extent, by francophone Quebecers, particularly those acting within the federal government and House of Commons. Quebecers participated fully during those constitutional conferences and negotiations as part of the Quebec delegation. The precise level of support in the Quebec National Assembly in favour of Patriation is not known due to the phrasing of the relevant motion by the Parti Québécois concerning that constitutional agreement. The system of Parliamentary government in Canada, as with most other democratic governments in the world today, does not require a popular referendum for constitutional amendments to be binding and legitimate. While it may be true that many Quebecers wanted something more or something different from the Amendment, one cannot conclude that Canada as a country or the 1982 *Constitution Act* are illegitimate, or justify separatism. While Trudeau's words in the course of one speech in 1980 concerning the commitment to change were arguably vague, his lifelong views on the matter were not, and Trudeau himself stated at that time in writing that no true reform could be achieved because of the existence of a P.Q. government dedicated to separation. Quebecers voted "No" in a second sovereignty referendum when there were no purported 'promises' of decentralization. It is simply impossible to conclude that the existence of a country or a constitution is illegitimate due to a vague phrase spoken on one occasion during a referendum on sovereignty concerning a province, especially given the circumstances. This conclusion is reinforced by the fact that Quebec was never betrayed during the Constitutional negotiation process leading up to the 1982 Amendment, it participated fully at that constitutional conference, and Quebecers participated meaningfully both as part of the federal and provincial levels of government.

Nevertheless, it is not a joyous matter that Quebec is still not a signatory to the 1982 Amendment while remaining bound by it, or that some Quebecers may have misunderstood the words of Mr. Trudeau during the course of a 1980 sovereignty referendum speech. However, these bases offer very weak support, if any at all, for separatism or sovereignty, which, in turn, is not even close to being proportional to the actual grievance. The critical test must be whether the Amendment and, indeed, all of Canadian federalism taken together, prevents francophone Quebec and Quebecers, in any real or substantial way and not just apparently, from preserving the French language or from promoting the flourishing of its society. The answer is no.

Nevertheless, the fact of constitutional battles, as well as the outcomes in 1982 and the failed quest for further accommodations in favour of Quebec led many to believe that Quebec as a province and people were being humiliated and rejected by the rest of Canada. Nothing could be further from the truth as any thorough investigation of Canadian federalism demonstrates. Still, the perception may remain that Canada and Quebec do not see "eye to eye" and cannot live together.

Perhaps, the least mentioned, but, most important concern of francophone Quebecers was the fact that although they are a majority within their province, the business life of that province was historically dominated by anglophones, be they Canadian or American. Given that francophone society became urbanized, industrialized and modernized at a rapid rate, and given that the language of advancement and, to a certain extent, of the workplace was English, this situation posed the greatest threat to the survival of the French language and to the flourishing of francophone society in Quebec. Until the 1960's, with little provincial government action in Quebec to promote francophones in Quebec's business world, it must certainly have appeared that federalism was not functioning well to protect the French language in Quebec and the needs of francophone Quebecers who, while constituting a majority in the province, were not even masters in their own house.

The realities of Canadian federalism demonstrate that Quebec as a province and society possesses sufficient powers and the ability to protect and provide for the flourishing of the French language, and of its francophone society. First and foremost, not only does its francophone majority control government in Quebec, but, through the action of Quebec governments exercising powers conferred by the Constitution, the dominance and flourishing of francophone business in Quebec was facilitated and achieved. The 'social justice' concern involving the imbalance between the French and English linguistic groups is rectified. With the language of business, work and the public sector in Quebec being predominately French, the major building blocks for the survival of the French language are in place. Furthermore, one must note the significant decline of the number and importance of anglophones in all aspects of Quebec life. Such decline in the weight of anglophone significance in Quebec also means a decline in the attractiveness of learning and using the English language by allophones or francophones to the detriment of the French language. As a result, francophone dominance in Quebec, including in the area of Montreal, was strengthened.

In response to Quebec's demographic anxieties in having the lowest birth rate in Canada, Quebec governments developed a demographic policy by configuring federal Family Allowance payments, and supplementing it with further incentives to encourage larger families. Through the Cullen-Couture Agreement, as extended by the McDougall-Gagnon-Trembley Accord, Quebec can encourage greater francophone or francophile immigration to that province and provide services to integrate immigrants.

The language of public primary and secondary school education in Quebec is predominately French and encompasses the vast majority of allophones and a large number of anglophones. This situation reflects a tremendous shift, particularly in terms of allophones. Students whose parents received an English language education in Canada may still receive an English language education. That constitutional protection of minority anglophone linguistic education rights is more restrictive than minority francophone rights existing outside Quebec and, therefore, reflects a distinct society characteristic of Quebec. Furthermore, it provides for greater protection of French speaking minorities outside of Quebec.

Notwithstanding recent case law, the imposition of a uniquely "French Face" in the outdoor and commercial advertising of Quebec is within the power of the Quebec government to establish, with or without the aid of the notwithstanding clause in the Charter. Given the immense political costs of overriding the Charter, such usages will be confined to situations that are deemed absolutely necessary. The impression is nevertheless left upon any observer walking on the streets of Quebec, including Montreal, that one finds oneself in a francophone society.

The language of culture and media in Quebec is predominately in French, which may be demonstrated through significant mediums such as books, newspapers, cinema, videocassettes, radio and television. Interestingly enough, broadcasting, be it radio or television, is a matter of federal jurisdiction and French language stations predominate in Quebec. There can, therefore, be no reasonable assertion that the language of culture and media create any real assimilatory pressures in favour of the English language. This conclusion is reinforced by the fact of francophone dominance in other areas of Quebec life.

To the extent that culture in Quebec is different from other parts of Canada, its survival and manifestation are protected. These are assured since francophones are the major consumers within the cultural market of that province, and francophones control that provincial government, including the power over education. Furthermore, educational broadcasting, the print media, and even the Charter, protecting the freedom of thought and liberty of expression, aid in the protection of culture in Quebec.

The real issue regarding the survival of language in Quebec and the flourishing of Québécois society relates to the greatest extent to francophone dominance in the political, social and economical life of that province, and has little to do with whether some Quebecers may feel themselves to be less distinct as a result of the modernization, urbanization and industrialization. It is clear that the Quebec of today is similar to other areas of Canada and is less distinct a society than it was in 1950. Indeed, what is ironic is that Quebec government initiatives themselves reflected a desire to meet the challenges of these transitional forces, in large part reflecting a pursuit for economic prosperity, making Quebec as a government and society less distinct, while at the same time many of the initiatives themselves were distinctive. However, it is through these initiatives that the survival of the French language and the flourishing of francophone Quebec society are ensured. Indeed, remaining in the "distinctive" 1950's mould, although an impossibility in the face of these forces, would likely result in a significant amount of francophone assimilation and may very well have undermined the flourishing of francophone society. "Feeling" distinct would, in reality, mean assimilation, whereas, the Quebec of today, although less distinct as a province and society, is well able and maintains a desire to protect its French language and to provide for the flourishing of Québécois society.

Nothing in Canadian federalism, the *Constitution Act, 1982*, including the Charter, or the decreased distinctiveness of Quebec francophone society diminished the willingness or desire of its francophones or the Quebec government to preserve the French language or to promote the flourishing of their society. Indeed, the evidence shows exactly the opposite, which was otherwise predictable. Francophone Quebecers possess a direct and intimate incentive to continue their efforts because their quality of life and prosperity are directly tied with doing so, and Quebec governments being responsible to their electorates are expected to pursue such fundamental goals. These goals are not just fundamental goals for Quebec, they are also fundamental for Canadian federalism as a whole. Indeed, the well-being and prosperity of all Canadians is a fundamental goal of Canadian federalism.

However, this cultural and societal convergence between Quebecers and other Canadians gave rise to a heightened sense of Québécois nationalism, particularly at the political and constitutional levels. Fundamental constitutional demands made by Quebec governments were often symbolic in view of the fact that the French language is well protected and francophone society is flourishing in Quebec. The demands for distinct society recognition are also symbolic. Although Quebec does not possess explicit distinct society recognition in written constitutional text, it does enjoy such recognition in practice, with adequate powers to preserve and promote their distinctiveness. Quebec's distinct society is recognized and entrenched in the Canadian constitution through the division of jurisdiction, the Charter, it is reflected in the federal government, and is reflected in intergovernmental agreements, as well as through federal policies. What is more important is that such distinctiveness exists and is protected in reality, regardless of what symbolic provisions may or may not state in constitutional text. Further fundamental accommodations or change in written constitutional text do not appear to be necessary at this time, at least on a fundamental scale.

Neither can it be said that substantial changes and accommodations in the overall functioning of the constitution were not made, or that Quebec's needs and concerns have not been addressed in that process. Substantial constitutional changes occurred in the course of Canada's progression from being quasi-federal to a truly federal country, with two levels of government co-ordinate (exercising divided jurisdiction) and independent. The division of jurisdiction itself would, over time, better reflect regional interests. Such significant decentralization occurred largely as a result of constitutional conventions and legal interpretations of the Constitution by the judiciary, particularly the Judicial Committee of the Privy Council. It is arguable that those judicial interpretations went too far in decentralizing Canada, and the technical and legalistic interpretations made were not adequately addressing functional considerations and problems encountered by contemporary society.

The second aspect of a federal system involves adequate resources to reflect jurisdiction. Judicial interpretations of the taxation powers defined limits to the seemingly limitless federal power. Additionally, through judicial interpretation and constitutional amendment, the provincial taxation power became very substantial.

In many respects from a federalism perspective, the constitution operates less in the way the judiciary says it does and more in the way determined by intergovernmental relations and agreements, especially in terms of constitutional convention and as a response to the issues involving jurisdictional overlap and interdependencies. Perhaps, the most significant aspect of Canadian federalism is that of fiscal federalism, involving government revenues and expenditures. The evolution of fiscal federalism demonstrates that Canadian federalism has successfully reflected the needs and interests of both levels of government, and better provided for the needs and interests of citizens to whom such expenditures are directed. As provincial spending responsibilities increased, so too did its revenue and not just through transfers and grants, but, significantly, through increased tax room.

The evolution of shared cost programs relating to social welfare, health care, hospital insurance and post-secondary education, while reflecting some centralization in the sense of involving federal spending in areas of provincial jurisdiction, also, reflected significant decentralization and provincial autonomy. Other special accommodations and distinctive agreements were made with respect to Quebec allowing it to opt out of those shared cost programs in return for additional tax room. This contracting out, in turn, allows Quebec greater control over its own personal income tax system.

However, due to the overall decentralization of the system, and through the actions of provincial governments, the extent of the distinctiveness of Quebec's arrangements and tax structure decreased. The declining relevance of basic federal tax and the imposition of surtaxes, deductions and incentives are making the other provinces more similar to a Quebec which never entered into a tax collection agreement with the federal government. From the perspective of autonomy, block finding is not really significantly more restrictive then contracting out. Thus, the criticism of the use of the federal spending power in the context of these programs is more a criticism of any federal involvement in important areas such as social welfare and health care, given that provincial autonomy is by and large not at issue.

Other examples of constitutional change and reforms occurred through constitutional amendment in the area of Income Security with respect to unemployment insurance, and old age pensions and supplementary benefits, including survivor and disability pensions. Again, Quebec's distinctiveness was recognized through the creation of the Quebec Pension Plan, which contributed to the flourishing of the new francophone business class in Quebec. Furthermore, significant non-constitutional renewal of the federation is occurring, particularly as an explicit federal policy in the 1990's.

Despite the scant public attention received, Canada is a federation that became highly decentralized over the years, often at the behest of and to address the needs and concerns of Quebec. These substantial changes in the workings of the constitution came about despite only modest changes occurring in constitutional text. To say that Quebec's concerns were not addressed, or that Quebecers and other Canadians possess irreconcilable differences compelling a breakup of the country does not make any sense and ignores the history, form and processes of Canadian federalism. Nonetheless, a perception is created that federalism is not working well.

The true purpose of a constitution is to limit and channel governmental authority and to provide a framework in which government may be adapted in light of future circumstances. This true and essential purpose is forgotten. Instead of assessing how, in reality, the constitution is addressing the needs and concerns of its citizens and government, for many, its value is derived from its symbolism. As a result, constitutionalism in Canada degenerated into a process of symbolism, status seeking and status anxieties by the relevant actors involved. Not surprisingly, amending the written text of the constitution is almost impossible. The process of status seeking that successive Quebec governments began and promoted signalled the death knell of the Meech Lake and Charlottetown Accords, and had nothing to do with the rejection of Quebecers or Québécois society.

In terms of the overlap of jurisdiction and the interdependencies of the two orders of government, the real issue is their management in key policy areas, or areas that give rise to substantial waste of expenditures. Such interdependencies arose in large part due to the theoretical and practical overlap found within the division of jurisdiction, particularly in an age of increased government activity, and the proliferation of issues never contemplated in 1867 cutting across jurisdictional lines.

It must be recalled that federalism works well in highly significant areas such as fiscal federalism, and, generally, works well in other areas. It is logically impossible for sovereignists and separatists to use the overlap issue to demand more decentralization and, yet, it is done. In areas where intergovernmental relations, and especially executive federalism, have been inadequate, new relations and structures may be required to address important concerns such as better economic integration in Canada, and the development of policies to facilitate Canada's economic competitiveness in the global economy. However, provinces, as well as the federal government, must be willing to discuss and to compromise based on principle to produce solutions. Symbolism and status seeking only get in the way as the substantial successes of federalism, as opposed to the failures of reform in written constitutional text, especially after the 1960's, demonstrate. Citizens will demand solutions and governments that do not participate may be left out.

Federalism is a symbiotic relationship of national and territorial communities, which gives salience to both. At the same time, in Canada, federalism is as much about governments as the communities they represent. The fact of institutionally created governments taking on a life of their own, the divided and overlapping jurisdictions they wield, the interdependencies that arise and the structures of governmental organization itself result in important effects for the processes and interactions within the federal system. On a systemic level, the Constitution of Canada set up a dynamic for competition between the two orders of government for more jurisdiction, to gain credit and avoid blame, as well as competing over citizen's conceptions of community. Yet, it would be wrong to say that relations in Canadian federalism are primarily or even mostly conflictual. Governments tend to collaborate far more than they fight.

Quebec is no different from the perspective of engaging in a process of competition than any other province and, indeed, it was Ontario that was the first real activist province. This competition allowed for the decentralization of Canada, but, now concerns are raised that provincial assertiveness has gone further than what principle might support, to the detriment of nationhood bonds, or seeking effective solutions to issues.

Federal-provincial competitions occur over a broad range of areas and at various levels. The variable of government leaders and party politics in Quebec contributed to a disproportionate effort and focus of public attention on the topic of the written constitutional text. Important public attention is, thus, diverted from the successes of federalism, and from identifying and improving areas not yet satisfactorily addressed by federalism, and especially executive federalism. Quebec governments are not the only ones responsible for this situation. Yet, the search for symbolism, status and the demanding of more decentralization is an embedded game in the party and electoral politics of Quebec; one that no party with aspirations of becoming the governing party in that province can presently ignore or reject.

This governmental competition underlies an even more profound process relating to the competition over citizen conceptions of community regarding which level or levels of community and/or government the citizen will view as natural and deserving of loyalty. The expansion of state activity in society and the economy draws citizens into a framework of national and provincial concerns.

It is quite natural that Quebecers would look to the territorial level of government in order to represent their interests and concerns for this is what that level of government is intended to do in a federal system. What is curious is that among a significant proportion of Quebecers who are separatists or sovereignists, there is not, simultaneously, a strong sense of national community. Opting for the separatism or sovereignty route would deny to Quebecers the deeply rooted Canadian part of their identities. Federalism is a form of government in which citizens simultaneously see themselves as members of the national and territorial communities. Indeed, a majority of Quebecers view themselves as part of both communities, are aware of the benefits thereof and see no need to choose between the two.

To a significant extent, the growing separatist or sovereignist sentiment, along with the corresponding decline of nationhood bonds relate significantly to the lack of visibility to Quebecers of the successes of Canadian federalism and the positive role of the national government and national community. In this way, the representatives of the national community have been outcompeted over the conceptions of community held by sovereignists and separatists in Quebec.

The successes of Canadian federalism are abundant and arise from the operation of the Canadian federalist system itself in respecting, accommodating and balancing each others' needs and concerns, as well as from the constitutional morality among Canadians and between their governments. Federalism is always changing to reflect those values. One of the unfortunate by-products of Canadian dismemberment would be the loss of this constitutional morality towards those outside the Canadian federation.

The conclusion that must follow from the evidence is that, ultimately, reasonable and substantial grounds do not exist justifying the dismemberment of Canada in favour of separatism or sovereignty. After thoroughly examining the history, form and process of Canadian federalism, the justifications that may have once appeared to be strong are revealed for the weak content for which they truly bear. Indeed, Canada's history and present existence should not be allowed to end with the triumph of illusion. Quebec francophones can be, and are, as much or more a people within Canada, as they can be outside of it, and that is the greatest lesson of Canadian federalism.

Notes

Introduction

1. Prior to 1982, the written Canadian Constitution was referred to as the *British North America Act*. In this book, the written parts of the constitution or the *Constitution Acts* will also be referred to as the "Constitution", whereas the entire constitution (both written and unwritten elements) will also be referred to as the "constitution".

Part I

Chapter 1

1. Sir Ivor Jennings, *Law of the Constitution*, 5th ed. (London: University of London Press, 1959), p. 134.
2. Donald V. Smiley, *The Federal Condition in Canada* (Toronto: McGraw-Hill Ryerson, 1987), pp. 7–11.
3. *Ibid*; Allan C. Cairns, "'The Embedded State: State-Society Relations in Canada," in Alan C. Cairns, Douglas E. Williams, ed., *Reconfigurations* (Toronto: McClelland and Stewart, 1995), p. 57.
4. J. Stefan Dupré, "Reflections on the Workability of Executive Federalism," in R.D. Olling and M.W. Westmacott, eds., *Perspectives on Canadian Federalism* (Scarborough: Prentice Hall, 1988), pp. 233–4.
5. *Ibid*, p. 233.
6. Cairns, p. 47.
7. Richard Simeon, *Federal-Provincial Diplomacy: The Makings of Recent Policy in Canada* (Toronto: University of Toronto Press, 1972), p. 175 .
8. *Ibid*, pp. 25–31.
9. *Northern Telecom Canada Ltd. v. Communications Workers of Canada*, [1983] 1 S.C.R. 733, at p. 741.
10. Smiley, p. 27.
11. W.R. Lederman, "Some Forms and Limitations of Co-operative Federalism," (Sept. 1967) 45 C.B.R. 409, 410.
12. *Ibid*.
13. Peter H. Russell, "Introduction," in Peter H. Russell, ed., *Leading Constitutional Decisions*, 3rd ed. (Ottawa: Carleton University Press, 1982), p. 21; Peter H. Russell, "The Supreme Court and Federal-Provincial Relations: The Political Use of Legal Resources," in Olling and Westmacott, eds., p. 94.

Part II

1. François Rocher, ed., *Bilan québécois de fédéralisme canadien* (Montréal: Ville-Marie Littérature, 1992), p. 7.

Chapter 2

1. *Le Français langue commune: Enjeu de la société québécoise.* Rapport du comité interministériel sur la situation de la langue française (Quebec: Ministère de la Culture et des Comminications, Québec, 1996), p. 54.

2. *Ibid.*

3. *Ibid.*

4. *Ibid*, p. 55.

5. *Ibid.*

6. Stéphan Dion, "Le nationalism et la convergence culturelle: Le Québec contemporain et le paradoxe de Tocqueville," in Raymond Hudon et Réjean Pelletier, eds., *L'engagement intellectuel: Mélanges en l'honneur de Léon Dion* (Sainte-Foy: les Presses de L'Université Laval, 1991), p. 300, citing Renée B. Danurand, "Peut-on encore définir la famille?," in Fernand Numont, ed., *La société québécoise aprés 30 ans de changements* (Québec, Institut québécois de recherche sur la culture, 1990), pp. 49–66.

7. *Langue Commune,* p. 52.

8. *Ibid,* p. 48.

9. *Ibid*

10. *Ibid.*

11. *Ibid.*

12. The region of Montreal, in the Interministerial Report, is taken to encompass Mirabel to the North, Notre-Dame-du-Bon-Secours to the South, Saint-Sulpice to the East and Vaudreuil to the West.

13. *Langue Commune,* p. 49.

14. *Ibid.*

15. In the study, Montreal Island also refers to Bizard Island.

16. *Langue Commune,* p. 49.

17. *Ibid.*

18. *Ibid,* p. 50.

19. One may note that the population figure given here for 1991 is not identical to that given for another study quoted in the Interministerial Committee Report. Compare *Ibid,* pp. 48 and 51.

20. *Le Français, Langue D'Usage Public au Québec en 1997,* Rapport synthèse, Conseil de la langue française (Québec: Ministère de la Culture et des Communications, Québec, 1999), p. 19.

21. *Langue Commune,* p. 55.

22. *Ibid,* p. 51.

23. *Ibid.*

24. For example, see Micheline Labelle and Joseph J. Lévy, *Ethnicité et Enjeux Sociaux: Le Québec vu par les leaders de groups ethnoculturels* (Montréal: Liber, 1995), p. 10.

25. *Langue Commune,* p. 52.

26. See *Ibid,* p. 54. It was estimated that a birth rate of 1.8 percent to be necessary for the rejuvenation of the anglophone population.

27. *Le Français, Langue D'Usage Public au Québec en 1997,* Rapport de recherche, Paul Béland, Conseil de la langue française (Québec: Ministère de la Culture et des Communications, Québec, 1999), pp. 46–47.

28. See Regean Lachappelle and Jacques Henripin, *The Demolinguistic Situation in Canada* (Montreal: Institute for Research on Public Policy, 1982), p. 196, cited in Roger Gibbons, *Conflict and Unity: An Introduction to Canadian Political Life,* 2nd ed. (Scarborough:

Nelson Canada, 1990), p. 49.

29. *Langue Commune*, p. 52.
30. *Langue D'Usage*, Rapport de recherche, pp. 46–7.
31. *Ibid*, Rapport de recherche and Rapport synthèse.
32. *Langue D'Usage*, Rapport synthèse, p. 9.
33. *Ibid..*
34. *Ibid.*
35. *Langue Commune*, p. 53.
36. *Ibid.*
37. *Ibid.*
38. See Richard Simeon and Donald Blake, "Regional Preferences: Citizens' Views of Public Policy," in Richard Simeon and David J. Elkins, eds., *Small Worlds: Provinces and Parties in Canadian Political Life* (Toronto: Methuen, 1980); see also Stéphan Dion, pp. 298–304.
39. Richard Simeon and David Elkins, "Conclusion: Province, Nation, Country and Confederation," in Simeon and Elkins, eds., p. 289.
40. See, for example, Christian Dufour, *A Canadian Challenge* (IRPP/Oolichan Books, 1990), p. 112; William Coleman, *The Independence Movement in Quebec, 1945–1980* (Toronto: McGraw-Hill Ryerson Ltd., 1986), p. 132.
41. Dufour, *A Canadian Challenge/Le défi québécois*, p. 111.
42. *Ibid*, p. 112.
43. Christian Dufour, *La Rupture tranquille* (Québec: Boréal, 1992), pp. 24 and 115.
44. *Ibid*, p. 70.

Chapter 3

1. W.J. Eccles, "The Preemptive Conquest, 1749–1763," in R. Douglas Francis and Donald B. Smith, eds., *Readings in Canadian History: Pre-Confederation*, 2nd ed. (Holt, Rinehart and Winston of Canada, Limited, 1986), p. 135; and, editors, comments at p. 125.
2. W.L. Morton, *The Kingdom of Canada* (Toronto: McClelland and Stewart, 1963), pp. 147–8.
3. Laforest, *De L'Urgence*, p. 14.
4. Some Quebec writers argue that the reason for this state of affairs was that the British realized if they were to profit from the colony, without expanding important military resources, they had to find a compromise. However, this view does not fully take account of the fact that the British could have dismantled any real French Canadian threat militarily prior to and during the years following the conquest, and it undervalues the sympathetic role of British Governors such as Murray, who refused to apply the Royal Proclamation of 1763, to its full force and effect.
5. See, for example, Fernand Ouellet, "The Insurrections," in Francis and Smith, eds., pp. 313–27.
6. See, for example, Jean-Charles Bonenfant, "The French Canadians and the Birth of Confederation," in Francis and Smith, eds., p. 480; *Royal Commission on Dominion-Provincial Relations, 1937*, Book I, Canada: 1867–1937 (Rowell-Sirois Commission), pp. 28–29.
7. A.I. Silver, *The French-Canadian Idea of Confederation, 1864–1900* (Toronto: University of Toronto Press, 1982), pp. 50 and 40.
8. Rowell-Sirois, p. 42.
9. See: *Ibid*, p. 43; Peter Hogg, *Constitutional Law of Canada*, 3rd ed., Vol. 1 (Toronto: Thompson Canada Ltd., 1992), p. 6-2.
10. Rowell-Sirois, p. 43.

11. Silver, pp. 105–107.
12. Mason Wade, *The French Canadians, 1760–1911*, Vol. 1 (Toronto: Macmillan of Canada, 1968), p. 395.
13. *Ibid.*
14. W.E. Hodgins, *Reports of Ministers of Justice and Orders in Council Upon the Subject of Dominion and Provincial Legislation* (Ottawa, 1896), pp. 693–94.
15. McCarthy was worried about the lack of cohesion in Canada and the perceived declining power of the federal government. For him, the root of the problem appeared to be the French Canadians. Accordingly, he advocated assimilation, and abolition of the French language.
16. *City of Winnipeg v. Barrett*, [1892] A.C. 1445 (P.C.), upholding the validity of the *Public Schools Act* (53 Vict. c. 38).
17. R. Ramality, *Honoré Mercier* (Montreal, 1936), p. 375, cited in Mason Wade, *The French Canadians, 1760–1967*, Vol. 1 (Toronto: McClelland and Stewart, 1971), p. 428.
18. Peter Waite, *Canada 1874–1896: Arduous Destiny* (Toronto: McClellend and Stewart, 1971), p. 211.
19. Henri Bourassa, *Le Devoir*, Sept. 8, 1914 — quoted in Rowell-Sirois, p. 92.
20. Masson Wade, *The French Canadians: 1760–1967*, Vol. 2, 1911–1967 (Toronto: Macmillan of Canada, 1968), p. 468.
21. "Quebec: A Brutal Escalation," *Time*, Oct. 19, 1970, p. 11.
22. "FLQ-outlawed – 240 Round Up," *Focus on Canada*. Waterloo: Fishers News Files Ltd., 1970.

Chapter 4

1. François Rocher, "Le Québec et la constitution: une valse a mille temps," in Rocher, ed., *Bilan québécois*, p. 20.
2. Rocher, in *Bilan québécois*, p. 8.
3. Christian Dufour, *Le defi québécois* and *La Rupture tranquille*.
4. Even pro-separatist writers in Quebec are in agreement that it is not enough to have the right of self-determination, there must also be good reasons for invoking its use. See, for example, Guy Laforest, *De L'Urgence: Text politiques, 1994–1995* (Québec: Boréal, 1995), p. 93.
5. See Kenneth McRoberts, *English Canada and Quebec: Avoiding the Issue* (North York: Robarts Centre for Canadian Studies, 1991), p. 7.
6. *Reference re Legislative Authority of Parliament to Alter or Replace the Senate (Senate Reference)*, [1980] 1 S.C.R. 54.
7. Donald V. Smiley, "A Dangerous Deed: The Constitution Act, 1982," in Keith Banting and Richard Simeon, eds., *And No One Cheered: Federalism, Democracy and the Constitution Act* (Toronto: Methuen Publications, 1983), pp. 74–75. The same author identifies the only major set of suggestions for basic constitutional change prior to the 1960's as the report emanating from the interprovincial conference of 1886, and the highly centralist thrust of the proposals of the League for Social Reconstruction in 1935. *Ibid*, p. 94.
8. *Senate Reference, supra.*
9. Alain Cairns, "The Politics of Constitutional Conservatism," in Banting and Simeon, eds., *And No One Cheered*, p. 49.
10. *Ibid*, pp. 49–51.
11. See Rocher, "Le Quebec et la Constitution: une valse a mille temps," in Rocher, ed., *Bilan québécois*, p. 25.

12. *Re Objection to a Resolution to Amend the Constitution (Reference re Quebec Veto)*, [1982] S.C.R. 793.

13. Rocher, "Le Quebec et la Constitution: une valse a mille temps," in Rocher, ed., *Bilan québécois*, p. 30.

14. J. Stefan Dupré, "The Future of Federalism: A Centralist Perspective," Business-Government Relations Seminar. The Canadian Chamber of Commerce, Calgary, Alberta. Oct. 24, 1990, p. 2.

15. A fall 1985 survey indicated that 35% of Quebec respondents supported sovereignty association; whereas, in the fall of 1987, that support jumped to 44%. Sources respectively: Louis Balthazar, *Bilan du nationalisme* (Montréal: L'Hegaxone, 1986), p. 197 and *La Presse*, November 30, 1987, B1, cited in McRoberts, p. 36.

16. Peter H. Russell, *A Constitutional Odyssey: Can Canadians Become a Sovereign People?*, 2nd ed. (Toronto: University of Toronto Press, 1993), p. 227.

17. National general news, September 20, 1994 13.08 Est, reproduced in Q.L., CP95, Document 2009508, p. 3.

18. *Ibid*, Document 2124957, p. 2.

19. *In re Reference by the Governor in Council Concerning Certain Questions Relating to the Secession of Quebec from Canada (Reference re Quebec Secession)*, [1998] 2 S.C.R., 217. Some might find it curious though that the Supreme Court spoke in terms of secession as being an amendment to the Constitution without giving greater analysis as to why the Constitutional amending formula was not applicable. It simply stated that the Constitution was silent on the ability of a province to secede. Furthermore, given that the Court was applying principles of the constitution and not constitutional provisions or constitutional convention, some may see the Court as giving more of a political rather than legal opinion on what actions would be more consistent with those principles and therefore desirable.

Chapter 5

1. Report of the Royal Commission on Bilingualism and Biculturalism, Pt. III, The World of Work (Ottawa: Queen's Printer for Canada, 1969); Yves de Jocas and Guy Rocher, "Inter-Generation Occupational Mobility in the Province of Quebec," C.J.E.P.S., XXIII No. 1 (Feb. 1957); John Porter, *The Vertical Mosaic* (Toronto: University of Toronto Press, 1976); see, also, Hubert Guidon, *Quebec Society: Tradition, Modernity and Nationhood* (Toronto: University of Toronto Press, 1988), pp. 53–56.

2. The Bilingualism and Biculturalism Commission, p. 16.

3. *Ibid*, pp. 20–22.

4. de Jocas and Rocher.

5. *Ibid*, pp. 66–67. The second generation of French would have 26% of its labour forces in the unskilled area, the British proportion would drop to 7%.

6. Porter, p. 92.

7. *Ibid*, p. 93.

8. *Ibid*.

9. *Ibid*.

10. *Ibid*.

11. *Ibid*.

12. Porter, p. 143. As the Trembley Commission reports, 66.43 percent of Quebec francophones lived in a rural setting, whereas 33.57 percent lived in an urban one. However, by 1951, the situation was completely reversed with 66.5 percent living in an urban setting and 33.5 percent in a rural one. See: Quebec (Province) Royal Commission of Inquiry on Constitutional Problems, Volume 2 (Province of Quebec, 1956), p. 60.

13. Porter, Table III, p. 94.

14. *Ibid*, p. 94.

15. *Ibid*, p. 143, quoting G. Fortin, Study Presented to Committee on Manpower and Employment, *Proceedings*, no. 22.

16. The Bilingualism and Biculturalism Commission, pp. 54 and 60.

17. *Ibid*, p. 77.

18. *Ibid*, pp. 33–34.

19. de Jocas and Rocher, p. 63; Porter, p. 98.

20. The Bilingualism and Biculturalism Commission, pp. 459, 460 and 462.

Part III

Chapter 6

1. Alain G. Gagnon and Khayyam Z. Paltiel, "Towards Maître Chez Nous: The Ascendancy of a Balzacian Bourgeoisie in Quebec," *Queen's Quarterly* 93/4 (Winter 1986) 731, 732.

2. *Ibid*, p. 733.

3. Matthew Fraser, Quebec Inc.: *French Canadian Entrepreneurs and the New Business Elite* (Toronto: Key Porter Books, 1987), p. 78.

4. Gagnon and Paltiel, pp. 733–4.

5. *Ibid*, at 734, citing Gilles Pacquet, "Entrepreneurship Canadien-français: Mythes et réalités," paper presented at the Colloquium of the Royal Society of Canada on Francophones in Canada, University of Manitoba, 3 July 1986, 30.

6. Gagnon and Paltiel, p. 735.

7. (L.Q. 1977, c.5).

8. Fraser, p. 95.

9. Gagnon and Paltiel, pp. 744–5.

10. *Ibid*, pp. 735–6.

11. See The Bilingualism and Biculturalism Commission, p. 472; and Gagnon and Paltiel, p. 740, respectively.

12. Gagnon and Paltiel, p. 740.

13. Fraser, p. 78; Gagnon and Paltiel, p. 734, quoting Bruce Wallace, "Controlling the Caisse," *Mcleans*, 5 May 1986, 40.

14. *Ibid*, at p. 743, citing Robert Bourassa as quoted in Wilson Anthony-Smith and Bruce Wallace, "Quebec's New Entrepreneurs," *Macleans*, 4 Aug. 1986.

15. *Langue Commune*, p. 221. The original text reads: "[l]a question de «justice social» ou «d'égalité des groups linguistiques» qu'on soulevait il y a vigent ans a été practiquement résolue."

16. *Ibid*, Graph 3.1.1, p. 65.

17. *Ibid*.

18. *Ibid*.

19. *Ibid*, p. 65.

20. *Ibid*.

21. *Ibid*, p. 67.

22. *Ibid.*
23. *Ibid,* p. 68.
24. *Ibid.*
25. *Ibid,* p. 72.
26. *Ibid.*
27. *Ibid.*
28. *Ibid.*
29. The Conseil appears to offer somewhat different figures than previous studies, but the confusion is cleared with its explaination that these percentages cannot be compared with previous studies since the structure of the questionnaires are different and the classifications made were a function of an indication of languages used in public and not a function of what one would say working habitually in French meant, nor to group workers into the categories most appropriate to the language of work. See *Langue D'Usage,* Rapport de reserche, p. 19, footnote 4; and Rapport synthèse, p. 31.
30. *Langue Commune,* Graph 3.1.5., p. 73.
31. *Ibid.*
32. *Ibid.*
33. *Ibid.*
34. *Ibid.*
35. *Ibid.*
36. *Ibid,* p. 99.
37. *Ibid.*
38. *Ibid,* p. 98.
39. *Ibid,* p. 99.
40. *Ibid,* p. 109.
41. *Ibid,* p. 112.
42. *Ibid,* p. 113.
43. *Ibid,* p. 122.
44. *Ibid.*
45. *Ibid,* p. 123.
46. *Ibid.*
47. *The National Finances,* (Canadian Tax Foundation, 1989), p. 8-12.
48. *Ibid.*
49. *Ibid.*
50. *Ibid,* p. 8-13.
51. *The National Finances,* (Canadian Tax Foundation, 1992), p. 9-6.
52. *Ibid.*
53. *Ibid.*
54. *Ibid.*
55. *Ibid.*
56. *The National Finances,* (Canadian Tax Foundation, 1994), p. 10-4.
57. *Ibid.*
58. *Ibid,* p. 10-5.
59. *The Finances of the Nation,* (The Canadian Tax Foundation, 1995), p. 9-6.
60. *Langue Commune,* Table 3.6.1., p. 154.

61. See, for example, *Langue D'Usage*, Rapport synthèse, pp. 22–25; and the public presentation of the Report *Le Français, Langue D'Usage Public au Québec en 1997*, by the President of the Conseil de la langue française, Madame Nadia Brédimas Assimopoulos, August 26, 1999.
62. (L.Q. 1977, c.5); as amended by (R.S.Q., c. C-11, 1993, c.40).
63. *Langue Commune*, p. 80.
64. *Ibid.*
65. *Ibid*, p. 92.
66. *Ibid*, p. 101.
67. [1984] 2 S.C.R. 66.
68. Labelle and Lévy, p. 164.
69. There has been controversy arising from the propensity of some school boards not to allow English to be spoken in school at all, including the hallways. Such a view is an example of demographic anxieties to an extreme.
70. *Langue Commune*, Table 3.5.1, p. 131.
71. *Ibid.*
72. *Ibid.*
73. *Ibid.*
74. *Ibid.*
75. *Ibid.*
76. *Ibid.*
77. *Ibid.*
78. *Ibid*, Table 3.5.2, p. 135.
79. *Ibid.*
80. *Ibid.*
81. *Ibid.*
82. *Ibid*, pp. 137–8.
83. *Ibid*, p. 138.
84. *Ibid*, Table 3.5.1, p. 131.
85. [1988] 2 S.C.R. 712.
86. *Reference re Quebec Secession*, at p. 29.
87. *Loi modifiant la Charte de la langue française*, (L.Q., c. C-11 1993, c.40).
88. (G.O.Q., Partie 2, Vol. 125, No. 43, Division II, 1993), p. 5564.
89. Jean-Pierre Bélisle, *Savoir pour Choisir* (Saint-Thérèse, SERDEV, 1992), p. 116.
90. R. *c. Enterprises W.F.H. ltée* [1999] J.Q. no 4586. Eleven years after the *Ford* decision, the Quebec government was required to discharge its onus of proof.
91. *Langue Commune*, Graph 3.3.1, p. 95.
92. *Ibid*, p. 96.
93. *Ibid.*
94. *Langue D'Usage*, Rapport de recherche, p. 24.
95. [1932] A.C. 304 P.C.
96. [1978] 2 S.C.R. 141.
97. *Langue Commune*, p. 216.
98. *Ibid.*
99. *Ibid*, pp. 164, 216.

100. Persons who claimed not to read books are in the following percentages: 23 percent francophones, 14 percent anglophones and 17 percent allophones. See *Langue Commune*, p. 160.
101. *Langue Commune*, p. 161.
102. *Ibid.*
103. *Ibid.*
104. *Ibid.*
105. *Ibid.*
106. *Ibid*, p. 162.
107. *Ibid.*
108. *Ibid*, pp. 163, 216.
109. *Langue D'Usage*, Rapport de recherche, p. 19.
110. *Langue Commune*, p. 216.
111. Jean-Guy Lacroix, "La culture québécoise face aux politiques culturelles canadiennes," in Rocher, ed., *Bilan québécois*, p. 318.
112. Frederick J. Fletcher and Martha Fletcher, "Federalism and Communication Policy: Communications and Confederation Revisited," in David P. Shugarman and Reg Whitaker, eds., *Federalism and Political Community* (Peterborough: Broadview Press Ltd., 1989), p. 387.
113. Marc Raboy, "Des vases non communicants: les communications québécois dans le système fédéral canadien," in Rocher, ed., *Bilan québécois*, p. 328.
114. Fletcher and Fletcher, p. 391.
115. *Ibid.*
116. *Ibid.*
117. Raboy, p. 333.
118. Louis Balthazar, "L'emancipation internationale d'un état fédéral (1960–1990)," in Rocher, ed., *Bilan québécois*, p. 159.
119. Kenneth McRoberts, *Quebec: Social Change and Political Crisis*, 3rd ed. (Toronto: McClelland and Stewart, 1989), p. 267.
120. Coleman, pp. 172–173, 180.
121. *Langue Commune*, pp. 89–90.
122. For example, see Robert McKenzie, "Leading the Charge for Quebec: Quebec City edgy as Bouchard assumes PQ Mantle," *Toronto Star* 18 May 1996.
123. *Langue Commune*, p. 124.
124. Labelle and Lévy, pp. 155, 156, 165 and 194.
125. Laforest, *De L'Urgence*, p. 89.
126. Dion, pp. 292–293.
127. *Ibid*, p. 294.

Chapter 7

1. Of course, the expression of one's culture should not be confused with actions undertaken purporting to further one's cultural or political views, for example, through violence and terrorism. In such a case governments have the legitimate right and ability to prevent those types of activities. Aside from that example, democracy, federalism and the Charter protect Quebec's culture and the French language.
2. See Dion, p. 299, citing Michel Beauchamp, *La communication et les organizations coopératives: le cas du Mouvement des Caisses Desjardins* (Boucherville, Gäetan Morin), 1989.

3. *R.W.D.S.U. v. Saskatchewan*, [1987] 1 S.C.R. 460.

4. *Société des Acadiens du Nouveau-Brunswick Inc. v. Association of Parents for Fairness in Education, Grand Falls District 50 Branch*, [1986] 1 S.C.R. 549.

5. Gibbons, *Conflict and Unity*, p. 82—citing the 1987 report of Canada's Official Languages Commissioner.

6. Michel Sarra-Bournet, "French Power, Québec Power: La place des francophones québécois à Ottawa," in Rocher, ed., *Bilan québécois*, pp. 209.

7. *Ibid*, p. 211.

8. See the statistics provided at *Ibid*, p. 213.

9. Cited by Minister Dion, "Minister Dion writes to Quebec Premier Lucien Bouchard regarding Federal Transfers to the Provinces", dated February 23, 1999.

10. See, for example, David Irwin and Gérard Bernier, "Fédéralisme fiscal, péréquation et déficit fédéral," in Rocher, ed., *Bilan québécois*, pp. 262–3.

11. It has been furthermore noted that if one adds the positive readjustment in equalization for the past three years, the increase in equalization over the next five years and the increase in CHST over the next five years, of the $21.7 billion in new transfers to the provinces, Quebec receives $7.4 billion or 35 percent. Ontario only receives 25 percent, while comprising 38% of the Canadian population. Minster Dion writes to Quebec Premier Lucien Bouchard.

12. Donald V. Smiley, *The Federal Condition in Canada*, p. 91.

13. No conclusion is expressed with respect to the desirability of constitutional change in the context of other states or polities, as vastly different considerations may apply.

14. See Max Nemni, "Canada in Crisis and the Destructive Power of Myth" 99/1 Spring (1992) *Queen's Quarterly* 222, 230.

15. *Reference re Amendment of the Constitution of Canada*, [1981] 1 S.C.R. 753.

16. Claude Morin, *Lendemains piégés: Du référendum à la "nuit des longs couteaux"* (Quebec: Boréal, 1988), p. 301.

17. *Ibid*.

18. Nemni, p. 230.

19. *Le Devoir*, 5 November 1981.

20. Nemni, pp. 230–1.

21. Morin, p. 301.

22. *Le Devoir*, 5 November 1981, quoted in Nemni, p. 231.

23. Morin, p. 301.

24. *Ibid*, p. 306.

25. There is a further highly contentious and emotional debate. Some argue that the Parti Québécois government desired the constitutional negotiations to fail. Trudeau charged that with a P.Q. government bent on separation, it was impossible to discuss real reform, but promised to use his energies to renew the constitution. This statement, if true, would tend to undermine the argument that Quebec did not consent to the 1982 *Constitution Act* and was left out, since its governing Party of the day never really bargained in good faith. Others have insisted though that Quebec neither intended, nor had the means to wreck constitutional reform.

There is conceivably some support for the suspicion that the Parti Québécois were not really bargaining with a view to achieving a reasonable compromise solution, for example, as evidenced through the actions and statements of Parti Québécois delegates in choosing to support the referendum option, or the fact that the P.Q. Party's ultimate goal was separation. To say that the P.Q. were democratically elected, as a justification for such a situation, if true, does nothing to deflect the severity of the circumstances. The beneficial dynamics of good faith negotiations would have been undermined.

26. Brian Mulroney's speech of 2 June 1989, as reported by Andrew Cohen in *The Financial Post*, 14 December 1990.

27. as quoted in Nemni, p. 227.

28. See, for example, Gil Rémillaird, "Legality, Legitimacy and the Supreme Court," translated by Terrance Hughes, in Banting and Simeon, eds., *And No One Cheered*, p. 201. The Supreme Court in *Reference re Quebec Secession* confirmed the unassailability of the *Constitution Act, 1982*.

29. *Patriation Reference, supra*, at p. 880.

30. R.I Chieffins and P.A. Johnson, *The Revised Canadian Constitution: Politics as Law* (Toronto: University of Toronto Press, 1984), pp. 80–1, 83. The King-Byng episode involved the Governor General, Byng, refusing to grant a dissolution of the House of Commons on the advice of the Prime Minister, King, which would have precipitated a general election. The reason for the refusal was that there had recently been a general election. In the unusual circumstances existing, the Liberals under King chose to stay in office despite having fewer seats than the opposition Conservatives. Faced with a vote of non-confidence due to a serious customs scandal, King asked for dissolution. The request was denied and Byng called on the Opposition leader Meighen to form the government, who was, himself, soon defeated, and King returned with a coalition government.

The second incident in which the Governor General refused to act on the advice of the Prime Minister related to the exercise of the appointment power. In 1896, after the defeat of the Conservatives under Tupper, Tupper recommended to Governor General Aberdeen the appointment of a number of prominent Conservatives to the judiciary and Senate. The Governor General took the position that although technically the Prime Minister was still in office, he was repudiated by the electorate and it would be inappropriate for him to find jobs for party supporters before the Liberal leader Laurier was sworn in.

31. *Patriation Reference, supra*, p. 888.

32. *Ibid.*

33. *Quebec Veto Reference, supra*, p. 816.

34. *Ibid*, p. 817.

35. See, for example, Marc Gold, "The Mask of Objectivity: Politics and Rhetoric in the Supreme Court of Canada," (1985) 7 *Supreme Court Review* 455.

36. Allan Cairns, "The Politics of Constitutional Conservatism," in Banting and Simeon, eds., *And No One Cheered*, p. 35.

37. *Ibid.*

38. See, *Patriation Reference, supra.*

39. Donald Smiley, "A Dangerous Deed: The Constitution Act, 1982," in Banting and Simeon, eds., *And No One Cheered*, p. 77.

40. Gérard Bergeron, "Quebec in Isolation," translated by Terrance Hughes, in Banting and Simeon, eds., *And No One Cheered*, p. 16, citing Prime Minister Trudeau in *Le Monde*, Feb. 7, 1982, reported in *Le Devoir*, Feb. 16, 1982.

41. *Quebec Veto Reference*, p. 815.

42. See, Sarra-Bournet, Tables 6A and 6B, at p. 212, source: Robert J. Jackson, *Politics in Canada*, 2nd ed. (Scarborough: Prentice Hall, 1990), pp. 444–445.

43. *Ibid*, Table 7A, p. 213. The francophone proportion of the population may be lower because the most recent census cited was 1981 and the francophone proportion of the population had been dropping, as the 1986 figures demonstrate.

44. Guy Laforest, *Trudeau et la fin d'un rêve canadienne* (Sillery: Septemtrion, 1992), p. 193.

45. Laforest, *De L'Urgence*, p. 27.

46. *Ibid*, p. 29.

47. Laforest, *Trudeau*, p. 197.

48. *Ibid*, pp. 36–38.

49. *Ibid*, p. 49.

50. Written by Trudeau in an open letter to Quebecers, cited in Michel Vastel, *The Outsider* (Toronto: Macmillan, 1990), p. 43.

51. However, the passage of an amendment that is clearly and irretrievably illegitimate, for example in being instituted through coercion or fraud, which is clearly not the situation in Canada before or concerning the passage of the 1982 Amendment, can not necessarily be justified by maintaining in a particular case that no real harm had resulted. Furthermore, if such gross illegitimacy had occurred in one circumstance it may occur in the future with harmful effects. Each circumstance must be examined in procedure and the substance of outcome to determine whether or not there was illegitimacy, the extent of illegitimacy and the extent to which the entire Constitution is thereby tainted.

52. See, for example, Dufour, *A Canadian Challenge*; Dufour, *La Rupture tranquille*; and Rocher, "Le Québec et la Constitution: une valse a mille temps," in Rocher, ed., *Bilan québécois*, p. 31.

53. Laforest, *De L'Urgence*, p. 35.

54. *Ibid*, p. 32.

55. *Ibid*, p. 57.

56. McRoberts, *English Canada and Quebec*, p. 24.

57. *Ibid*, p. 25.

Chapter 8

1. K.C. Wheare, *Federal Government*, 3rd ed. (London: Oxford University Press, 1953), p. 11.

2. *Liquidators of the Maritime Bank of Canada v. Receiver-General of New Brunswick*, [1892] A.C. 437 (P.C.).

3. *Ibid*, p. 442.

4. See *Hodge v. The Queen* (1883), 9 A.C. 117 (P.C.); *British Coal Corp. v. The King*, [1935] A.C. 500 (P.C.).

5. *In re the Initiatives Referendum Act*, [1919] A.C. 935 (P.C.).

6. On the other hand, under the Constitution of Canada, the provinces have no authority to formally interfere with the exercise of federal jurisdiction.

7. R.C.V. Vipond, "Constitutional Politics and the Legacy of the Provincial Rights Movement in Canada," *Canadian Journal of Political Science* 18 (June 1985) 267, 276.

8. Sir John A. Macdonald, *Report on Disallowance: Why the Rivers and Streams Bill Was Disallowed*, (May 17, 1881).

9. Vipond, p. 286.

10. *Ibid*; Christopher Armstrong, *The Politics of Federalism: Ontario Relations with the Federal Government, 1867–1942* (University of Toronto Press, 1981), p. 26.

11. Hogg, p. 22-15.

12. *Ibid*, p. 22-18.

13. *Lochner v. New York*, 198 U.S. 45, 76 (1905), per Holmes J., dissenting.

14. See for example Graham Hughes, "Rules, Policy and Decision Making," (1968) *Yale Law Journal*, 411.

15. Concerning the three JCPC periods, see Patrick Monahan, unpublished analysis.

16. In the United States, by 1890, the "due process" clause of the Bill of Rights' 14th Amendment became an important tool for the protection of private property and vested interests. The restriction on the State in infringing life, liberty and property without due process became much more than a procedural guarantee; it became a large reservoir of individual rights including the liberty to contract. At the basis of this restriction was a shared conception of law among older conservatism, entrepreneurs, politicians and the legal elite in which a set of legal relationships was conceived as between citizens, citizens and the state, the legislature and the judiciary and federalism, each being quantifiably distinct and operating legally according to quantitatively distinct principles. Each set of relationships was an example of delegation of legal powers absolute within their sphere and the judiciary's role was to police the boundary. The case of *Lochner v. New York, supra,* signified the height of substantive due process in holding that fixing maximum hours that bakers could work was an interference with the freedom to contract, which could only be interfered with in cases of material danger to public health or to employees.

17. See *Edwards v. Attorney-General for Canada*, [1930] A.C.124, 132 (P.C.).

18. Garth Stevenson, "The Division of Powers in Canada: Evolution and Structure," in Richard Simeon, ed., *The Division of Powers and Public Policy* (Toronto: University of Toronto Press, 1985), p. 101.

19. [1988] 1 S.C.R. 40.

20. [1989] 1 S.C.R. 641.

21. [1896] A.C. 348 (P.C.).

22. (1882), 7 A.C. 829 (P.C.).

23. For example, see G.P. Browne, *The Judicial Committee and the British North America Act*, (Toronto: University of Toronto Press, 1967), p. 83.

24. *Hodge v. The Queen, supra.*

25. "Rational connection", "integral part", as well as other formulations have been used to justify the encroachment on provincial jurisdiction by a valid federal statute. For a summary, see *General Motors v. City National Leasing, supra*, pp. 670–1.

26. *Irwin Toy Ltd. v. Quebec (Attorney General)*, [1989] 1 S.C.R. 927 at p. 958.

27. *Ibid*, p. 964.

28. [1995] 3 S.C.R. 453 at pp. 48–2.

29. Hogg, p. 16-18.

30. [1946] A.C. 193, 205 (P.C.).

31. [1922] 1 A.C. 191 (P.C.).

32. [1923] A.C. 695 (P.C.).

33. [1925] A.C. 396 (P.C.).

34. *Fort Francis, supra*, 703–4.

35. *Ibid.*

36. [1976] 2 S.C.R. 373.

37. *Labatt Breweries v. The Attorney-General of Canada*, [1980] 1 S.C.R. 914, 945.

38. *Crown Zellerbach, supra*, at p. 432.

39. (1881), 7 A.C. 96 (P.C.).

40. See, for example, *John Deere Plow Co. v. Wharton*, [1915] A.C. 330 (P.C.).

41. See *Proprietary Articles Trade Association v. The Attorney-General for Canada*, [1931] A.C. 310 (P.C.).

42. See *Reference re National Products Marketing Act*, [1936] S.C.R. 398; affirmed in [1937] A.C. 377 (P.C.).

43. *Reference re the Farm Products Marketing Act*, [1957] S.C.R. 198.
44. See *Carnation Co. Ltd. v. Quebec Agricultural Marketing Board*, [1968] S.C.R. 238; and *Central Canadian Potash Co. Ltd. v. the Attorney-General of Canada v. Government of Saskatchewan*, [1979] 1 S.C.R. 42.
45. See *Carnation Co., supra*.
46. *Attorney-General for Manitoba v. Manitoba Egg and Poultry Association*, [1971] S.C.R. 689.
47. [1943] A.C. 550 (P.C.).
48. [1958] S.C.R. 626, at 642.
49. [1971] S.C.R. 543.
50. On a simple level, a substantive provision creates a right or a group of rights; whereas, a remedial provision allows for some enforcement of or a protection regarding a right or group of rights.
51. *General Motors v. City National, supra*, at pp. 668–9, 683.
52. *Ibid*, p. 669.
53. G.V. La Forest, "The Allocation of the Taxation Power under the Canadian Constitution," 2nd ed. (Toronto: Canada Tax Foundation, 1981).
54. See *Reference re Agricultural Products Marketing Act* (1978), 84 D.L.R. (3d) 257 (S.C.C.) - involving a federal enactment purporting to authorize provincial marketing boards to impose levies.
55. See *In re Insurance Act of Canada*, [1932] A.C. 41 (P.C.).
56. [1924] A.C. 328, 342 (P.C.).
57. [1932] A.C. 41, 53 (P.C.).
58. *In re Insurance Act of Canada, supra*, stands for such a proposition.
59. *Attorney-General for Canada v. Attorney-General for B.C.*, [1930] A.C. 111 (P.C.).
60. *Attorney-General for Canada v. Attorney-General for Ontario (Unemployment Insurance)*, [1937] A.C. 355 (P.C.).
61. Hogg, p .6-2.
62. (1887), 12 A.C. 575 (P.C.).
63. [1943] A.C. 550 (P.C.).
64. [1978] 2 S.C.R. 545.

Chapter 9

1. Jean H. Guay et François Rocher, "De la difficile reconnaissance de la spécificité québécoise," in Rocher, ed., *Bilan québécois*, p. 64.
2. See Jean Mercier, "Bilan québécois du féderalisme canadien: perspectives d'un administrativiste," in Rocher, ed., *Bilan québécois*, p. 185 citing economists writing for *L'Analyste*.
3. See, for example, *Angers v. Minister of National Revenue*, [1957] Ex. C.R. 83; *Winterhaven Stables Ltd. v. Canada (Attorney-General)* (1988), 53 D.L.R. (4ᵗʰ) 413, [1989] 1 W.W.R. 193, leave to appeal to S.C.C. denied (April 13, 1989), Doc 21262, [1989] 3 W.W.R. ixxi, 55 D.L.R. (4ᵗʰ) viii; *Ref re Canada Assistance Plan*, [1991] 2 S.C.R. 525; and *Eldridge v. British Columbia (Attorney General)* (1997), 151 D.L.R. (4ᵗʰ) 577 (S.C.C.).
4. Dupré, unpublished analysis.
5. La Forest, p. 30.
6. *The National Finances*, 1992, p. 16-2; La Forest, p. 30.
7. *Ibid*.
8. *Ibid*.

9. *The National Finances*, 1994, p. 9-23; *Federal-Provincial Fiscal Arrangements Act*, 1966-7, 14-15-16 ELIZ. II, c. 89.

10. *National Finances*, 1994, p. 9-23.

11. *Ibid*, p. 9-24.

12. *The National Finances*, 1988-89, p. 16-6.

13. *The National Finances*, 1994, p. 9-22.

14. *Ref re Canada Assistance Plan, supra*.

15. *The Finances of the Nation*, 1995, p. 9-7.

16. It is arguable that under the *Budget Implementation Act, 1995*, which gives effect to the Canada Health and Social Transfer, the prohibition of minimum residency requirements is the only condition that affects social assistance given that the *Canada Assistance Plan Act* is repealed. Accountability would then rest at the provincial level. However, there is nothing preventing intergovernmental agreement to promote shared principles and objectives in this area if desirable, which is one of the purposes of the Canada Health and Social Transfer. On the other hand, provincial flexibility is also seen as desirable.

17. See Paul Barber, "The Development of Major Shared-Cost Programs in Canada," in Olling and Westmacott, eds., at p. 212, quoting Magnus Gunther and Richard J. Van Loon, "Federal Contributions to Post-Secondary Education: Trends and Issues," in David Nowlan and Richard Bellaire, eds., *Financing Canadian Universities: For Whom and By Whom?* (Toronto: OISE Press, 1981), p. 161.

18. *The National Finances*, 1994, p. 9-20.

19. *Ibid*.

20. This figure was obtained from discussions with officials from the Department of Finance, Federal-Provincial Relations Branch.

21. *The National Finances,* 1994, p. 9-20.

22. Harvey Lazar, ed., Canada: The State of the Federation, 1997: Non-Constitutional Renewal (Kingston: Queen's University–The Institute of Intergovernmental Relations, 1997), p. 13.

23. See Minister Dion, "The Contrasting Evolution of our two Federations," Speech to the Canadian-American Centre University of Maine, Orono, Maine (March 19, 1999).

24. Keith Banting, "The Past Speaks to the Future: Lessons from the Postwar Social Union," in Lazar, ed., pp. 51–4.

25. *Towards a New Canada*, The report of the Canadian Bar Association on the Constitution, (Montreal: The Association, 1978), cited in La Forest, p. 34.

26. Lazar, in Lazar, ed., p. 3.

27. Ibid, p. 7.

28. See, for example, Banting, in Lazar, ed., p. 62; and Harvey Lazar, "The Federal Role in a New Social Union: Ottawa at a Crossroads," in Lazar, ed., p. 121.

29. Lazar, in Lazar, p. 115.

30. Robert Howse, "Searching for Plan A: National Unity and the Chrétien Government's New Federalism," in Lazar, ed., p. 323.

31. Lazar, in Lazar, ed., pp. 121–122.

32. Howse, in Lazar, ed., p. 323.

Chapter 10

1. *Task Force on Canadian Unity* (Ottawa: Minister of Supply and Service, 1979), p. 29.

2. Dufour, *A Canadian Challenge*, p. 158.

3. Peter H. Russell, *Constitutional Odyssey*, p. 75.
4. See Raymond Breton, "The Concepts of 'Distinct Society' and 'Identity' in the Meech Lake Accord," in K.E. Swinton and C.J. Rogerson, eds., *Competing Constitutional Visions: The Meech Lake Accord*, (Toronto: Carswell Co. Ltd., 1988), p. 9.
5. See, for example, Richard Simeon, "Meech Lake and Visions of Canada," in Swinton and Rogerson, pp. 299–300.

Chapter 11

1. Armstrong, p. 4.
2. Garth Stevenson, *Unfulfilled Union: Canadian Federalism and National Unity*, 3rd ed., (St. Catherines: Gage Educational Publishing Co., 1989), p. 74.
3. Vipond, pp. 267–8.
4. *Ibid*, p. 275.
5. *Ibid.*
6. See for example Thomas O. Hueglin, "Federalism in Comparative Perspective," in Olling and Westmacott, eds., pp. 24–25. In Canada, federal-provincial interdependence exists alongside provincial autonomy unlike the situation in the United States in which interdependence has succeeded autonomy and intergovernmental relations have replaced classical notions of federalism. See Vipond, at p. 290, citing Richard Simeon, "Constitutional Development and Reform," in Michael S. Whittington and Glen Williams, eds., *Canadian Politics in the 1980's* (Toronto: Methuen, 1981), p. 246.
7. R.A. Young, Phillip Faucher and André Blais, "The Concept of Province Building: A Critique," in Olling and Westmacott, eds., p. 141.
8. *Ibid.*
9. Vipond, p. 292.
10. *Ibid*, p. 294.
11. See Pierre Trudeau, "Values of a Just Society," in Lloyd Axworthy and Pierre Trudeau, eds., *Towards A Just Society* (Markham: Penguin Books Canada Ltd., 1990).
12. Even these universal mobility rights may be somewhat balkanized, for example, by non-discriminatory laws of general application and reasonable residency requirements within a province with respect to public social services, as well as being subject to affirmative action programs in a socially or economically disadvantaged province, if the rate of unemployment in that province is above the Canadian rate.
13. Stevenson, in Simeon, ed., p. 110.
14. *Ibid*, p. 92.
15. Kenneth Norrie, Richard Simeon and M. Krasnick, *Federalism and Economic Union in Canada* (Toronto: University of Toronto Press, 1986), p. 52.
16. Patrick Monahan, Lynda Covello and Nicola Smith, *A New Division of Powers for Canada* (Background Studies, No.8), (North York, Ontario: York University Centre for Research on Public Law and Public Policy, 1992), pp. 17–18.
17. *Interprovincial Co-operatives Ltd. and Dryden Chemicals Ltd. v. R.*, [1976] 1 S.C.R. 477, referred to in Monahan, *et. al.*, *ibid*, p. 13.
18. *Crown Zellerbach, supra.*
19. Frederick J. Fletcher and Donald C. Wallace, "Federal-Provincial Relations and the Making of Public Policy in Canada," in Simeon, ed., pp. 164–5.
20. Monahan *et. al.*, *A New Division of Powers for Canada*, p. 10.
21. Stevenson, in Simeon, ed, p. 113.

22. Norrie, Simeon and Krasnick, p. 142.

23. Mercier, "Bilan québécois du fédéralisme canadien," in Rocher, ed., *Bilan québécois*, p. 191.

24. Fletcher and Wallace, p. 131.

25. Cairns, "The Embedded State: State-Society Relations in Canada," in Cairns and Williams, eds., p. 35.

26. *Ibid*, p. 60, citing Hugh G. Thorburn, *Group Representation in the Federal State: The Relationships between Canadian Governments and Interest Groups*, Volume 69 of the research studies prepared for the Royal Commission on the Economic Union and Development Prospects for Canada (Toronto: University of Toronto Press, 1985), pp. 60–62.

27. Stevenson, in Simeon, ed., p. 92.

28. *Ibid*.

29. Cairns, "The Embedded State: State-Society Relations in Canada," in Cairns and Williams, eds., p. 60.

30. Norrie, Simeon and Krasnick, p. 143.

31. Fletcher and Wallace, p. 132.

32. Albert Breton, *Competitive Governments: An Economic Theory of Politics and Public Finance* (Cambridge: Cambridge University Press, 1996).

33. Dupré, "Reflections on the Workability of Executive Federalism," in Olling and Westmacott, eds., p. 236–7.

34. Paul Barker, "The Development of the Major Shared-Cost Programs in Canada," in Olling and Westmacott, eds., pp. 213–214; Dupré, "Reflections on the Workability of Executive Federalism," in Olling and Westmacott, eds.

35. Dupré, "Reflections on the Workability of Executive Federalism," in Olling and Westmacott, eds., p. 235.

36. *Ibid*, p. 236.

37. *Ibid*, pp. 236, 248.

38. Smiley, p. 89.

39. Donald Smiley, "An Outsider's Observations of Federal-Provincial Relations Among Consenting Adults," in Richard Simeon, ed., *Confrontation and Collaboration: Intergovernmental Relations in Canada Today* (Toronto: Institute of Public Administration of Canada, 1979), p. 110.

40. Lazar, in Lazar, ed., p. 31.

41. Francis and Smith, eds., *Readings in Canadian History: Post-Confederation*, 2nd ed., p. 1.

42. Donald F. Warner, "The Post-Confederation Annexation Movement in Nova Scotia," in Francis and Smith, eds., *Ibid*, p. 7.

43. David Elton, "Federalism and the Canadian West," in Olling and Westmacott, eds, p. 350.

44. Daniel Latouche, "The Constitutional Misfire of 1982," in Banting and Simeon, eds., *And No One Cheered*, pp. 103–4.

45. *Ibid*, p. 105.

46. Alain G. Gagnon and Joseph Garcea, "Quebec and the Pursuit of Special Status," in Olling and Westmacott, eds., p. 304.

47. *Ibid*, p. 305.

48. *Ibid*.

49. *Ibid*, p. 307.

50. Rocher, "Le Québec et la constitution," in Rocher, ed., *Bilan québécois*, p. 24.

51. Gagnon and Garcea, p. 309.

52. *Ibid*, p. 313.

53. Cairns, "The Embedded State: State-Society Relations in Canada," in Cairns and Williams, eds., p. 39.

54. See, also, Simeon and Elkins, in Simeon and Elkins, eds., p. 289; and Samuel V. La Selva, *The Moral Foundations of Canadian Federalism: Paradoxes, Achievements and Tragedies of Nationhood* (Montreal: McGill-Queen's University Press, 1996), p. 189.

55. The figures were obtained from discussions with officials in the Federal-Provincial Relations Division of the Federal Department of Finance.

56. David Irwin and Gérard Bernier, "Fédéralisme fiscal péréquation et déficit fédéral," in Rocher, ed., *Bilan québécois*, p. 256.

57. Minister Dion's letter to Premier Bouchard, dated February 23, 1999.

58. The figures were obtained from discussions with officials in the Federal-Provincial Relations Division of the Federal Department of Finance.

59. Organized and well financed interest groups are in a different position as they can obtain the relevant expertise.

60. La Selva refers to the *péquiste* agenda to achieve a sovereign Quebec as an attempt to erase from collective memory the proud Canadian national identity held by Quebecers. See La Selva, p. 99.

Conclusion

1. Laforest, *De L'Urgence*, pp. 88–89.

INDEX

DATE DUE

NOV 0 7 2000		
OCT 2 8 2002		
AUG 2 1 200 JAN 0 2 2006		

HIGHSMITH #45230